THE BERKSHIRE COTTAGES

A Vanishing Era

BY CAROLE OWENS

anne & Tom
Summer 1987

The Berkshire Cottages, A Vanishing Era

Library of Congress Catalog Card Number: 84-71191

ISBN 0-918343-00-3

Published by: Cottage Press, Inc.
Box 1265
Englewood Cliffs, New Jersey 07632

Book Design by: Madeline and Harvey Hersh

Cover by: Robert DeLage © 1980

To Granny, born November 17, 1895.
This one is for you, old girl…
The first one
was always meant for you.

ACKNOWLEDGEMENTS

Supporting materials for this book came from all over the eastern seaboard. Whether the materials are reproduced or quoted herein or used as background information, they added immeasurably to the dimension of the book. For the tireless researcher, a great deal remains chronicling the Gilded Age in the Berkshires. It took three years to amass that portion which is reflected here. Although it does not represent the entire body of information available, even this portion could not have been collected without help. I want to express my appreciation to Peter Barash in Washington, D.C.; Elizabeth Banks of the Frederick Law Olmsted National Historic Site; Margaret Chevian at Providence Library; Susan Halpert at The Harvard University Houghton Library; the reference librarians at the Englewood Library in New Jersey; the New York City and Boston Public Libraries; the staff at the Essex Institute in Salem, Massachusetts; Paul Ivory, Susan Frisch Lehrer, and Kathleen Oppermann at Chesterwood, Stockbridge and Denis Lesieur at the Berkshire Athenaeum and the Lenox Library; Ann and Jerry Kelly at Linwood; James Parrish in Pittsfield; and Alfred Branam, Jr. in Philadelphia who was a superb finder of rare photographs and generously shared them with me. Special thanks to Polly Pierce of the Stockbridge Library Historic Room for her knowledge and special charm, and to Robert DeLage for his talent, commitment to the history of the cottages, and his willingness to share. A special thank you to David Frank who quite literally hung from pipes in the ceiling to "get the picture"; Jackie Kinney who, I believe, types a hundred words a minute; and my sensitive friend and manuscript reader, Sally Snyder.

"History is not only to be found in books or in the eaves of old buildings but most of all in the memory."

There would be no book without the wonderful present-day residents of Lenox and Stockbridge who consented to be interviewed and share memories, opinions, diaries, letters, and photographs. There is certainly another book of equal weight to be written about the rich and varied experience of chatting with the descendants of both the "upstairs and downstairs" of the Berkshire cottages.

Olivia Stokes Hatch shared all of the above with me and more. She shared her pride in her heritage. She was a constant encouragement sending post cards with additional tidbits as she thought of them over two and one half years. I had imagined handing her the first copy of the manuscript to read. I regret that Mrs. Hatch died before it was finished, and that I cannot say to Mrs. Hatch, along with all the others listed below, thank you.

Miss Anna Alexandre, Mrs. R. Breck, Mrs. Margaret (S. T.) Church, Mr. and Mrs. Edward Daley, Ms. Mary deLasko, Mrs. Adele Emory, Mrs. Joseph Franz, Mr. William Osgood Field, Mr. Alexander T. Halpin, Mr. J. D. Hatch, Mr. Eugene Jappron, Mrs. Wenzel Krebs, Mr. William J. Leary, Mrs. G. K.

Livermore, Mr. Leo Lincoln, Mr. Edward Mahanna, Mr. George Mole, Mrs. Persis Morris and the late Mr. Stephen V. C. Morris, Mr. J. Graham Parsons, Mr. Joseph J. Fignatelli, Mr. Jeffery Platt, Mr. Helaire Regnier, Miss Rosamond Sherwood, Mr. Joseph Walsh, Mrs. H. G. Wilde.

The final form of this book was made possible by the unique talents and resources of a special group—my family.

Promotion:
Robert Owens

Editor:
Dr. Jerome Schein

Business Advisor:
Herbert Owens

Photograph Editor:
Fritzi Owens

Design Consultant:
Raleigh Schein

Research Assistants:
Todd and Joseph Ehrlich

Their talents were blended with those of a fine group of professionals:

Editors:
Elizabeth Montgomery and Claudia Chyle Smith

Graphic Designers:
Madeline and Harvey Hersh

Photographers:
David Frank and Mimi MacDonald

Photo-Reproduction:
The Snap Shop, Great Barrington

Map Maker:
Vaughn Gray

Printer:
David Gordon

PHOTOGRAPHS

Arrowhead—Berkshire County Historical Society

Berkshire Eagle

Boston Public Library

Edith Wharton Restoration

Essex Institute

Frederick Law Olmsted National Historic Site

Great Barrington Historic Commission

Lenox Library

Library of Congress

Original Photographs by:
Todd Ehrlich
David Frank
Mal Guralnick
Sherman E. Hall
Paul Ivory
Mimi MacDonald
Carole Owens
Robert Owens
William Tague

Private Photographic Collections of:
Miss Anna Alexandre
Mr. & Mrs. Edward Daley
Mrs. Adele Emory
Mr. William O. Field
Mrs. Nancy Goldberg
Mr. & Mrs. J. D. Hatch
Mrs. Jane Foster Lorber
Mr. & Mrs. Stephen Morris
Mr. John Nichols
Mr. J. Graham Parsons
Riverbrook School
Seven Hills Resort
Miss Rosamond Sherwood

Providence Library

Stockbridge Library

Trustees of Reservations

TABLE OF CONTENTS

FOREWORD: TO THE TRAVELER

I wrote this book for the simple reason that I wanted to read it. When I came to the Berkshires for the first time in 1979, I was thrilled by what I saw and tantalized by what I did not see, could not find, but had been told was there: ***"The Berkshires has been a famous summer resort for over a hundred years. It was the country seat of the very rich and powerful during the Gilded Age. Before that it was called the American Lake District—home of the great poets and authors. Remnants of the past are all around you."***

That year I was the traveler; seeing enough to believe what I had been told, but only enough to whet the appetite, not to satisfy. I wanted a guide to tell me who built what, when, why, and for how much. I wanted a map to show me what was hidden behind the walls of greenery, and where the nineteenth-century driveways into the Gilded Age lay off the twentieth-century roads. I wanted to go back in the evening to my room at the inn and read stories and anecdotes that would give me a glimpse into the life in the opulent settings that were the Berkshire cottages. There was no such book for sale. I looked, searched old book stores, made a nuisance of myself at the Stockbridge Library Historic Room. I found luscious crumbs but never a whole meal. So I wrote it myself like the hungry person forced to cook at midnight.

Both Lenox and Stockbridge were founded in the 1700s. Between 1880-1910, at the venerable age of one hundred plus, Stockbridge and Lenox experienced a building boom that changed the landscape and the economy of the area. Stockbridge seems to have had deeper roots and hardly swayed in the effort of supporting the building boom of the Gilded Age. Lenox seems to have become Lenox during the period and still reverberates with the memories and relics of the era. The most outrageous structures that best elucidate the state of mind of the late 1800s were built primarily in Lenox; so Lenox had more of a shock to absorb. It was a rush of carnival-like activity that left great architectural monsters behind in what had been Puritan woods and simple farm lands.

The manners and social gatherings decorated the age as surely as the tapestries. During that period, newspapers, magazines, and books dealt with every bit of social minutiae in the Berkshires. Columns in the newspapers had Stockbridge and Lenox datelines as well as Newport, Bar Harbor, Tuxedo Park, Saratoga, and later, Palm Beach. Names were misspelled, titles were granted by the fourth estate, dates for the building of cottages, locations, and even the name of the builders were often wrong. Society events were reported upon when possible and invented when necessary. It was an age never lacking for a superlative. At times, the errors were the result of the difficulty in getting information from a very exclusive upper class, and at other times the errors were calculated to prevent the truth from standing in the way of a good story. Some of the mistakes have been handed down from generation to generation.[1] If libraries, newspapers, and chroniclers of the day made errors, so did this twentieth-century traveler. Wherever possible, errors have been corrected and hopefully new ones have not been made.

The builders and the caretakers of the great estates—those that gilded the age and those that polished it—were the subject of news stories then, and are the subject of daydreams and drama now. Never since the demise has the era or the people been treated quite seriously. The age has been criticized into ignominy or dramatized into fantasy. The relics of the age and the stories take on the aspect of set and plot in some period play. The times seem so different from our modern age as to be pure drama or melodrama. "History is written by the victors." The historians have been part of our current middle-class America. The age of elegance and gilt and uncountable wealth has been treated as an entertaining parenthesis to the history of America. I have tried to treat the subject matter seriously and factually; not as an entertaining aside, but as the antecedent of our world today. The era was colorful, gay, and brief. The end of the era was catastrophic; world war followed by world-wide depression followed by world war. The age is over. The possibilities are to preserve our heritage, what is left of it, or, alternately, allow it to decay and vanish forever.

Part II of the book is a guide to the Berkshire cottages from one traveler to another. It is meant to enrich your visit by allowing you to be successful if you choose to go on a hunt through the Berkshire Hills for historic treasures. If you have come to Stockbridge or Lenox looking for gems of a past era, the last section of this book is your map.

PART I: A VANISHED ERA

1

THE VILLAGES

"Every Lenox has its Stockbridge."

Cleveland Amory: *The Last Resorts*

Courtesy of the Stockbridge Library

The Stockbridge Railroad Station circa 1893

As the road turns and dips into Stockbridge, you pass the Stockbridge railroad station. At that point, your path crosses the past. If you are arriving on a Friday afternoon for a weekend, you are repeating a social ritual that was replayed at that railroad station countless times in the last century. Only your method of transportation has changed. Then, the train spewed and hissed into the station. The screech of metal on metal could be heard on the porch of the Red Lion Inn as the train pulled in to discharge its passengers. They came up from New York and down from Boston: the cottagers. You can no longer watch as the doors swing open, as the cottagers and their weekend guests, the members of Gilded Age Society and the hopefuls, alight. You will not see the liveried footmen waiting beside the carriages or the rainbow of satin dresses, but, it is the gift of the villages to the twentieth-century traveler, that the station appears as it did in 1891, the third to be built on the spot since the train came all the way up to Stockbridge. Enough is left of the sights those travelers in the other century saw, and the places they visited, that, with just a modicum of assistance, during your stay in the Berkshire Hills, you can stand in two centuries at once.

From 1880 to 1920, as a summer colony of the American economic elite, the villages had, if not their finest, surely their most colorful era. The tiny villages played host to the most powerful men and women of their age. Alternately called the American aristocrats, the power elite, and the robber barons; they were the arbiters of taste, the geniuses of nuance, the purchasers of civilization, the proponents of prejudice, the power brokers. For the forty-odd years that they reigned, they were the permanent elite. Any tale of the Berkshire cottages is also the story of the builders and a period of history.

Cottage was the superb misnomer used by the builders. The cottages have been more accurately described as great beasts and leviathans; structures whose parts were "the peaks and turrets of outrageous fortune."[1] The people who built these great houses were powered by great wealth and a uniform idea, they were the elite, the celebrities of their day. If all of their names are not familiar today, it is not because they were unknown then. They affected American politics, law, and religion. They became diplomats affecting international relations. They were the captains of industry and the bankers for the country. It is possible to admire the fruits of their labors, the country cottages and the city homes, the museums, theaters, and art collections, without knowing who they were. It may be sufficient to know that as a group, these people powered their age: their every wish was someone's command; their every social move was of public interest; their decisions in their work places affected lives and American life. The tale of the Berkshire cottages is a tale of people and places. Although the places are all in the Berkshires, the names belong to many parts of the country, especially New York.

In New York City, after the Civil War, an idea was forming. By the late 1800s, New York City was the undisputed capital of the United States in every way but politically. From Wall Street, from the vantage point of the tip of an island, men looked out across the country. They saw an abundance of everything. There was no dearth of natural resources, production, or manpower. The industrial revolution had put the machinery in place, and a national transportation system moved it around. There was no popular philosophy, religious or governmental, to foist a monkey-wrench into their machinery. There was no war to divert attention or energies. Whether the optimism guided the use of the resources, or the abundance of resources created the optimism, did not matter. The optimism was the foundation of the idea. The idea, like the era, was both simple and superlative: to be the best. America would emulate and surpass Europe. New York would rival Paris, London, and Vienna. The architects of this idea were the financial princes of New York.

A Berkshire resident and descendant of one such man said, "My grandparents didn't have to be embarrassed in front of Queen Victoria nor anyone on earth. They were perfectly capable." If they were the power in New York, which in turn fueled a country that was becoming a major power, of whom would they stand in awe?

The simple idea was reinforced on all sides. No obstacle stood in the way. No loud or persistent voice was heard to refute it. The press only wrote of the tallest, the biggest, the grandest, and the best. The optimism was reinforced by the belief that the resources were limitless and so were the opportunities for people. Just north and east of Wall Street were the newest and poorest of Americans, the immigrants from every country on earth who had struggled to reach the land of promise. Further uptown, to the east were the homes of some of the oldest and most respected American families. Next door were great mansions built as symbols of the financial success possible in America. The mansions were closer to the center of the island, preempting the position of the older families. As they continued to build, they continued to move up the island. Above, theaters, opera houses, parks, museums, libraries, and clubs were built to attest to the wealth, culture, and society, the finery, of the New World. The city spread north as if to say, "There is still room for more people to move up the island from the teeming tenements; to succeed and build." New York was a visual explication of the American dream.

Highlawn House
circa 1910

Courtesy of the Library of Congress

By the 1880s, the architects of the idea were literally builders. Simultaneously with building their city palaces, they built their country seats. Spreading out from New York, they superimposed on the Hudson, the Berkshires, and Newport the symbols of the same idea. The builders of the Berkshire cottages came up from New York. They played as they worked with the same optimism, superiority, and competitive spirit. They had the unchallenged integration of energy, purpose and action that is often youthful and always successful. They rolled into the Berkshires powered by an idea. The power of the train was only the symbol of the real energy driving them. They rolled into and over the Berkshire Hills, and, not for the first time in history, the residents lined the streets and waved flags of welcome at the conquerors.

Barrington House

Courtesy of the Stockbridge Library

The villages of Stockbridge and Lenox are, and always were, charming in their own right; both have a history that predates the arrival of cottages. The history of Stockbridge prior to the Gilded Age can be divided into four parts: prior to 1737 when it was Indian land called Housatonic; the colonizing by white missionaries after 1739; the colonial period which saw the gathering of great religious orators and those concerned with the founding of a new nation; and after 1830, the literary period.

The territory of Housatonic, including Stockbridge, was purchased from the Indians "in consideration of four hundred and sixty pounds, three barrels of sider [sic] and thirty quarts of rum." It was, therefore, more expensive than Manhattan Island.

The first missionary to Stockbridge was Reverend John Sergeant who built his Mission House in 1739 on what is now called Prospect Hill. (Today the Mission House is a historic site on Main Street.)

Jonathan Edwards had a parson's salary of six pounds in "lawful money" plus twenty-five loads of wood from his white congregation and eight sleigh loads of wood from the Indians. His daughter Esther earned her wedding gown by embroidering cloth and painting fans for wealthy Boston matrons.[2] She married Reverend Aaron Burr who was much her senior. Rules were rigid and there was a nine P.M. curfew. Reverend Burr became President of Princeton University, and their grandson Aaron "had, in later years, a way of staying out after nine."[3]

Main Street,
Stockbridge in winter

Courtesy of J. Graham Parsons

In 1774, the County Congress, or the Berkshire Convention, met at Stockbridge Tavern under the sign of the red lion with the green tail. (Today it is The Red Lion Inn, Main Street.) Mark Hopkins and Theodore Sedgwick presided. They voted not to consume any goods manufactured by the British. It was one of the first such formal actions in the colonies.

After the Revolutionary War, when defense of a homestead was a less pressing issue, residents were willing to move from the Hill to the Plain. "Great men of Stockbridge" like Theodore Sedgwick and Jahleel Woodbridge built their homes along Main Street. The Sedgwick home still stands today. Woodbridge's "Laurel Cottage" is gone.

The Literary period was born in Theodore Sedgwick's home where his daughter Catherine wrote ***New England Tales.*** It was widely read and literati sought Catherine first in the Stockbridge home of her father and later at her brother's home in Lenox.

Lenox history prior to the Gilded Age can also be divided into four parts. However, they seemed to bloom and fade rather than flowing smoothly one period into the other. First, there was the time of Chief Yokun and the Indian tribes. Then, in 1750, the first white man settled in Lenox. The town was formed combining lands granted to the Quincy family plus four thousand acres granted to individuals who had given up their land for the Indian

Courtesy of the Stockbridge Library

Main Street, Stockbridge

mission at Stockbridge. The Indians disappeared from Lenox. In 1767 the town was incorporated and named Lenox after the English Duke of Richmond, Charles Lennox. The third period was marked by the arrival of judges and lawyers and those who had business with the county court as Lenox became a Massachusetts shiretown in 1787. Six years later, Reverend John Hotchkin founded what would later be the Lenox Library, and in 1803, he founded the Lenox Academy for Boys.

Among the new arrivals in 1820 was Charles Sedgwick, clerk of the court. When Catherine moved from Stockbridge to Lenox to live with her brother, the salon she had attracted moved with her. Charles' wife, Elizabeth Dwight Sedgwick, began her famous

Two views of Main Street, Lenox

Courtesy of the Lenox Library

school for young ladies in Lenox. Charlotte Cushman and Jenny Jerome (later, Lady Churchill) were among her students. The Berkshire Coffee House was a warm and welcoming place to sleep and eat. (Today it is the Curtis Hotel on Main Street.)

In 1868, after a protracted battle, the court was moved from Lenox; Pittsfield became the seat of Berkshire County. Lenox quieted down and waited. The next period did not so much arrive in the person of Samuel Gray Ward as it was foreshadowed. In 1841, and again in 1844, Mr. Ward purchased land to form the first great estate, Highwood. Although the land was primarily in Stockbridge, and although by timing and by his own proclivities he belonged to the literary period, still he has been granted the title, "The First Berkshire Cottager."

Courtesy of the Stockbridge Library

Laurel Cottage

The list of residents and guests of Lenox and Stockbridge in the early nineteenth century reads like a crib sheet for an American history course: Henry Wadsworth Longfellow, Mark Twain, Herman Melville, Nathaniel Hawthorne, Theodore Roosevelt, Daniel Webster, Oliver Wendell Holmes, Aaron Burr, William Cullen Bryant, the Sedgwicks, and the Fields: David Dudley, Cyrus, Stephen J., and Stephen. A list of later residents reads like the syllabus for an Arts and Letters Survey Course: Daniel Chester French, Owen Wister, Matthew Arnold, Frederic Crowninshield, Frank Crownin-

Courtesy of the Berkshire Eagle

Andrew Carnegie

shield, Edith Wharton, Henry James, Joseph Choate, Thomas Shields-Clarke, Susan Metcalfe, Lydia Field Emmet, Robert Emmet Sherwood and Rosina Emmet Sherwood.

Why did they come? One reporter explained: "In the early nineteenth century, Stockbridge was on a main route to the stagecoach line between Boston and Albany, and eight coaches a day, four each way, made regular stops."[4]

Literally, the stagecoach brought them, but it is hard to imagine that men and women of such stature simply went where the coach went. Some were born there. Others came for inspiration, but as inspiring as the countryside was, they also came for the society. In part, one brought the other. The population was more concentrated then than now, and it was concentrated in New England. The Berkshires was a rare gem of natural beauty that was also easily accessible. Because of the beauty and the people who came to the Berkshires, it became known first as "The American Lake District." During that period, Nathaniel Hawthorne, Henry Wadsworth Longfellow, Henry Thoreau, Robert Lowell, and William Cullen Bryant all paid tribute to the area.

From the little red farm house on Stockbridge Bowl, Nathaniel Hawthorne wrote: "The sunsets of winter are incomparably splendid, and when the ground is covered with snow no brilliancy of tint expressible by words can come within an infinite distance of the effect. Our southern view at that time, with the clouds and atmospherical hues, is quite indescribable and unimaginable; in the various distances of the hills that lie between us and the remote dome of the Taconic are brought out with accuracy unattainable in summer."[5]

Mr. & Mrs. Anson Phelps Stokes at Shadow Brook

Courtesy of Olivia Stokes Hatch

When Thoreau achieved the summit of Mt. Greylock, he wrote that he found himself: "...in the dazzling halls of Aurora playing with the rosy fingers of dawn...There were immense snowy pastures, apparently smooth shaven and firm and shady vales between the vaporous mountains; and far in the horizon I could see where some luxurious misty timber jutted into the prairie...."[6]

Courtesy of the Lenox Library

Cricket Team at Elm Court (seated second from left, Carlos deHeredia; seated to the right of Mr. deHeredia, the British Ambassador, Sir Mortimer Durano; seated extreme right, W. D. Sloane; standing extreme right, his son-in-law, William B. Osgood Field)

From his land at the oxbow on the Housatonic in Stockbridge Longfellow wrote: "What a lovely place! On three sides shut in by willow and alder hedges and the flowering wall of the river; groves clear of all underbrush; rocky knolls and breezy bowers of chestnuts; and under the soil, marble enough to build a palace. I build many castles in the air, and in fancy many on earth."[7]

Longfellow was more than poetic, he was prophetic. By the 1880s, the marble was indeed being used to build castles called the Berkshire cottages. While lack of funds drove Hawthorne and Melville out of Lenox and Stockbridge, it was wealth that carried the new wave into the area. If the stagecoach brought the earlier luminaries, the railroad brought the later. During the Gilded Age, a list of the cottagers and their guests reads like the index of ***The Robber Barons:*** the Vanderbilts and the Astors, Marshall Field, Mark Hopkins, Andrew Carnegie, George Westinghouse, J.P. Morgan, Harry Payne Whitney, and Mark Hanna's son, Dan. The list is not one of people prepared to be off the streets at nine P.M. It was an odd intrusion of new mores and unknown riches into the old New England Puritan villages.

"Do you recall entertaining any famous guests?"

"Well, yes, I'm sure we must have done."

The interviewer pushes for details, "Can you think of anyone in particular?"

There is a pause, "Well . . . "

The interviewer searches for a name so well known as to represent a period of history, not just a person. "For example, did you ever entertain F.D.R.?"

"Oh, well, Frankie, yes. He was always about the place. Of course, he was a cousin."

So the interviewer learns by the effective tool of embarrassment that anyone who one has ever heard of or should have heard of was there—in the Berkshire cottages.

The cottages themselves are as much a part of the story as the people who built and occupied them.

Courtesy of The Museum of Fine Arts, Boston

Portrait of Theodore Sedgwick by Gilbert Stuart

"Shadow Brook, yes, I remember it, it was like a great leviathan laying curled on the hilltop; lit up at night, it looked like a great ship afloat."

Why did the great and powerful, the rich and famous, set these great beasts and vessels down in the Berkshire woods? There are so many reasons given that the number belies the accuracy of any one. They say they rolled in on the rails and on the wealth that they had amassed. They say they came to the Berkshires because of the literati that had preceded them. They say that ten came because of the one that had come before the ten. They say that land was cheap. (But it rose from fifty dollars an acre to one thousand dollars an acre when Society began to buy.) They say the beauty of the Berkshires was captivating. They say it was perfect for carriage rides. They say the fall foliage brought them.

Edith Wharton at The Mount

Courtesy of Edith Wharton Restoration

In 1894, ***Scribner's Magazine*** reported that people came to the Berkshires for the drives; it was not a horsey area in the sense of Saratoga. It was for the carriage set. ***Scribner's*** reminded the reader that the fall foilage was known everywhere and cuttings were even sent to Europe as gifts.

Courtesy of the Berkshire Eagle

Henry Wadsworth Longfellow

In order really to understand the times, one must accept the point of view of the people of the time. It was not an introspective world concerned with motivations and underlying causes. It was not the psychological world of today. It was a material world. Who you were was determined by what could be seen. When one influential matron of society wore a pink gown to the opera, another equally influential matron objected, sighing as she asked, "What does she mean by that?"

The twentieth-century reader may be confused, but the nineteenth-century matron was quite certain: the objection was to the color pink. A "proper" gown would have been grey or white or black. The question: what does she mean by that was exact, because something was meant by everything one did and said and wore and built and didn't say and do and wear and build. It was a time when "keeping up with the Joneses" was not a general phrase symbolic of an attitude in life—it meant literally keeping up with the Jones family of New York City, the parents of Edith Wharton nèe Jones.

It was a time when one serious reporter explained to his newspaper readers, "The automobile will catch on so that people can follow the Vanderbilts."

At leisure they competed as surely as at empire building but for a different goal: the stuff of society, the symbols of success. They turned to Europe to borrow the symbols—French clothes and English country houses. They fanned out from New York City, the undisputed center of American finance, to Newport, Long Island, the Adirondacks, and the Berkshires. What took them to the Berkshires was partly the need for somewhere to go.

First, then, the Berkshires were close to New York City, the undisputed center of their social and financial world. Second, neither Stockbridge nor Lenox had ever been an industrial center, an unacceptable prelude to the establishment of a country seat. Moreover, the villages had won the reputation as the home of authors, painters and poets, jurists and clergy, therefore, a respectable group predated the millionaires. Third, a serious consideration for a group that traveled "in season," at a time when those two words expressed one complete thought, was that the Berkshires bloomed at the right time. June and July were spent at Newport by the sea; August in Saratoga for the waters and the horses; November in New York City for the theater. The Berkshires fit neatly between Saratoga and New York City. It fit between them geographically and on the calendar. September and October were spent in the Berkshires for the fall foliage. Last, there was land and plenty of it, an important point, because to establish a country seat, a true cottage, one must meet certain criteria. First

Courtesy of the Lenox Library

Catherine Sedgwick

and foremost, a cottage could never be the primary residence. Second, the house and grounds must conform to the more-than formula: the house must have more than twenty rooms situated on more than thirty acres.

Of course, the Berkshires are breathtakingly beautiful. Like Paris, like few other places on earth, the scenery is intoxicating. In a time before mass-produced technological entertainment, a time when a black and white photo was the nearest relation to the television or a movie, looking was an entertainment.

As ***Scribner's*** characterized it, "Lenox ***was*** for the simple reason that nature had fitted it so to be."

Henry James described the Massachusetts Berkshires as "the land beyond any other in America, today, as one is much reminded, of leisure on the way to legitimation, of the social idyll, of the workable, the expensively workable, American form of country life."[8]

So finally the social dictum came in 1893: "The well regulated society can no longer neglect a visit to Lenox during some part of the season than he can omit to observing Lent or to speak French at table."[9]

It no longer mattered whether the families who came lent social acceptability or the area was acceptable so they came. The Berkshires had arrived and taken its place alongside Newport. Here they built their cottages at Newport by the Sea and the Inland Newport. Newport ceased to identify a town in Rhode Island, and became a generic term identifying summer colonies of the elite.

When Cleveland Amory wrote, "Every Lenox has its Stockbridge," he meant that every neighborhood that achieved social standing had an adjoining area, second best, that sprang up to handle the overflow, the hangers-on, the wishers and the wishers-well. The description is a trick of vantage point. Beginning in the twentieth century and traveling backward, one comes to Lenox first, but beginning in 1737, you must meet the gentle First Families and the literati in Stockbridge before you continue to Lenox to meet The Four Hundred. As Stockbridge seems to have evolved out of the roots of American history and won its place on the map by its longevity, Lenox appears to have exploded onto the map one day (almost literally) in a time of social and industrial explosions—post-Civil War America. Lenox history telescopes on forty of the most powerful years in the shaping of the country—1880-1920 Lenox was subsumed by the cottagers, while Stockbridge tried to hold its ground.

Finding where Stockbridge ends and Lenox begins physically is more difficult than finding the spiritual divide. The physical border is obscure and meandering. The granddaughter of Anson Phelps Stokes, the wealthy and socially prominent builder of the largest of the Berkshire cottages, Shadow Brook, was asked, "Wasn't Shadow Brook actually in Stockbridge?"

"Yes," she said, "all but the gatehouse which was actually in Lenox. Of course there was some snobbery about Lenox, but actually I think they took the Lenox address from practicality. They were physically closer to the town of Lenox and used the Lenox post office."

The psychological difference between the two towns is clear cut. To explain it, at the height of the Gilded Age, Joseph Hodges Choate, a prominent lawyer of New York City and Naumkeag, Stockbridge, said, "In Lenox you are estimated, in Stockbridge, you are esteemed."

As you cannot walk down Main Street in Stockbridge without tipping your hat to your heritage, you cannot walk through Lenox without tipping your hat to American progress. You are reminded of the ghosts of Lenox and Stockbridge by the relics they left behind. The men and women who changed America from an agrarian society and a country cousin to world leader, to an industrialized country of international standing, came to the Berkshires. Lenox went from being the county seat of Berkshire County to the country seat of the American aristocracy. The builders were those individuals who have been called so many names for so many years that the only certain fact is their undisputed importance. They were fascinating in their day, and even if we have forgotten some of their names, their way of life has never lost its fascination for us. It was as if the carnival came to town, filled the villages with color and excitement, touched every aspect of life, and then left.

The reasons for their leaving are as numerous as those given for their coming. Income tax changed the way people could live. World War I changed the way people felt. The automobile drove America into the twentieth century. Ironically, these much maligned and often admired people were inventing a new century and like all those who do their job well, they worked themselves out of a job. They invented a new way of life that rendered their way obsolete. As one Newport cottager recalled:

> I remember a man who made his living by bringing people past the gates of our Newport home and I could hear him telling the spectators, "Their front doors weigh 200 pounds, and they eat ice cream every day." Now everyone eats ice cream every day.[10]

When we can all eat ice cream, the ice cream eaters lose their fascination and their lofty place among us. Yet the symbols of another time, of a way of life that included more than ice cream, stand in the country houses of the Berkshires. Many of them stand silent, as if still maintaining the values of the people who built them. People who would never dream of allowing a face to appear at the window or a voice to float out into the yard. They were not above show, but the show was part of the initiation rite into the group to which they wanted to belong. It was an exclusive group. Multiplying the "First Families" times the dollars, they became The Four Hundred. Or, with the dollars, the nouveau riche bought a berth in the American social upper class. As after each of the previous periods of history, after the Cottage Period the villages were sleepy again, but it was a sleep disturbed by dreams of its most

Courtesy of Miss Rosamond Sherwood

Robert Emmet Sherwood

colorful period.

From almost any vantage point along the roads in Lenox and Stockbridge, a glimpse of the estates is possible. They sit off and up on hilltops. They are like objects sought in a dream where all your faculties are slightly impaired. You know they are there, but you can't quite see them. They are screened by trees, obscured by the angles of the road and the hills. They are at the end of tree-lined drives. Then all at once, one of the cottages stands out for an instant like a penny flashing in the high grass.

"Look at that!" the twentieth-century man says. Beleaguered by income tax and the rising price index, hassled by escalating fuel costs, rolls of pink insulation, and the workman who patiently explains why it is impossible to install the storm windows before April, he asks his wife, "What is it?"

"It's a school or a hotel," his wife guesses.

"Is it? Maybe it's a convent. Look at those grounds, it must be a private club."

"Well," the wife considers, "maybe it's a house."

The husband is certain, "***That*** is no house."

Note to the twentieth-century traveler: it has been all those things, but first it was a Berkshire cottage.

2

TWICE TOLD TALES

We like a story all the better for having heard it two or three times before.

Nathaniel Hawthorne:
The Wonder Book

Courtesy of the Berkshire Eagle

Lenox Post Office circa 1894

ach of the locals is a minor historian by right of physical possession. But the tales of the Berkshires are unlike other 'mountain lore.' On the streets of Lenox and Stockbridge, they stop to tell you, "The cottages, now they were something to see." They don't refer only to the great summer residences that met the criteria of the more-than formula, but to the cottagers as well who had to meet certain criteria of social standing, style, and showmanship. If asked, the locals will tell you how the great mansions came to be called cottages. Before the private residences were built, visitors stayed at the Curtis Hotel. The wealthy and prestigious hotel guests were housed not in the main building, but in roomier and more private quarters; these were called the cottages. When these same yearly visitors built their mansions, the names that had signaled their special status were still used to describe them. Their summer quarters were cottages, and they were the cottagers. The elite were a small group well known to one another. They influenced economic and political decisions over dinner. A description of the Lenox post office that appeared in ***Scribner's Magazine*** in 1894 attempted to show the importance

of the Society that had gathered in Lenox:

> ...Twice and even thrice a day you may find yourself at this point of interest. Everyone goes there, and there, at one time or another between morning and evening, you may be pretty sure of meeting everyone you know.... It is a cross between a Casino and a country store.... One who once tarried in Lenox was heard to remark that he considered the office of post-master in Lenox to be the most desirable social position in the United States....[1]

The postmaster of Lenox would be certain to meet and pass a remark or two with the social elite every day; more than the average man could hope for. The idea of mingling with the great men and women of the day was a heady one in 1894. As distant and unapproachable as the elite were from the average man in New York City, that is how close they were to the townspeople when they got to the country. The stories the townspeople tell about the celebrities of the last century are not the ones found in the newspapers in New York City at that time. In villages the size of Lenox and Stockbridge, population 1,845 and 2,089 respectively in 1880, the elite were seen at close range, and no man is a hero to his valet.

History circulated like so many pieces of stationery swirling in the wind around the door of the old Lenox Post Office. The letters were sent by the financial princes in residence and came from the presidents of the United States.

In 1872, a young Teddy Roosevelt visited Lenox. He had relatives there, and it was thought that the mountain air would be healthy. He wrote: "Dear Barnie, I arrived here last night safe and sound.... For lunch in the cars, I had eight sandwiches and twenty-four peaches. The asthma has left me.... Uncle Hill says he is glad I have come, because he wants somebody to talk and swim with.... Tell Hattie to be sure and feed the turtle in the kitchen window. Your own brother, PeeWee."

In 1888, President Chester Arthur wrote to accept the honor of dedicating Lenox's Trinity Church. On land acquired on Kemble Street, the new church was built by and for the members of the summer colony. Just across the street from the church stood the Frelinghuysen cottage built in 1881 by Frederick T. Frelinghuysen, President Arthur's secretary of state from 1881-1885.

In 1889, President Grover Cleveland wrote that he would be in Lenox to participate in the dedication of Sedgwick Hall. Two years earlier, in the first presidential wedding to take place in the White House, 50-year-old Grover Cleveland had married Miss Frances Folsom of Pittsfield, the 22-year-old daughter of his former law partner.

In 1892, Anson Phelps Stokes, in the midst of building Shadow Brook, the largest of the Lenox/Stockbridge cottages, wrote President Cleveland inviting him to dinner. Mr. Stokes, a multimillionaire and philanthropist, copied the response into his journal:

> Dear Mr. Stokes, I thank you very much for your courteous invitation to dine on the 15th...and am exceedingly grateful for the

> considerate manner in which your invitation is [worded]. It could not be necessary to assure you that I would greatly enjoy meeting you and your guests [but] I have made up my mind that I must forego such pleasures. If, as you suggest, my health is drunk in my absence, I hope that it may be coupled with the wish that strength and wisdom may be given me to meet the expectations of those who have trusted me.[2]

In 1897, President William McKinley wrote to accept an invitation to dine at the Lenox cottage, Wyndhurst. John Sloane, builder of Wyndhurst, and his brother, William of Elm court, were the owners of the W. & J. Sloane Furniture Stores.

In 1902, PeeWee, now President Theodore Roosevelt, was back in Lenox. This time the trip was not good for his health. The president was nearly killed when his horse and carriage were struck by a trolley car.

The locals spin the yarns, embellishing the landscape with the humor or sadness of human behavior. Not the least of storytellers was once the postmaster in Lenox. The man who held the coveted position, recalls: "In 1917, you know, Andrew Carnegie lived over at Shadow Brook. His secretary would collect the industrialist's mail everyday. I still remember him telling me, 'Andrew Carnegie gets twice this much mail each day at his New York address.' Everyday he'd pick up the mail, and everyday that's what he'd say to me. That's so's I'd know how important Andrew Carnegie was! I thought that was silly. Then, I remember Honorable Henry White. He married Emily Thorn Vanderbilt after Mr. William Sloane died, and they lived over to Elm Court. He used to come in the post office every year when he'd come up from New York, and he would say, 'What's going on?' That's what I got a big kick out of. Gad, you know, there he was on top of the world—Ambassador and everything—and he comes in asking ***me*** what's going on in the world. I used to love that."

The Honorable Henry White

Courtesy of William O. Field

Storytelling is an art, not a science. We learn as much from tall tales as we do from short facts. Tales are neither fact nor fiction. They are memory, and memory is neither, and memory is both. The teller of the tale believes firmly that his account is true, but memory never serves exactly and what we recall is never quite as it happened. Like fiction, it is colored and shaped by the teller; like fiction, it encompasses the process of selection and the processes of shading and emphasis. The tale becomes the property of the teller as memory does, as fiction does, yet the tale is based upon or at least illuminates some fact. The following stories echo down the halls of the mansions today even if they never echoed in fact or in the first place. They are retold here not because they are true, but because they have been told so many times in the Berkshires as to become part of the mountain lore, and because what they may lack in accuracy, they make up in giving a flavor to the times.

The dimensions of the world of the American aristocracy between 1880 and 1920 were enormous. Private ballrooms would accommodate a number calculated in the hundreds. The porch circling the Aspinwall Hotel in Lenox was one mile. Shadow Brook had one hundred rooms, and Elm Court had ninety-four. Cottages were sited on estates of up to nine hundred acres. It is easy to make a direct hit when aiming criticism at so large a surface. It's a job that could be done by even the clumsiest among us, and it was done by the clever and the clumsy alike. However, the aim of the local historian, and teller of tales of the cottage era, is not to criticize, but to explain to the outsider what life during the cottage period in Lenox and Stockbridge was like.

The stories can be grouped. There are those that explain the dimensions. The locals would like the listener to be awestruck by the numbers and be set to imagining what it was like to live with such arithmetic in people, rooms, and dollars. Such stories make the wealth that only a few amassed more palatable to the many by entertaining them. There are the stories that expose the eccentricities or the special gifts of the wealthy, and thus satisfy a yearning that many have to discover that the very rich and powerful were also strange or different. Last, there are those stories that tell secrets, and therefore, do more than set the listener to imagining life inside the city palaces and country cottages, these stories seek to expose that life.

Courtesy of Mrs. Olivia Stokes Hatch

Weekend guests at Shadow Brook 1896. Mr. Stokes is in the rear, standing against the front door, in a white hat. Mrs. Stokes is seated in front of him to his right.

Stories of Dollars and Dimensions.

It is difficult to argue about the wording of a telegram that was never sent. However, it has been done over the years. It is said that shortly after Shadow Brook was completed in 1893, Anson Phelps Stokes, Jr., sent his mother the following telegram: "Arriving this weekend with Class of 96." Anson Stokes Phelps, Jr., attended Yale and was a member of the Class of 1896. Did the junior Mr. Stokes mean that he was arriving with 96 people, or all the members of the Yale Class of '96? In either case, the story goes, his mother responded: "Already have house guests. Try to bring not more than 50."

The daughter of the supposed sender of telegrams, and granddaughter of Mrs. Stokes says, "My husband and I have heard that story in every country in the world that we have visited except in Russia."

The story has lived so long because of a single fact: Shadow Brook was so enormous a country estate that the telegram could be believed. Whether the Class of '96 was a hundred men; or the junior Mr. Stokes was bringing 96 men; or honoring his mother's wishes, he altered his plans and brought fifty, the story lives because no one doubts that the house could accommodate them.

Some years later, someone thought to ask Bishop Stokes whether he ever had sent such a telegram. He wrote back to the Stockbridge librarian that he never had. The last word belongs to the lady of the house. When asked by her granddaughter, "Did father send such a telegram?" Mrs. Anson Phelps Stokes of Shadow Brook replied, "No. But I could see the opportunity for the joke." Indeed that lady more than any other could see the opportunity, having run the largest household in America, or the largest of the resort cottages, or at least the largest in the Berkshires, depending upon the reporter and the date of the report.

The tale is a good one because like all tales it illuminates the truth even if it doesn't tell it. Whereas the truth, one suspects, is that where you stand depends on where you sit, and if your "seat" occupies half a mountain, the view is quite different. So that for illuminating a way of life and a point of view, the truth, or in this case the true telegram, is the better one.

Mrs. Olivia Stokes Hatch, the granddaughter, offers a true story to replace the one she has taken away. "The real telegram came not ***to*** my grandmother, but ***from*** her to her architect, H. Neill Wilson in Pittsfield." She wrote with the anxiety of the home builder who doesn't want to make a mistake and find out too late. The builder of the hundred room estate was worried about space. She telegrammed, "Please make each room one foot larger in every direction."

Size alone gives insight into the life-style of the Gilded Age, but the dimensions of the cottagers' world also included the number, the seemingly endless number, of ways they devised to spend their money.

Courtesy of Miss Rosamond Sherwood

Miss Olivia Stokes
painted by
Lydia Field Emmet

Wheatleigh is an Italianate cottage built by H.H. Cook in 1893. It was built, the story goes, as a wedding present for his daughter when she married Carlos deHeredia. The American real estate tycoon was so happy that his daughter had married a Spanish Count and brought a title into the family that he hired Frederick Law Olmsted, Robert Swain Peabody, and John Goddard Stearns to create the appropriate setting for the couple. Behind the Italianate cottage, Wheatleigh, the Stockbridge estate of "Countess" deHeredia, is a lovely tower. Tales of all sorts have clung without effort to its varied lines. It is so unusual a structure that one mystery writer used it as the site for the climax of her first thriller.[3] But the tale that has stuck the longest had to do with Mrs. deHeredia's love of dogs, and gained the structure the name: The Poodle Tower.

"Guess what that is?" the fun-loving local begins, pointing to the Tower.

Wheatleigh, the estate of
Mr. & Mrs. Carlos deHeredia

Courtesy of the Providence Library

How you respond depends upon your imagination, your love of the game, or what else you have to do; but you will end, as we all do, by saying, "I can't guess. Tell me."

"Why, that's the Countess' mausoleum for her poodles."

Just think, you are urged, of people who had so much money that they could construct such a thing for the sole purpose of burying their dogs. What better proof need you, the critic asks, that their animals lived better than the American poor? What better proof do you need, the supporter asks, that they were an American aristocracy that lent charm to every aspect of life?

"First of all," a descendant of John Jacob Astor clears the air, "Mrs. deHeredia was not a Countess and never called herself one. That's something the press made up. Anyone who wandered into Lenox in those days was handed a title. Silly."

A woman who is in fact a Countess explains, "I don't know exactly what happened there, but I can tell you the possibilities. Carlos and Georgie Bruce Cook met in Cuba. If he was a Cuban, of course he would not have had a title. But if he was Spanish, the Spanish deHeredias were titled. His title may not have been transferable to his wife, or, like many other Spanish aristocrats, he may have lost his title and fled to Cuba. In any case, even if the title were also hers, one does not use titles in America, you know."

"Oh, no," her footman confirms, "Mrs. deHeredia didn't like being called Countess." He pauses and, not wanting to cheat his former mistress of one cent of the credit due her, he adds, "There ***was*** a coat of arms in the front hall that went from ceiling to floor, to be sure." He goes on to clear up the Poodle Tower. "It was a water tower, you know. That story got started because the animals were buried down behind it. Do you realize I had to bring a dead cat up from New York so it could be buried there?" He answers himself, "Yup. Cat named Mocha. There were a variety of dogs buried back there, poodles and the last ones were cocker spaniels. They are all down there behind the water tower."

One needs to understand, the story tellers seem to say with every breath, the amount of money available to these people.

Mr. Carnegie purchased Shadow Brook in 1917. He died there in 1919. One day, walking his grounds, he came upon his superintendent. Some work was being planned and the superintendent explained that it might cost as much as $300,000.

"Why, man, it would take me a month to save that much money!" Mr. Carnegie exclaimed to his $450 a year superintendent.

It's impossible to check the facts of the story since the only two men present are now dead. "But," asks a local history buff, "does it matter if the story is exactly correct if the figures are? That man spent $3,000,000 renovating Shadow Brook, and I couldn't see what was wrong with it in the first place."

If the annual income figures alone are not the stuff that dreams and stories are made of, you are asked once again to ponder the dimensions. The hundred-room Shadow Brook was situated on 738 acres. The ninety-four room Elm Court was on a larger estate, including Highlawn Farm (first a part of Elm Court and later the estate of the Sloane's daughter, Lila Field), it sat on more than nine hundred acres. The numbers, simply stated, are hard to comprehend, like the figures associated with the national debt, asked to define it, one simply says, "big." If the proportions still escape you, think of it this way, the ground floor of some of these houses covered one acre. Then, of course, they rose two, three, and four stories. If that doesn't help, the story tellers urge you, try this:

"I know for a fact how many windows there were at one of the

Courtesy of the Providence Library

The Entrance Hall at Wheatleigh
with coat of arms worked into tapestry on the rear wall

estates [Ananda Hall] because I installed every one—well, all but six—there were one hundred and fifty-six windows."

"A coach and four could go up one of the grand staircases."

"Edith Wharton described her thirteen-by-fifty-two foot entrance hall as small but well proportioned."

"In those private ballrooms they could accommodate three to four hundred guests, and when Elm Court was turned into an inn for awhile, the dining room sat fifty."

Or, perhaps size is always best described by a story. In exasperation, one rainy day, Mrs. Anson Phelps Stokes importuned, "Children, please, go up to the attic and ride your bicycles." She was the mother of nine children.

The Eccentric and the Gifted.

One of the grandchildren of the Sloanes of Elm Court says, "I remember going to Erskine Park. I couldn't have been more than six. I remember sitting on George Westinghouse's lap. Erskine Park was a beautiful place. The roads were white and the bridges across the man-made ponds were white. The house was not all white, I don't think, but it seemed to be."

Some of those who worked at Erskine Park recall the estate and Mrs. Westinghouse, but with a slightly different feeling.

"She didn't want to look out her window and see black roads so she had white crushed marble brought in, tons of it, so that the roads would be all white. The inside of the cars had to be white. Everything had to be white to suit her. Today you could have some psychologist tell you why. I can't tell you why, but Mrs. Westinghouse had to have everything white." There is a pause, and then a confidence, "It was mental though, I'll tell you that. Anyone will tell you that."

Everyone remembers the same estate and no one can forget its whiteness. Did Mrs. Westinghouse have an obsession? Now here is the stuff that tales of the super rich are made. Poor Mrs. Westinghouse. Perhaps we ought to call a psychologist to do a posthumous analysis. What tales we could tell of obsession, depression, deep-seated guilt, and what fun speculating on the root causes. But the key to Mrs. Westinghouse's "obsession" is not to be found in psychology text books, but architectural books.

The World's Columbian Exhibition was held in 1893, the year that Erskine Park was built by Mr. and Mrs. George Westinghouse. If, during the 1890s, there was any question left what style would dominate the gilded age, it was answered with finality by the World's Columbian Exhibition, held at Chicago in 1893.[4]

The Westinghouses were there. George Westinghouse had installed the entire power and light system for the Exhibition. As Mrs. Westinghouse viewed the Exhibition, she could understand why it was called "The White City." The Exhibition changed architectural design and decoration. It affected ideas about use of color.

Mrs. Westinghouse envisioned and executed indirect lighting for the first time in a private home. Outside, she puttered around in one of the first cars (electric) while equestrians looked on and wondered. She was a modern lady and quick to pick up on architectural shifts in taste made at the Exhibition in 1893 and the color that symbolized them, white. She was no more eccentric than anyone who seeks to be modern.

Courtesy of the Lenox Library

White marble bridge over man-made ponds at Erskine Park

Not long after Erskine Park was built, she was asked by her doctor to leave the Berkshires for health reasons, and she did. The property was purchased by Mrs. Margaret Emerson McKim Vanderbilt. It is ironic that coming up the drive, Mrs. Vanderbilt pronounced Erskine Park "horribly Victorian" and had it razed. Mrs. Vanderbilt built Holmwood on the site. Some have argued that Holmwood was not in the best tradition of Berkshire cottages and not the equal of the cottage destroyed. All agree that Mrs. Vanderbilt, later Mrs. Baker, succeeded in achieving her goal: Holmwood is clearly not Victorian. With a stroke of final justice for the past owner, Mrs. Vanderbilt had it painted white.

Frederick Law Olmsted

Courtesy of the Frederick Law Olmsted National Historic Site

The roof and the sections of the cottages that we glimpse through the trees as we wind around the roads of the Berkshires today are the free-standing nineteenth-century equivalent of a twentieth-century media event. All the high-tech gilt you can imagine from Las Vegas to Hollywood to Broadway is an echo of the first show-stoppers. The production had its set designers, like architects McKim, Mead and White, Peabody and Stearns, and Richard Morris Hunt or landscape architect, Frederick Law Olmsted. It had special effects like the art, furniture, gowns, silver and china bought and brought back to this country from Europe. It had its stars like the Astors, the Vanderbilts, and the Morgans. It had its producers like Ward McAllister in New York and Newport, and Frank Crowninshield in New York and Stockbridge.

Frank, born in 1872, was the son of artist, Frederic Crowninshield. As a young boy, Frank had been educated by private tutors in Italy where his father was director of the American Academy in Rome. He arrived in Stockbridge with his parents, a brother and sister, in 1886. Even at fourteen years old, "Crownie" displayed the panache that would cause ***The New Yorker*** to call him "the last of the species" when he died in 1947. The "species" was as common a thing in 1886 as it was apparently rare in 1947, a gentleman.

Courtesy of the Berkshire Eagle

George Westinghouse
of Erskine Park

In Stockbridge in that year, Nathalie Sedgwick was very impressed by the changes in her village. The Sedgwicks were a prominent Stockbridge family, but that was something quite different from the wave of prominent families moving in from New York and Europe.

> Outside was slowly creeping into the village. Summer people were buying places... down the street the big family of Joseph H. Choate was going to build on a hill... the Matthew Arnolds took the house where the Musgraves used to give us supper on the lawn. Worshipping over the banisters I used to watch Matthew Arnold come into the hall of the old house, in striped trousers and black coat, to call on Laura. When Frank Crowninshield, a man of the world at 14, appeared in front of the hotel [The Red Lion], took off his hat with a gesture, my harmonious line was broken... he brought out the bumpkin in all of us. Playing beanbags at children's parties, the way he said, "that side's troubled with the dropsey," and picked up a bag easily, is fixed in my memory as the first sophisticated humor. His coming was

good for us. We village children had the place too much to ourselves.... on the near outskirts of Stockbridge, the Crowninshields built a house [Konkaput Brook] Main Street sported a yellow casino...the Choate's new stone mansion [Naumkeag] on the hill bellied over the valley... it was more like a city house inside, run by a machinery of easy effort unkown.[5]

Nathalie Sedgwick may have been one of the first women of Stockbridge taken by "Crownie," but she was far from the last. A ninety-year-old woman who has lived in Stockbridge all her life recalls that Frank Crowninshield was a handsome and genial flirt whom all the women adored; many hoped while all wondered whom he would marry. "Crownie" subscribed to Lord Chesterfield's advice: compliment beautiful women for their wit and ugly women for their beauty. In fact, Frank Crowninshield never married. He invested himself in his work as editor of ***Vanity Fair***, a job he was particularly suited for, and which called upon his talents as tastemaker, critic, sophisticate, and nurturer of the egos of some of the best writers of the day, men and women alike.

In New York, the law firm of Butler, Evarts, Southmayd and Choate balanced the legal briefs of precedent-setting law cases concerning income tax, trusts, railroads, and Society divorces with aplomb. In Stockbridge, Charles Butler, Charles F. Southmayd, and Joseph Hodges Choate built cottages. For those who seek confirmation that the Gilded Age was a time filled with people to be judged harshly, the locals offer tales of Mr. Charles F. Southmayd. For those who want to hear that the very rich were also very clever, stories of Mr. Choate are told.

Courtesy of Miss Anna Alexandre

Frank Crowninshield with the ladies at the Berkshire Hunt in 1901

Nathalie Segwick Colby in ***Remembering*** begins the acquaintance with Mr. Southmayd.

> When he had indigestion and was put on a diet of water and milk, with gruel for high spots . . . he ordered all his precious liquors up from the cellar and had them emptied out in front of the house on the gravel. Thousands of dollars worth soaked into the old world—enough to inebriate and send it reeling and out of its orbit! He wouldn't have minded that as much as to have had his wine run in another man's veins.[6]

Now before those who are comforted by learning that the super rich were mean become too smug, Ellery Sedgwick, editor of ***The Atlantic,*** continues the story in ***The Happy Profession:***

> Before I leave Mr. Southmayd, I want to pay his memory a personal tribute which I have carried in my heart for 60 years. . . . There came a summer day when my father said to me, "Ell, if I am to save the old house, I must borrow $7,000 and I have decided to ask Mr. Southmayd for it." . . . I see my father with the desperate look of the dead or doomed visible across his face. We were homeless; I had little doubt of it. Then suddenly the doorway flung open and out came my father, his ruddy face glowing with happiness. There was no need for words, but as we trotted home, my father kept exclaiming: "What a kind man! What a good man!" Mr. Southmayd, it seemed, had made everything easy. . . . The full extent of Mr. Southmayd's generosity my father never knew.[7]

Ellery Sedgwick explains that Mr. Southmayd left the meadows put up as security against the loan in his will to a surviving Sedgwick.

Whether mean or generous, remembered as both, and notwithstanding the fact that Mr. Southmayd was said to look like a character out of Charles Dickens, no one doubted that he was brilliant. It is no easier to judge any of the cottagers than it is to make a clean-cut decision about Mr. Southmayd. So, allowing the example of Charles Southmayd to put the forming of harsh judgments to rest, the tales continue.

It was Mr. Southmayd that prepared the briefs on which Mr. Choate pleaded his case against the income tax in 1894. Mr. Southmayd held the idea that the right of property was the foundation of all civilized government, and that, therefore, the Act of Congress instituting the income tax would require an amendment to the Constitution. When the law firm, in the person of Joseph Choate, argued the case successfully in front of the Supreme Court, it was ruled unconstitutional. Until the Constitution was amended by ratification of the Eighteenth Amendment in 1913, the wealthy had legal discretion over income in amounts unheard of since. Mr. Choate had won the case that created and supported the times in which he and Mr. Southmayd lived. When he was asked about Mr. Southmayd's contribution, Mr. Choate said, "Most men are endowed with only five senses. Mr. Southmayd has a sixth—the sense of property."

Courtesy of the Berkshire Eagle

Joseph Hodges Choate
dressed for a costume ball

Joseph Hodges Choate may be remembered for many things in New York City where he was named the First Citizen of New York before he died in 1911, and abroad where he was Ambassador to the Court of St. James, but at home in Stockbridge he was best recalled as a wit. He was an affable fellow, of whom Ellery Sedgwick was said to be jealous for Choate's ability to say the outrageous and walk away unscathed.

When asked to contribute for a fence to enclose the local graveyard, Mr. Choate declined saying, "No one on the outside wants to get in, and no one on the inside can get out." When asked, "If you were reincarnated, what would you come back as?" Choate responded, "I would come back as Mrs. Choate's second husband."

When poor Mr. Southmayd, shaken by a visit from the Gentleman Burglar, refused to open his Stockbridge home for the season, Choate advised him "either to maintain a garrison or get married and support a wife. I don't know which would be the surest safeguard."

On October 20, 1901, Anson Phelps Stokes wrote in his journal: "We hired for a week a house at New Haven where we entertained several guests for the Bicentennial—the Honorable Joseph H. Choate and Mrs. Choate and Mark Twain."[8]

Choate and Twain were great friends. When Samuel Clemens died eight years later, it was Joseph Choate who delivered the address at the memorial meeting at Carnegie Hall. Choate must have been as pleased with his Stockbridge reputation as a man who could make people laugh, as he was of his accomplishments in

New York, Washington, D.C., or London, for he said of Mark Twain that he had made men better by making them laugh and that to make men happier and better was the only real triumph.

The Choates almost forsook their plans to build in Stockbridge. Early in the project there was a problem with getting water to the house. David Dudley Field was president of the Hill Water Company, and Choate complained to his wife in a letter, that the lawyer, Mr. Field, was so busy and important a man that he could not arrange to see him. David Dudley Field may have been hard to find in New York, where he was called the Father of the New York Penal Code, but, in Stockbridge, he was quite accessible as a member of an old Stockbridge family, "the fabulous Fields." His brother Cyrus had laid the transatlantic cable, his brother Stephen Johnson was a Supreme Court Justice, the last to be appointed by Abraham Lincoln, and nephew Stephen Dudley was an inventor who built the first electric train and ran it around his front yard in Stockbridge because he could not get the financial backing to run it anywhere else.

Cortlandt Field Bishop
in his automobile

Courtesy of the Berkshire Eagle

The lawyers met in Stockbridge, and the water problem was settled. The Choates built their cottage, Naumkeag, across the road from David Dudley's cottage, Eden Hill. Although no one is sure what the exact nature of the problem between the two lawyers was, the result is clear, the inimitable Mr. Choate ended by being master of Naumkeag and president of the water company.

Cortlandt Field Bishop was a man well-equipped with talents, eccentricities, and passions. When he was seventeen, his father, David Wolfe Bishop, inherited the bulk of the vast combined fortunes of John David Wolfe, the hardware merchant, and the tobacco fortune of Pierre Lorillard reputedly the first man ever to be called "millionaire." His family owned, in addition to their New York home, the cottage Interlaken. After marrying a member of The Four Hundred, Amy Bend, Cortlandt owned the Winter Palace in Lenox, and later built Ananda Hall. A man who never had to work, neither was he a man to sit idle. He financially backed the American Art Association in New York which later became Parke-Bernet, and became involved as a buyer of antiquities in Europe. His passion was the automobile. At a time when P. T. Barnum thought it appropriate to place a car in the center ring of the circus so the patrons could get a look at one, Mr. Bishop was motoring around the world. The automobile was so odious to the horse and carriage set in Lenox that each morning the butlers would call Mr. Bishop's butler and ask on which roads Mr. Bishop would be driving his car. The butlers could then inform the ladies of the house so that they, in their carriages, could avoid those roads. It was entirely on Mr. Bishop's account that the town of Lenox passed a law to limit the speed of an automobile to fifteen miles per hour. Later, to accommodate the equestrians, he published his route for the following day in the local paper.

The large pages of the guest book at Shadow Brook were often irresistible to the anonymous wit and the would-be poet. The following entry was dated May, 1898, and the writer probably had Mr. Bishop in mind.

In the days of the coach and the horn;
Which days, alas! Now are gone,
To [illegible] about,
They used no doubt
The coach and four, and tira lira! the horse!
To the days of the steam and the car
In which busy days we now are
To travel around
They use roads, iron bound,
The steam engine, toot toot! and the car!
But what matter the stupid old car,
When fresh air and good horses are ours,
And along the old roads,
They pull many young loads,
For light hearts and good spirits are ours.
Ha! Ha! What good spirits are ours! C.R.B.

Once, standing outside of the post office, Mr. Bishop was approached by the boy who was paid five dollars a week to deliver special delivery mail. The boy handed the letter to Mr. Bishop explaining that it was for him. "You are paid to deliver special delivery mail to my door," Mr. Bishop told the boy. So saying, Mr. Bishop got into his automobile, drove home and stood outside the front door of the Winter Palace waiting for the boy to come on his bicycle with the letter.

Tales of Crime and Passion.

No one debates that the Gilded Age and its cottages rested predominantly in Lenox, and so when the crime-of-the-century, Berkshire style, took place, some erroneously placed it in Lenox. If the cottagers centered in Lenox, why not the tales? No self-respecting burglar, folk logic has it, would root around the perimeter (in Stockbridge) when the treasure was housed (or cottaged) in Lenox. So the Gentleman Burglar and his exploits are placed in Lenox. Because we seem to strain ourselves to import a British eccentricity along with other European treasures to adorn our American aristocracy, the hostesses whose houses were not robbed are reported to have complained. Given the eccentricities of staggering wealth, the story goes, it would seem something of an insult not to be selected to be robbed. Did the oversight imply that the jewels were paste, the artwork copied, the coffers empty? Worse, absent a visit from the Gentleman Burglar, one might be left out of the conversation at the dinner table. One didn't like to lose the telling of a good story. This was no small matter in a society where one of the sins was to bore, and by extension not to entertain. So for congruence and the logic of the thing, tales placed the Gentleman Burglar knocking politely at the door and bidding entrance to cottages in the town of Lenox.

However, the Gentleman Burglar was Stockbridge's own, Nathalie Sedgwick recalls.

> ***One night a burglar entered Mr. Southmayd's second story and went off with his wallet. Alick [Sedgwick] read the notice of a reward in the post office. "$1,000 for apprehending the villain." Alick set a number of traps but the burglar omitted the Sedgwick house stealing jewels at all the other Stockbridge homes near around: Mrs. David Dudley Field had a hand-to-hand struggle with the same marauder; the burglar stole the jewels of an old maid opposite. The only man who had ever been in her bedroom, he melted her frozen libido. "He took everything away from me so quickly and gently, it was a pleasure." she testified.***
>
> ***The New York Times**, *September 10, 1893 gave a full page account: Stockbridge Is Under Arms—Terrified By The Acts Of A Mysterious Burglar. The once quiet peaceful town now sleeps with barred doors. The watchmen in the streets and the detective on the alert—A tall man with arching eyebrows**

and a mesmerizing voice the cause of the alarm—His visits during the summer season—One very thrilling experience... at that instant a sight confronted her [Miss Stetson] that drove every drop of blood in her body to her heart and paralyzed her with fright. Standing in the doorway was an apparition unearthly in its appearance, intensified in its ghostly outlines by the flickering lamp it held in its muffled hand. Six feet and over in height, looking taller and more spectral by the shadows heaving around it, a derby hat pulled far down over the forehead, a man's hemstitched handkerchief drawn tightly over the lower part of the face and secured behind the ears, the figure before her could not have imbued her with more terror had she seen it come up out of the grave. In the right hand, also muffled, gleamed a revolver; both feet were bandaged with towels.... [I]n relating the episode, Miss Stetson said, "The instant he spoke, the tension snapped and I was myself again. The voice was low, musical, soothing, mesmeric in its effect. The change from the stifling silent presence to the talking human being was like the passing of a refreshing summer breeze."

"I want your money" he finally said.... "I have none," replied Miss Stetson. "I only came to stay the night with my friend because she is afraid of you."... He crossed the hall and entered Mrs. Swan's apartment.... "I have a pistol," she exclaimed.

"So have I" he replied, deliberately advancing towards her. ... "You had better give me that pistol," he said in a quiet decisive way, "You might hurt yourself with it."

"I can't give it to you," she cried. "It is borrowed."

"Very well," he replied. "I will take it from you, because you might hurt yourself and I will leave it downstairs."... He then walked over to her dressing case and picked up her rings.

"Won't you please leave that one?" she cried. "It belonged to my mother. I prize it highly."—thinking it was an emerald of rare beauty.

He nodded his head and replaced the ring on the silver tray. But she had made a mistake. It was a diamond ring he had had in his hand, and in the morning she had found it where he had laid it. The emerald was gone—its actual value was $750. As an heirloom it was priceless. He stripped her pocketbook of its contents, amounting to $80. Then he walked over to her desk. "Where is the key?" he demanded.

"I don't know. I have been thinking where I could have laid it. The visit was so unexpected that I am unable to collect my thoughts. If you let me up, I may find it."... As he left Mrs. Swan's bedroom she asked, "Don't you think you might seek some other employment?"

[He then returned to Miss Stetson's room and demanded her watch. She said she had none.]

"On your honor?" he said, raising his eyebrows.

[He next visited the home of Mrs. David Dudley Field.]

A piece of black silk now covered his face... She maintained her grasp around his neck and was lifted until her feet were clear of the floor.... "You will get hurt!" he exclaimed quietly, exerting himself to the utmost to shake himself free. "You will hurt yourself. Keep quiet. You will get hurt." Across the room and into the hall, the struggle continued. She hanging on with the frenzy and desperation of despair... her shrieks in course of time had awakened Mr. Field's valet, who now rushed into the hall, pistol in hand.

"Shoot!" cried Mrs. Field to the astonished valet who stood paralyzed to the spot, not five feet away. "Don't mind me! This man is a robber and he has my watch."

With a sense of the proprieties that was delicious, even if it were untimely, the valet cried, "I must get my wrapper" and departed for that indispensable article—to a valet—of wearing apparel... The next morning, Stockbridge, and, for that matter, the whole of the Berkshires had something to talk about, and they have been talking about it ever since. Mr. Charles Butler promptly offered a reward of $500 for the arrest and conviction of the burglar, the authorities added $500 more, and Mrs. Field $200. The state detective came over from Lee and promptly said, with a sagacity of a clever detective, that the big reward spoiled the case, for the robber would hide his light for a time under his bushel... the general verdict was that the robberies were committed by a person, one who was thoroughly conversant with the structure of the houses and the habits of the occupants. The argument was further strengthened by the fact that he not only disguised his face, but covered his hands and feet as additional precaution against detection... several points indicated the burglar to be a novice. He used no regular burglar tools and no skeleton key. He cut out no windows or panels of doors, climbed no piazzas, and had broken open no cellar doors.... All his victims bear witness to the soothing voice, almost mesmeric influence of his voice. Before... his coolness, deliberation in word and act, impressed some with the suggestion that he was a professional man fairly conversant with human nature and the temperament of women. Illiterate and educated agree on this point. When Miss Stetson deliberately called him back in order to catch a glimpse of his eyes, she noted that his dress was that of a gentleman, that his clothing was of mixed material and of fashionable cut, that his three-button cutaway coat fitted his figure to a nicety, and that his trousers were of a quiet pattern. He wore a white shirt. His eyes were dark and mild and soft in expression. His ears were small and shapely, and his hair closely trimmed and dark colored. His figure was erect and was carried with dignity and ease. It was also noted that he invariably drove off in a buggy and his horses were fast.[9]

The nineteenth-century reader understood that the reporter for the ***New York Times*** had described a gentleman. Miss Stetson is credited with giving him the title: "The Gentleman Burglar." With every timely indication of a gentleman of 1893, imagine the dismay when the burglar was apprehended. He was Thomas Kinsella, a stone cutter employed by Joseph Choate in 1885 while building his estate, and a man who shot his mother in 1887. He was a Stockbridge town resident. The town tax assessor lists his assets as totalling $1430. That included a house, barn, mountain lot, and brick yard valued at $200, $230, $800, and $200 respectively. His tax bill is marked paid.

A descendant of Thomas Kinsella and present day resident of Stockbridge does not believe that the story of the Gentleman Burglar ended with the arrest of Thomas. It is his belief that it was a ring of men and that only Thomas was caught. That would mean that each description of the Gentleman Burglar might have been of a different man and finally was just a description of the myth.

Courtesy of the Providence Library

The Swann House, Stockbridge. It was houses like this one on Main Street that the Gentlemen Burglar visited.

Grenville Lindall Winthrop of New York and Groton Place, Lenox, was descendent from John Winthrop who came to America in the 1630s as the first governor of the Massachusetts Bay Company. Shortly after their arrival in the new world, they changed the company to a commonwealth, and John Winthrop, the Puritan squire of Groton Manor, Suffolk, became the first governor of one hundred freemen and a commonwealth. Mr. Grenville Winthrop would not permit his daughters any male companionship.

As footman at Wheatleigh, Eugene Jappron, says, "I remember answering the phone, and it was Mr. Grenville Winthrop's butler. Mr. Winthrop wanted the guest list for Mrs. deHeredia's dinner party before he would let his daughters attend. He was very careful about where his daughters went. But they came to Mrs. de Heredia's."

Stephen Morris, the son of Newbold Morris the builder of Brookhurst, continued to spend summers at the cottage well into the twentieth century. He recalls that Mr. Winthrop was an intellectual, a gentleman, and an art collector. He doesn't know why Mr. Winthrop treated his daughters as he did.

A man who lived in the village of Lenox and worked at a garage recalls, "Mr. Winthrop was a nice man. He must have had a reason. I just don't know what it was. One night the Misses Winthrop couldn't get anyone to drive them, and they wanted to go out to dinner, so they called me. They asked if I would take them. Mr. Winthrop went with us. He rode along, he asked if I would go back for them at a specified hour, and he rode with me to pick them up."

Some say that his wife died in childbirth, and he feared if his daughters married, the same fate would befall them. Some say Mrs. Winthrop died insane and her husband sought to stop the insanity with her generation by precluding the daughters from marrying. One who speaks as if he knows says that the doctor who treated Mrs. Winthrop in a psychiatric institution told Mr. Winthrop to prevent the girls from marriage and childbearing to avoid their mother's fate. A contemporary and friend of the sisters says that all the rumors have some grain of truth. Mrs. Winthrop suffered a postpartum depression from which she never recovered and it deepened into a chronic condition. Mr. Winthrop sought both to avoid insanity in future generations and to protect his daughters. Understanding of mental disturbance was in its infancy, and he did receive advice and guidance that encouraged his behavior.

The elopement of Kate and Emily Winthrop made the front page of the ***New York Herald Tribune*** and most other papers. They married who they knew—the chauffeur and the poultry man. (At Groton Place they kep chickens, this man was hired to tend them.) It was a shock to everyone that these closely guarded ladies married at all, but it was a scandal that they married beneath them.

Miss Anna Alexandre, daughter of the builder of Spring Lawn, a Lenox cottage, and a contemporary of the girls recalls, "Oh, when they married there were headlines, and they were big black ones. No one could talk of anything else."

One of the marriages, that to the chicken man, was very successful. They lived in Richmond and raised horses. You can still rent a horse and carriage from their farm. The other marriage ended in divorce. For years after, the rumors continued to fly. The daughter whose marriage was successful had been disinherited, and the other daughter reunited with her father when she left the chauffeur. Contrarily it was written that the successful marriage was accepted by Mr. Winthrop when the first grandchild was born, and the other daughter was disinherited. The only ones who didn't care who inherited or who didn't, were the daughters. Each was a millionairess in her own right by inheritances from their mother and paternal grandmother. In fact Grenville Winthrop's will states, "I give, devise, bequeath and appoint any and all property over which I have the power of appointment... to divide the same into two equal shares..." for his daughters Kate and Emily.

Issues of sanity and marriage played roles in another family drama in the cottages. Amy Bend was one of the few women to appear on the list of Four Hundred without her father or mother also appearing. She was a young woman of quality and beauty. When she married Cortlandt Field Bishop, it was a romantic match of beauty, adventure, and wealth. The commentators on Society, said at the time their marriage would be a continuous Grand Tour. When Beatrice was born, the daughter became a co-traveler to the amazement of Victorian ladies.

In ***A Life in Two Worlds,*** Beatrice Bishop Berle tells her own story, but before the book was published, it was the subject of many a whispered tale.

Courtesy of Miss Anna Alexandre

Miss Anna Alexandre (left) fishing at the Mahkeenac Boat Club, 1904

Photography by Carole Owens

Groton Place,
the Grenville Winthrop cottage

"Imagine," it frequently began, "a mother who would not speak to her own daughter."

We live in a psychological world where understanding of the mysteries of mental strain or disorder are common subjects over lunch. That was not always the case. When Beatrice consulted a relative and prominent psychiatrist, Austen Riggs, about her mother's behavior, it was a scandal. To accept that anything might be wrong with her, was counter to everything Amy Bend Bishop knew or understood. The situation was tense beyond any fictional melodrama of the day, but the daughter was not disowned until she married.

Interestingly, the discrimination, that was so much a part of the maintenance of social position, ruled against Adolph Berle. Interesting, because Adolph Berle was a member of Franklin Delano Roosevelt's "Brain Trust," an ambassador, assistant secretary of state and an acknowledged contributor to plans to lift America out of the Depression. The social 'cut' was practiced in the world of The Gilded Age. When the wrong was egregious enough, the person was cut, that is, that person no longer existed. Beatrice Berle was married without her parents present and neither ever spoke to her again. Dr. Beatrice Berle, who became a psychiatrist, had not only lived in two worlds, but, as she lived at a time of social transition and was an exceptional woman, her life foreshadowed the changes to come in America.

Whether or not these ingenious people were "only rich"—duplicitous and classless—who had to import culture from Europe and marry good breeding and good family names; with the perspective of a hundred years, we know they formed a tradition which is now our heritage. The judgments and the criticisms are a mere whine—irritating but almost inaudible—against the roar of the accomplishments. You cannot make a call, go to work, plan a trip, turn on a light to read a book or turn off a light to watch your television or a movie, listen to a radio weather report in order to decide whether to put snow tires on the family car, without bowing to the past and to those who invented it. Regardless of the judgments leveled over the years, two facts stand out: they could do it and they did do it. That is perhaps the most instructive reason that they built country seats in the Berkshires. They were a people that had the freedoms of burgeoning technology, a spirit of invention, and great wealth. They had education, energy, and optimism. The combination made a great deal possible; it was the age of the possible. The patriarchs of these distinguished families built forever. The country house was a family asset to be passed down intact from generation to generation. Ownership was a solid and absolute state of things that twenty-thousand word wills regulated.

Today, a scant one hundred years later, very little is left. What is, is transformed. They built for all time and like Ozymandias crumbling in the desert, what they built is now demolished, destroyed, transformed. It makes some of us smug: the symbols of their wealth and power are crumbling. It makes others sad: their lives and those symbols also had the trappings of fantasy and that fantasy intrigues us. Upon reflection, neither quick emotional response is satisfying. The considered response is that their loss is our loss. They were builders not just of houses but of commerce, transportation, communication. They were the policymakers and the makers of pictures and verse. They were, for all their faults and prejudices and triumphs and contributions, our heritage. We cannot dismiss them without dismissing our own history.

Courtesy of the Berkshire Eagle

Library, Groton Place

3

TO THE MANOR BROUGHT

The Vanderbilt divorce seems to have stirred to their depths not only the 400 but the 400,000…

Joseph H. Choate:
Letter, March 5, 1895

hen the city officials changed the drive through Central Park from a two-way to a one-way street, Mrs. Emily Thorn Vanderbilt Sloane White of New York City and Lenox, responded with great energy and disapproval. In fact she took it personally. "But," she sputtered, "how will one wave to one's friends if they cannot pass in the other direction?"

When Alva divorced William Kissam Vanderbilt in New York City, it was news on the front page of every paper from the ***New York Times*** to midwestern weeklies a thousand miles away. The settlement figures were tossed around and debated with more energy than is necessary to discuss national defence spending. And the search for the name of Mr. Vanderbilt's correspondent was approached as seriously as a search for the mother lode.

It is easy to treat the cottagers simply as a source of entertainment, but to understand any one of the Berkshire cottagers individually, it is helpful to understand the Gilded Age aristocrats as a group. The wealth amassed by these people was so outrageous that it was consistent to believe any story about them no matter how outrageous. Furthermore, they were the accepted arbiters of taste; they set the standard. Regardless, and perhaps because of, the fact that the standard was unattainable by the average person, the public was hungry for every scrap of news. Everything the power elite of the Gilded Age did was of national interest.

The elite were not unaware of the impact they had. In fact they expended their vast resources in a concerted effort to impress. At the same time, Mrs. Hamilton McKown Twombly, Emily Thorn's sister, selected footmen who were tall and efficient enough to stand around her, in a carefully planned configuration, so that no one could catch a glimpse of her when she went out in public. On December 26, 1893, Anson Phelps Stokes wrote in his journal:

> Costume dinner dance at our house which about 120 were present. Newton had arranged with a Boston photographer to take a photograph of this dinner (of course not for publication). Newton had been at a private fancy dress ball in Boston where this man had been employed. The next day, the photographer came and told me that while he was at lunch, a copy had been stolen and taken to the ***New York Herald,*** which was going to publish it. I had grippe and could not leave the house, but sent Newton to the office of the newspaper where he was told that it had already been printed. John E. Parsons, Esq., the eminent lawyer succeeded, however, in stopping the publication by

firmly notifying the publishers of the paper that the publication would be against my wishes and against my rights.[1]

Since Newton was his son, Anson trusted him. Betrayed, by accident or design of the photographer, Anson asked John E. Parsons to correct the matter. Parsons was not just any lawyer. He was the owner of a neighboring Berkshire cottage, Stonover; the second husband of Mrs. David Wolfe Bishop who owned another cottage in the neighborhood, Interlaken. By that mariage, Parsons became the stepfather of Cortlandt Field Bishop of the Winter Palace, Lenox. He was a friend and a social peer, a man who would understand the gravity of the situation. If time and energy, imagination and funds, were expended to set standards of taste and impress others by the standards set, why was publication of a veritable picture of success against Mr. Stokes' wishes? Why would Florence Vanderbilt Twombly deny the public a glimpse of the splendor in dress and equipage that she had sought to attain? While only the achievement of an elegant lifestyle could put you into the social register, publicity about that achievement could expunge your name. The Gilded Age aristocrats, as a group, performed only for one another.

American Architect and Building News

Salon at Bellefontaine 1899

American Architect and Building News

Dining Room at Bellefontaine 1899

Courtesy of Jane Foster Lorber

Entrance Hall at Bellefontaine 1899

It was November, 1981. The afternoon sun cast long shadows across the beautifully proportioned living room. It was fitting to note the proportions since the builder, Charles Astor Bristed, once said that although Lakeside was not the largest of the Berkshire cottages, it was the best proportioned. In 1894, ***The New York Times*** described Lakeside as, "One of the finest cottages being built in Lenox this season . . . Its dimensions are 120 by 80 feet. The architecture is of the colonial style. The interior finish will be very much like other cottages, having hardwood floors, oak ceilings in the halls, and oak and mahogany in the finishing of the other rooms. The main hall is large and well lighted and will have a handsomely carved staircase."[2] Sitting in the living room eighty-eight years later, the setting was unchanged as was the ownership. Charles Astor Bristed's daughter had been discussing her experiences in the Berkshire cottages, and those of her friends and relatives. Then she paused and said, "I don't think this is terribly interesting, do you?"

The question is asked by a direct descendant of John Jacob Astor on one side and Theodore Sedgwick on the other. With her lineage assured regardless of the criteria used, her question hangs in the air. No one answers. No one presses the question. The gulf silently widens between one who can remember a certain lifestyle, and one who can only imagine. It is the gulf between one who believes in, and was shaped by, a way of life, and one who only seeks to write about it. The question is never answered, the moment passes, and the interview continues.

The question hadn't really been offered for the purpose of eliciting an answer. She knew the answer. It was a red herring foisted into the machinery with the hope of jamming it. The great granddaughter of John Jacob Astor still reflected and was motivated by the values of an age past; by a social rule that stated, "A lady's name appears in print only three times in her life: when she is born, when she marries, and when she dies." The habit of protection that motivated Mr. Stokes and Mrs. Twombly, lived on in this small, elegant woman long after the age and most of its participants were dead. What was it that had motivated them? What were the rules of the social elite, and what was the dear prize that assured adherence even years later?

Before the Civil War, a millionaire was rare in America. Many who had wealth were landed and had made their money through agriculture. The United States was not viewed by the rest of the world as a power or even a particularly enviable civilization. In the thirty years after the Civil War, there was significant change. Four thousand and forty seven millionaires emerged in the United States. Only eighty-four of those millionaires had amassed their fortunes through agriculture. The new breed was engaged in industry, trade, railroads, real estate, and banking. Not an aristocracy in the strict sense, they were surely a plutocracy.

The simplest definition of power is the ability to exercise your will over the resistance of others. By direct control or captivation, these families had power. They touched and changed every aspect of American life. The new plutocrats were the masters and directors of the economic revolution that was changing the face of America. Externally, they intended to transform America from a mere country cousin to a world leader. The very rhetoric of politics, the law, and religion supported their efforts and viewpoint.

Courtesy of Jane Foster Lorber

Library at Bellefontaine

When Charles Darwin set out in the Beagle, his intention was to explain the origin of the species not their interactions. When Herbert Spencer applied Darwin's biological theories to man and his society, he articulated the philosophical underpinnings for this powerful incursion into every aspect of American life. Spencer's works, 368,000 volumes, sold in the United States far more than in his native England. Americans found special fascination in Herbert Spencer's work. They recognized the industrial struggle around them as a struggle for survival. They readily accepted that survival was at stake and that natural selection had awarded the most to the best specimens among them.

Spencer applied biological concepts, especially the concept of natural selection, to social principles and justified the unimpeded struggle for existence on the ground that 'survival of the fittest' made for human progress.[3]

Henry Ward Beecher was a well-known Presbyterian minister and writer of his day. His pulpit was Brooklyn's Plymouth Church, and he had a country house, Blossom Farm, in Lenox. He applauded Spencer's Social Darwinism. He wrote to Herbert Spencer, "The peculiar condition of American society has made your writings far more fruitful and quickening here than in Europe."[4] Beecher, like many of his colleagues, had found Social Darwinism a handy philosophy to explain the religious right of the rich to their riches: God had rewarded the most fit with the most wealth. The theory was doubly useful in that it not only deified the rich, it vilified the poor: the poor were so because of their unfitness.

For all their unimpeded forward motion and power, the super rich still had a problem. Somehow their new status, and the nation's, had to be represented. Proud, wealthy, optimistic, and energetic, they dotted the landscape with the symbols of their newfound stature. They were inveterate builders. To quote Russell Lynes, in ***The Tastemakers***, they were men and women "to whom display and ostentation were a highly competitive game... They invested more money in the erection of dwellings as any of the royal families of Europe, the Bourbons excepted."[5] The word game should not be misunderstood; it was deadly serious. The reward for winning was power and prestige. They were following the great economic theorist, Max Weber, whose dictum was that although economic power is the result of how much money one accumulates, status and social honor can only be acquired by how the money is spent.

In 1901, Andrew Carnegie published ***The Gospel of Wealth***. In it he laid ground rules for spending. He said that wealth was to be

Courtesy of the Lenox Library

Drawing Room of Ventfort Hall

used first to sustain oneself and set an example, and next "to provide modestly for the legitimate wants of those dependent upon him." The excess was seen as a sacred trust "which he is called upon to administer in the manner, that in his best judgement, is best calculated to produce the most beneficial results for the community—a man of wealth thus becoming the mere trustee and agent for his poor brethern, bringing to their service his superior wisdom, experience and ability to administer, doing for them better than they would or could do for themselves."[6]

Carnegie voiced the class obligation of the blessed for the lesser classes. The result was that all the things a twentieth-century person thinks of as publicly owned and paid for by taxes, were privately granted. Noblesse oblige created museums, universities, hospitals, parks, schools, and libraries.

Carnegie did not, however, overlook "the first duty of a man of wealth"; the responsibility to provide for his own style of living. Carnegie ended his treatise by accepting his wealth as his by right of superiority. He accepted, as did Beecher and the church, the government and the people, the right to be rich. That was the necessary underpinning that allowed for the colossal show of wealth that created the summer colonies of Stockbridge and Lenox. The wealth was an acknowledged badge of superiority. It certainly was not to be hidden, but in a variety of ways to be conspicuously expended. Among other houses, Carnegie purchased the hundred-room summer cottage, Shadow Brook. He and his peers not only provided for the community, they built into their own houses, for personal use, all the things we think of as public spaces—ballrooms, museums, libraries, squash courts, art galleries, music rooms, school rooms, bowling alleys, tennis courts, formal gardens, and sufficient dining and sleeping space for a respectable inn. The elite had taken the first steps toward solving the problem of how to create an American aristocracy.

Drawing Room of Wheatleigh

Courtesy of the Lenox Library

Wealth was a consideration, but money seemed a capricious and thoughtless child running to the lap of some, deserting others. The old families did not necessarily become the "right families." Fate discovered the granddaughter of a signer of the Declaration of Independence sniffing into her mended handkerchief over the fact that ***The*** Mrs. Astor was "three generations from a trader!" Yet Mrs. Caroline Schermerhorn Astor was the Grand Dame of New York Society, and she was excluded.[7] If the nouveau riche had no problem that one generation would not solve, and if the fine houses and the money to build them was not the whole initiation rite, how did one get membership and exclude others? To the members of that society at that moment, houses were important but not sufficient. In fact the bald expenditure of money was not enough. An aristocracy had to be a closed circle of special people. There had to be stringent rules for inclusion and exclusion.

Loggia at Brookside

Courtesy of Mr. John Nichols

Thorstein Veblen published ***The Theory of the Leisure Class*** in 1899. Veblen was never a man to be entertained in the halls or by the people whose lifestyle he sought to explain. Born on a Wisconsin farm, Veblen was ultimately a critic of the aristocrats, but first he was a keen observer. He was less interested in establishing the right of a superior class to amass wealth than he was in observing how they spent it and why. Veblen's premise was that once there is ownership, there is the ability to accumulate goods. Public esteem is directly associated with accumulation. The more one accumulates, the more esteem one is awarded. The result is a competition for the accumulation and the winners are due the most esteem.

The basis on which any good repute in any highly organized in-

Courtesy of Mr. John Nichols

Dining Room at Brookside

Courtesy of Mr. John Nichols

Music Room at Brookside

Entrance Hall at Brookside

Courtesy of Mr. John Nichols

dustrial community ultimately rests is pecuniary strength; and the means of showing pecuniary strength, and so of gaining or retaining a good name, are leisure and a conspicuous consumption of goods.[8]

If good repute rested on how you spent your money, consumption was not the light, fanciful, ignominious, nor faintly amusing business it has been reported to be. It was serious—and it was tricky—business. The goods conspicuously consumed had to be valuable and tasteful.

> He [the man of wealth] was no longer simply the successful, aggressive male... In order to avoid stultification he must also cultivate his tastes, for it now becomes incumbent upon him to discriminate with some nicety between the noble and the ignoble in consumer goods.[9]

Mr. Southmayd was wrong when he instructed Joseph Choate that it was sufficient and proper to accumulate and hold onto his money, and Joseph Choate Knew it. (See p. 217) Indeed, it was not

Courtesy of Mr. John Nichols

Formal Garden at Brookside

enough to accumulate and spend money. Everyone who was anyone—or hoped to be—was involved in what Edith Wharton called "the complex art of civilized living."[10] ***How*** you lived was as important as where, and was indistinguishable from who you were and whether you fit in. In order to garner public regard, one had to accumulate, discriminatingly consume, and "then put it in evidence."[11] It was easy to become overly enthusiatic and miss the point exactly as Mrs. Westinghouse of Erskine Park did when she folded a hundred dollar bill into the napkin of each of her dinner guests. Mrs. Westinghouse put it in evidence, but sometimes one just got it wrong. The penalty was stultification and embarrassment. These two were to be judicially avoided as was the third of the sins, notoriety. The public was not the proper judge of acumen; the guests at dinner, your peers, must judge. All rules governing the conduct of the wealthy and the display of wealth were pointed at one aim: to establish an American aristocracy.

Given that the esteem of an individual was dependent upon his social position and social acceptance, the list of The Four Hundred acceptable guests takes on a new meaning. When Ward McAllister made his list, it is said, several thousand New York matrons took to their couches swooning in shock and depression. Who was in and who was out (or in this case, who was on the list and who was off) was no small matter. In 1893, when Ward McAllister published The Four Hundred, he thought he had uttered a last word in social acceptance. But in late 1700s, Mrs. John Jay had written her "Dinner List." There was almost no duplication of names on the two lists.

Mrs. Jay's list represented the American First Families; the families who had made their money and their mark prior to the Civil War. It was they who were visited and invited to Mrs. Jay's home to dine on the delicate white imported china with the tiny gray flowers and the gold intertwined double-Js in the center. In a truly stratified society with an aristocracy extant, how long one had money and how long it had been since one actually worked for it, were more important than the money itself. From Mrs. Jay's list to Ward McAllister's list, only four generations had elapsed. Even in so short a time, compared with the longevity of European aristocracies, the lists did not repeat.

Moreover, the men who amassed the great wealth in America, worked for it. As they were building their palaces, they still worked. If you had enough money and the desire to enter Society in America, given time, you could do it. Without the traditional process of status being determined by bloodline; money, and the appearance of being a lady or gentleman, was enough to make one a lady or gentleman, but it was not enough to exclude others. The idea of an American aristocracy was a vital goal, and it

Entrance Hall at Brookhurst

Courtesy of Mr. Stephen Morris

Library and Bedroom at Brookhurst

Courtesy of Mr. Stephen Morris

Architect's rendering of Stonover

Courtesy of the Providence Library

was unattainable.

For all the folderol, Americans did not originate aristocracy, they borrowed it. Like a borrowed article of clothing, it didn't quite fit. One made do. The clothes, the art, the architecture, the professions of landscape and building architects were copied or brought from Europe. Still, when the treasures and symbols were set down on American soil, there was an uneasy tension: the feudal lord, the king, were not the historic bulwark of the American aristocracy, but the Constitution and the Fourteenth Amendment. They could amass wealth and accumulate material symbols of civilization. They could exhibit discriminating taste by buying Worth gowns and Brewster carriages, creating Olmsted gardens and country seats, but they could not create a class of noblemen whose status was assured by birth. They could not borrow from Europe that which would assure their status, so a Yankee lady from Stockbridge grumbled at the "silliness and the waste," even the comedy, of several liveried footmen "loafing around Bellefontaine when a single efficient maid might have done as well."

At no time was the tension between families in social position and families trying to assume a position resolved. Even the "old" families lost some of their resolve to exclude the nouveau riche and married them. If Ward McAllister's misconception about his list was folly, it was a folly shared by a whole upper class. Each new elite believed in himself. Each new composition of social upper crust fought against the new insurgents, and each failed. But it made the process no less real, nor the power of the ruling elite any less powerful. It was only that it was for the moment, and change was certain. The fluidity of the upper class made the ability to determine membership in the group difficult. The answer was the

Courtesy of the Lenox Library

A Four-in-Hand driven by Mrs. Field of Highlawn House with her parents, Mr. & Mrs. W. D. Sloane of Elm Court, in rear seat

creation of a complex array of rules to govern social behavior. It turned the members of the world of the visited and the invited into masters of nuance, adherents to style in both dress and manner. Speech was an indication of station not simply a means of communication. The rules were very clear to everyone who belonged to the status circle, and persuasive enough to still affect the behavior of a great grandchild on a November day in the twentieth century. The whole complex system of manners and expenditures were meant to close the magic circle of the American aristocracy to the unwanted. Finally, with this last bit of rigor added to all the rules governing the display of wealth, the plutocracy hoped to close ranks and create a solid and distinct Society even absent the expedient of class by birth.

A woman with whom one could spend many an enjoyable afternoon, as much for her own wit and charm as for her impressive relatives who include Franklin Delano Roosevelt and Henry James, tries to explain membership in this exclusive group.

"There was a social prescription—what was expected."

The interviewer hastens to ask for the exact elements of the prescription.

"Good behavior was the order of the day, but it was completely natural. Not put on in any way." She answers. "[Others] didn't know the rules of the game. [The members of society] spoke differently —a sort of lingo of the class. Others copied it. It was a very select company of people. They didn't have to feel embarrassed before Queen Victoria or anyone. They were perfectly capable."

She is having some difficulty specifying, not because she doesn't know the rules of social acceptability, but because she knows them so well. They were woven naturally into her everyday life, and it is difficult for her to pick the individual threads out of the pattern.

"Clothes, of course. Some made their valet wear their clothes for a while [so they wouldn't appear too new]—shabby chic in the country." She tries it the other way around, "I would have known almost at once if someone didn't belong. There was a nervousness. How he spoke and what he said."

Courtesy of Mrs. Adele Emory

Mrs. W. D. Sloane feeding her poodle, Cocoa, buttered toast, 1905 (Elm Court in rear)

It was all form. Not form without substance; the form was the substance. If all the specific indicators of class evade the lady, the core of the issue does not.

"I could tell in five seconds of being introduced if one belonged. The servants—they could tell in three."

"Oh, yes. I could do that," a former servant says. What would he look for? "Oh, it's in the manner and the approach."

After he had retired, the former servant was offered an unusual proposition by a cottager.

"He was a brilliant man—graduate of Harvard—studied abroad and all. His wife—he tried to make me believe she was this and that. I thought, 'who are you kiddin'?' Then ***she*** came to me, and she wanted me to teach her the manners I had learned from my experience in the grand houses. I had to tell her how to sit—back straight, both feet on the floor of course, and hands in the lap—and walk. Some had such a regal walk." He sighs. "All the while, you had to look like you knew what you were doing. Dinner manners, yes. Clothes, of course. You could always tell from the fit and the fabric, of course. I had to teach her practically everything."

The etiquette books of the period were articulate on this important subject of "the best society."

> There are many in our best society that resemble the saying: "One man is born as good as another, and a great deal better than some." This assertion has a foundation in one of the great truths . . . [some] acquire a aire [sic] of dignity and distinction . . . they really offer a higher standard of elegance and culture . . . encourage an improvement in manners and stimulate the growth and spread of refined taste.[12]

The book then fills 567 pages describing acceptable behavior in

Courtesy of Mrs. Adele Emory

The Hammond sisters in a buckboard at Elm Court, 1905

every conceivable situation including a section headed "Immortal Life." It does not describe acceptable behavior in heaven, the section purports to know how you get there. The angle of the extended hand, the changing position of a lady's eyes as the subjects of conversation change, the proper way to remove yourself from the dinner table are described, justified, and the consequences of error are spelled out. It was no laughing matter. It was a time when far from a dirty word, discrimination was a virtue sought.

"They were protecting a way of life that was terribly pleasant. I approve of the change," she explains at the end of the interview, "but when we rebelled against and progressed past the nineteenth-century social prescriptions, we both gained and lost. We lost a way of life and values, now all we can do is remember. It is terribly interesting."

Mr. & Mrs. W. D. Sloane
at Elm Court
(Man on the right unidentified)

Courtesy of William O. Field

So in the late afternoon, a cousin of FDR and Henry James inadvertently answers a descendant of John Jacob Astor when on another afternoon the latter had asked, "I don't think this is terribly interesting, do you?"

We can satisfy ourselves that we had, in fact, an American aristocracy. Whether you define it as the literary and political contributors of this country amassing or marrying wealth at one point in our history or whether you are satisfied that wealth itself can form an aristocracy, authorities agree we had one. Its reign was brief, because at the same time in America's history that Social Darwinism supported the aristocracy, William James' theory of Pragmatism found a following; as new factories formed so did labor unions. The social fabric was not quite as uniform as it may seem when perceived from a distance. Distance tends to blur features and soften differences. In fact, the aristocracy could not go on intact. The eventual dissolution of the Society of the Gilded Age

Courtesy of the Lenox Library

Mr. Giraud Foster
at home at Bellefontaine

Two views of the library at Elm Court taken in 1910 by W.B.O. Field

Courtesy of Mr. William C. Field

was built in.

William Dean Howells wrote about the aristocracy: "Until very recently we had no such class, and we rather longed for it. We thought it would edify us, or, if not that, at least ornament us; but now that we have got it, on certain terms, we can hardly be sure it does either."[13] Seemingly dubious about the value of an American upper class, he went on to say that, "This is the most dramatic moment, the most psychological moment which has ever offered itself to fiction." Howells, Dean of American Letters, critic, poet, prolific writer, was suggesting that the best possible subject for the great American novel was the American aristocracy: "I should be content if he [the author of the proposed work] would portray the life of our leisure class... he would appeal to the widest general interest... Our appetite for everything that relates to the life removed from the life of work is almost insatiable."[14]

Howells correctly reflected the dual nature of the American attitude toward Society. Unclear if it had any merit or had edified the country in any way, he was anxious to know every tidbit about how they lived. Howells who considered the upper class the best subject for the great American novel, also wrote a poem wherein the "lordly men and women" danced upon a polished floor that covered over and was supported by the writhing bodies of millions of suffering and dying people. The duality was not to be resolved. Not in America. The upper class was at once disdained and sought after. Aristocracy was not to flourish in American soil. The speed, the progress, the readiness for change, all supported by the upper class, undid it. If America has a truly native equivalent, it is not a borrowed aristocracy, but our own homegrown celebrity. No American was "to the manner born," and without that biological assurance of social stratification, wealth, acquisition, and ritualized social intercourse were doomed to fail the ultimate test. But for some forty years, "lordly men and women" believed no less in their own power and the power of the rules they had set down. They danced in the city mansions and country cottages on the polished wood floors that testified to their exclusivity and discrimination.

4

DISCRIMINATING DIVERSIONS

No more fiendish punishment could be devised than that one should be turned loose in society and remain absolutely unnoticed by all the members thereof.

William James
The Principles of Psychology

ntertainments were quite serious because they established worth, identity, and station. The social events were the place wherein one's presence, manners, taste, and pecuniary strength were tested and attested to, and rank was established. Everyone knew where he fit in and what those all important rules of conduct were. Almost all upper crust humor was based on that common understanding. The turn of the phrase was funny when it elucidated the obvious condition of things. A story that was funny when told for the first time at the turn of the century, did not produce so much as a grin when it was retold over eighty years later at a tour of The Mount, now the Edith Wharton Restoration in Lenox:

> Mr. Wharton, late for a dinner in Newport, hopped a ride on a milk wagon. He was seen doing so by a nouveau riche. The young man said to Wharton later, "If I were you, I wouldn't have done that." Mr. Wharton replied, "I wouldn't have done that, if I were you."

Each person knew his position and its relative position. The lower the rung on the social ladder, the more careful one had to be of doing the right thing. Mr. Wharton turned a phrase that made the obvious clear and devasted a man trying to criticize him. In short, Wharton put each of them in their relative social places.

It was a simple society—small, closed, blessed, and powerful—meant to go on forever. They attended the same schools, colleges, clubs, and churches. One summered where others did, and went to Europe "in season." If you belonged, you went where and when you would find your peers. All went to the "best places," the definition of which was rather circular. Places were the best because the best people were there, and if the best people were there, those became de facto the best places. To be excluded from membership in the social circle was to be excluded from a whole way of life. One only ***knew*** the right people; they were the only ones present. Business and politics were conducted with those who were there. It was a matter of material, spiritual, and psychological well-being to be, literally, inside the right place at the right time.

It is not surprising then to find so many of the social elite together in the Berkshires. Of course we cannot expect to find everyone of prominence in the last century in permanent residence in the Berkshires. Some only visited. Others, born there, departed. Marshall Field, for example, left the Berkshires in 1856 to make his fortune in Chicago, although he credited his five year's experience as a clerk in Deacon H. G. Davis' dry goods store in

The Mount

Pittsfield for his later success. Still, one long time resident and member of the summer colony's old guard believes, "My dear, everyone in the world came here. Berkshire County. We knew everyone would be here sooner or later." By everyone, she really means the members of the club. For a time and in the country, they came together and did all the aristocratic things they could think of with élan and a serious appreciation that social regard hung in the balance.

Given the general demeanor of the nineteenth-century Society, it is no surprise to find that the entertainments rigidly followed the clock, the calendar, and convention. Social events were not unlike Worth gowns. Charles Frederick Worth was born in England in 1825. At twenty years of age, he went to Paris as a shop assistant selling dress goods. He never left. From 1858 until his death in 1895, Worth ruled fashion in Paris; to rule fashion in Paris was to rule fashion in the world. Called the founder of haute couture, his dresses were lavish and fanciful creations. Each dress was exquisite and so expensive that ***Harper's Bazaar*** called him "the arch demoralizer of women." Each gown was also apparently unique, but that is the point at which his gowns become an analogy for the social events to which they were worn. "Worth established a system of standard interchangeable components so that one pattern piece could be used for innumerable designs."[1] Regardless of the surface differences, the underlying structure of the social life followed the accepted pattern. Individual expression when entertaining was tolerated, and even applauded, but only if it was decoration of, not divergence from, the pattern.

Part of the secret charm of the country was the latitude allowed in diverging. Young ladies did ride across the Berkshire Hills with young gentlemen unchaparoned, a thing unheard of in the city. The demand for formality was less stringent in the country, but in the country, as in the city, the pattern held. Sherry's usually catered lawn parties. Tents were pitched for dancing on the lawn. The Mahkeenac Boat Parade, the Lenox Horse Show and the Berkshire Hunt were annual events. Mr. and Mrs. Anson Phelps Stokes had an annual New Year's Eve house party, and notwithstanding the story about the ninety-six house guests, the photos taken at the 1895 and 1896 parties show only thirty-four guests. The cottagers arrived in Lenox and Stockbridge and drove about leaving cards. When they left, they paraded on foot through Stockbridge's Ice Glen or rode through the streets of Lenox in the Tub Parade.

The Tub Parade closed the Lenox season. Parades so precisely suited the gentry, that one critic wrote: "Their chief interest was in parade; parade of horses, carriages, clothing and costly entertainment."[2] Indeed, it was so, but it was not necessarily decadent. The Tub Parade embodied all their love of competition and show and jollity. Coaches, tallyhos, landaus, surreys, carts, and the horses were bedecked with flowers and paraded up and down. They moved at a sedate pace. Judges awarded prizes to the best. Who knows if the best rig was determined by quantity of flowers and equipage or quality, or if quantity was the mark of quality. Fault the cottagers for anything but never for stinting; wheels, harnesses, horses, and ladies all were covered with thousands of flowers grown on the estates. Whether riding or lining the road, everyone was out, to watch or be seen. It was the bidding of farewell to the

Harper's Magazine, September 22, 1886

The Tub Parade

The Casino

Courtesy of the Stockbridge Library

season at Lenox. Until the turn of the century, it was the final production at Lenox and everyone loved it—players and audience.

A contemporary account describes the event:

> The famous Tub Parade of Lenox, in spite of its name, has nothing to do with the lavandieres along the Seine in Paris. It is an array of decorated two-wheeled pony carts equipped and driven by women and children, and is given in September, the last month of the Lenox season, partly that its adornment might include the first glory of the autumnal leafage—the crown of Berkshire Glory. Under the vaulted elms of the village street... the dainty vehicles come trundling along in the wake of brisk little garlanded, cockaded, and beribboned ponies.... Upon the decking of these dainty chariots, and upon the harmonious toilets of their occupants, is bestowed such choice care as to make the whole array seem fit for the marriage of some prince of elf land. At a given signal from the marshal on horseback, the procession is set in motion... the charioteers meeting afterwards for tea and compliments in the drawing room of one of their leaders.[3]

The equivalent in Stockbridge to the Tub Parade was a parade through Ice Glen at night. Ice Glen is so called because it is sheltered and remote enough for ice to remain there even in August. In 1895, the Ice Glen Parade was described by a participant as follows:

> In point of seniority, the Ice Glen Procession at Stockbridge, Massachusetts, and the Tub Parade at Lenox should be awarded first place among the festival pageants undertaken and carried out by the cultivated class of society. We drove over to "the loveliest village of the plain" from Lenox, her rival loveliest village of the hills, to rendezvous at night fall with a gay party of people in fancy costume, in an open grassy space at the entrance

> to the glen. . . . The host of revellers was marshaled, I remember, by a fair leader clad in stars and stripes wearing a liberty cap and carrying a long alpenstock tipped with an American flag. In no ballroom, under no gas or lamp or candlelight, could have been produced the effect of that fantastic group of torch-bearers among the scattered boulders at the mouth of the glen. . . . A procession being formed, led by a band of musicians, we penetrated the forest gloom . . . the scene was wonderfully fine. The Parade ended with a bonfire.[4]

In an 1890 journal entry, Anson Phelps Stokes recreates his season at Lenox.

> I was elected director of the Lenox Club and president of the Mahkeenac Boat Club and vestryman in Trinity Church, Lenox. We greatly enjoyed ourselves at Lenox. . . .
>
> Col. Auchmuty had long led the flower parade which had become a notable annual function at Lenox but when he could no longer ride, I had, at his suggestion, been appointed to lead which I did for a number of years. . . . The ladies, assisted by the gentlemen friends, dressed their village carts with flowers in much taste.
>
> This was a very good autumn at Lenox—probably the greatest season they ever had there. We got a tent from New York to use as a dancing room for a ball which we gave at Homestead.[5]

Mr. Stokes social position in Lenox is attested to by the formal positions he was awarded. Following his own dictum, "when in the country Episcopalian," he was vestryman of the Trinity Church. He was also marshal of the Tub Parade. He pitched his striped tent on the back lawn of Homestead, the house built by the Appleton sisters that he rented before building Shadow Brook, and danced with his guests on the lawn and ate a feast prepared by Sherry's. Not only a member of the Lenox Club, he was named a director.

The Lenox Club was the mandatory country counterpart of the city club. A gentleman had to be "proposed by one stockholder and seconded by another." A single "black ball" excluded him. The club offered golf and tennis and a place for gentlemen to gather. "No games of hazard, faro, loo, poker, or any other round or banking game or any game which the Board of Governors shall interdict, shall be played in the Clubhouse; nor shall any game of any description whatever be permitted on the premises on Sunday; and the house shall be closed at 12 P.M. every night, unless ordered to be kept open for special occasions by the Board of Governors."[6]

The Club had an annual July 4th luncheon which Anson Phelps Stokes recalls in his journal as both impossible to avoid and equally impossible to suffer through.

The Stockbridge counterpart was perhaps the Casino, but it was less exclusive and was more of a tea house, dance hall, theater, and place to annually exhibit art. Golf was as popular in Stockbridge as it was in Lenox. But while the tennis courts were on the grounds of the Casino, the gold course was down Main Street. Women went to the Casino in the afternoons for tea. It was not a place reserved for men. It more resembled the functions served by Sedgwick Hall in Lenox, now the town library, than the Lenox Club. Far from offering the tedious luncheons Anson Phelps Stokes describes, the Casino offered light entertainment.

The Casino was built in 1887 by Messers. Choate and David Dudley Field. The architect was Stanford White. As it was being completed, an editorial appeared in the local press warning that dissipation as a result of the presence of a "casino" in Stockbridge could only be avoided by prudency. The editor hoped that demoralization which was the result of too much gaiety and entertaining would be avoided. Margaret (Peggy) French Cresson of Chesterwood saved a program from the Casino dated 1913 and written by Frank Crowninshield of Konkaput Brook, Stockbridge, and ***Vanity Fair*** magazine, New York. Not an example of the wit and sophistication for which "Crownie" was known, the program perhaps captures the spirit of the Casino, and gives insight into the nature of the feared gaiety and entertainment.

> The Salome dance has been omitted owing to the tender sensibilities of some of our eldest families.... The President of the Casino is in the audience!!! Let there be no loud or boisterous laughter!!... [The program lists nine offereings, the fourth is titled "Rip's Return."] A heart rendering interpretation of Mr. Van Winkle's reappearance in town after a twenty-year slumber in Ice Glen. By special request of the Ladies, Mr. Van Winkle will be unaccompanied by a dog. [Confident perhaps that the show was superior to the program, Crowninshield closes.] Good Night. Thank you for your dollars.

Social gatherings in the country were often out-of-doors, and centered around the popular sports of tennis, golf, riding, hunting, boating, croquet, fishing, the gymkhana, and dog and horse

Courtesy of Mrs. Olivia Stokes Hatch

The Shadow Brook Boat House on Lake Mahkeenac

The Gymkhana at Tanglewood

Courtesy of the Berkshire Eagle

shows. As the Tub Parade was supplanted by the Berkshire Hunt, so the Ice Glen Procession was replaced by the Lake Mahkeenac Boat Parade. The Berkshire Hunt was a typical fox hunt over the rolling hills of various estates including Highlawn, Bellefontaine, Blantyre and Overleigh. The horse shows might include both saddle horses and carriages. The Hunt and the Mahkeenac Boat Parade soon closed the season, as in past years the Tub and Ice Glen Parades had. The Boat Parade was a waterborne Tub Parade. Boats were decorated with flowers and paraded from the Boat Club around Lake Mahkeenac, now more commonly called Stockbridge Bowl. The water parade was described as "a glimpse of Arcadia: the flowery chain of boats gliding between verdant banks dotted with wild flowers and grazing cattle." A gymkhana is a series of races, and so it was at Tanglewood, but the ladies raced pet pigs and geese and chickens.

Two stylized social rituals were "afternoons at home" and "leaving cards." Mrs. Wilde recalls, "Calling hours were in the afternoon. When my sister and I were little, Mother had horses. The children were sat in the back of the wagon and Mother would go visiting. She liked to take us along because then she didn't have to stay too long. She could say that the children were out in the carriage. You often went and left your card. You did not necessarily want to see anyone. Sometimes you hoped that no one was 'at home' so you could just drop off a card and leave. Calling was the 'etiquette' thing to do."

All cottages had at-home days which they would indicate either by writing the day on the corner of their visiting card or by sending an invitation, one of which read, "Mr. & Mrs. Daniel Chester French will be at home, Wednesday, September 18, 1911, at 4:00, at Chesterwood, to show for the first time Mr. French's latest sculpture, his plaster model of Abraham Lincoln."

A day written on a visiting card indicated a general ongoing welcome to visit on that day. W. D. Sloane was at-home Thursdays and enjoyed squash or golf. Mrs. deHeredia was at-home between 4:00 and 7:00 on Sundays for tea. Like the deHeredia's, one could always drop in at the Field's between 4:00 and 7:00 on the at-home day. However, one knew that tea was served at 5:00. So it was impolite, unless specifically asked for tea, to arrive at 5:00. One came either before or after 5:00.

Cards were left without a visit to indicate arrival or departure in town. In the latter case, the left hand corner of the card was folded over in the European fashion. If there had been a death, the card was bordered in black. Cards were also left as a thank-you for a dinner attended. The rule was that one left a card as soon as possible, usually the following morning, or at least within the week. One card was left for each adult female in the household.

Mr. Morris recalls, "It was a chore. One called it 'leaving cards on,' and it was best to go at 3:00 to assure that the household was out or resting. I once left six cards because there were six women in the household. Everyone laughed. There must have been a limit, and I exceeded it. I think I made a mistake there, had it on my conscience ever since."

Among all the ritualized events, the dinner party was preeminent. There had been something of a Puritan revolt at the beginning of the period that brought city aristocrats to the New England countryside. It had to do with the lateness of the fashionable dinner hour. Ministers preached that a serious rend in the moral fabric was caused by dining at eight. Perhaps the ministers' position can be understood if one thinks of dinner as following a workday, at six. To those believers in the work ethic, late dinners, and late and constant entertainments were the stuff of a leisure class and

Courtesy of the Berkshire Eagle

The Berkshire Hunt

A social gathering on the lawn of Bonnie Brae

Courtesy of Mr. J. Grahm Parsons

therefore suspect. In fact, the gentlemen in America differed very significantly from their European counterparts in that they did work. They toiled less and reaped greater rewards than the many, but the privileged few in America did work. They also favored fashionable entertaining, and ministers who did not preached moral decay as evidenced by late dining. The matter was soon dropped from sermons, and dinner parties continued to begin at eight o'clock.

Stephen Morris was too young a man, during the Gilded Age, to have been invited to a dinner party at Elm Court ordinarily, but he found himself there because a grandson his age was visiting, He recalls the event as "terrifyingly stiff and formal." According to the proper manners, one never turned down a dinner invitation without good cause. The invitation and the response were written. Once accepted, the invitaiton required attendance in all cases short of death. There were rules prescribing the hour that one arrived and took one's leave. There was a protocol for announcing dinner and walking to the dining room. Once at the table, one spoke first to the person seated to one's right and then to the person on one's left. The degree of formality was indicated, in part, by the number of servants.

"Mr. Morris, at a formal dinner at Elm Court, was there really a footman behind every chair?"

Courtesy of Mr. J. Graham Parsons

Boating on Lake Mahkeenac, 1907

"No, not so many as that, but almost, and enough so you never had to do anything for yourself."

Given that as a measure, then Elm Court was even more formal than Bellefontaine, but not by much. No other Berkshire cottage touched those two in the realm of formal dining.

"Although Mrs. deHeredia lived formally at Wheatleigh," Mr. Morris says, "dinner parties there were fun and informal." Comparisons of the cottages are often made now because they were made then. The comparisons underlay the competition. For the loyal footman at Wheatleigh, the issue is that long after the age is dead, gone, and all but memory and ashes, the competition between cottages is still alive, and for Eugene Jappron's money, his lady, Mrs. DeHeredia, has won.

The footman explains, "Why, over there [Elm Court] when Mrs. White was finished eating, that was it, they didn't pass again. At Wheatleigh, we passed and passed until the dish was all gone. Everyone wanted to be invited to Mrs. deHeredia's."

Mrs. Wilde, Emily Sloane White's granddaughter, smiles and says, "I remember grandmother ate awfully fast. And when she had house guests, as soon as she would finish eating, the footman would clear the table and take the dishes away. So, if you were a slow eater, you never got to finish your meal."

Agreement that Wheatleigh was less formal offers a chance to understand the degree of formality and ritual that characterized the entertaining. Olivia Stokes Hatch recalled a dinner party she attended at Wheatleigh. But to understand the events as she did, an introduction to the ritual of the dinner party is useful.

Everyone, from Edith Wharton, at the turn of the century, to Russell Lynes, looking backward in his 1949 book ***The Tastemakers,*** made it clear that society was in a developmental stage from 1880 onward. To possess great wealth without taste and bearing was obscene. That meant rules were necessary. The least desirable behavior was one that offended. The offense might be to a person, or much worse, to the ideal of civilized living. Etiquette books were important because they concretized and left small margin for the developing Society to err. Many etiquette books, respected at the time, dealt seriously and at length with the dinner party because it was the most important of social occasions, the true test of manners, wit, and membership. Here are examples from two books:

> If during a dinner party [there is] an accident, instantly introduce a topic of conversation that will direct the company's attention to a totally foreign subject.[7]

> A master or mistress should refrain from speaking to their servants at dinner, let what will go wrong... No matter what may go wrong, a hostess possessing "savoir vivre" will never seem to notice it. By passing over it herself, it will escape the attention of others very frequently.[8]

Mrs. deHeredia liked to give dinner parties from time to time

Courtesy of the Lenox Library

Two views of the Dining Room at Wheatleigh

for young ladies whom she would have expected to know the rules. At this particular dinner, the then Miss Olivia Stokes looked up and saw a bat on the curtain. Miss Stokes felt it was not a moment to act precipitantly. She felt it was equally important to do something that would result in the bat's removal from the dining room, as it was to do nothing that would create disequilibrium.

Mrs. Lila Sloane Field of Highlawn House driving out to "leave cards"

Courtesy of Mr. William O. Field

After much pantomiming by Miss Stokes, her hostess comprehended the situation. Mrs. deHeredia signaled to the footman.

"Miss Stokes says there is a bat on the curtain," Mrs. deHeredia whispered without looking herself at either the bat or the footman, Eugene Jappron.

"Oh yes, I remember that," he says, and takes over the story as he had that night taken the problem in hand. "Now there is only one way to get a bat out of the house. So first I turned on the lights on the piazza and then turned off the lights in the dining room—but only for a moment—and the bat followed the light out the door and that was that. Oh no, none of the ladies shrieked, they wouldn't have done that. In fact, no one moved. Except that the dining room was dark for a moment, dinner was not interrupted."

Even at Mrs. deHeredia's, no amount of "fun and informality" would have been allowed to interfere with the smooth running of a dinner party. Fun was a result of a congenial mix of people and witty conversation.

No one remembers the conversation as particularly sparkling in Lenox. "Oh, yes, in Stockbridge the conversation was bright, but Stockbridge was always literary. I almost want to say it was dull at

Courtesy of Mr. William O. Field

Afternoon "at home" at Elm Court. 1905

1905 at Elm Court (second from right, Mrs. W.D. [Emily Thorn Vanderbilt] Sloane; extreme right, Joseph Hodges Choate; rear, second from right, Mr. W. D. Sloane)

Courtesy of Mr. William O. Field

dinner in Lenox, but then, it was beautiful to see." The sparkle was in the eye. One dressed for dinner. The dishes, linens, and glassware shone. The choice foods and wines, the liveried servants, and the flower arrangements created the ambiance at the dinner party. The table decorations were often very impressive.

There were flower shows where the women displayed their talents at flower arranging and the extent of their gardens. At one such event in Lenox, the judge was Edith Wharton. There was a carry-over into the houses, where great attention was paid to the attractiveness of the dinner table flowers. Not infrequently, the flowers were not just lovely, but carried a theme appropriate to the guest of honor or purpose of the event. On one such occasion, the great expansiveness and zeal that characterized the age got completely out of hand.

In 1897, President and Mrs. William McKinley were entertained at Wyndhurst by Mr. and Mrs. John Sloane. Anxious to impress their guests of honor, the Sloanes put great effort into the table decoration. It was an elaborate flag and eagle made of flowers on a contraption that, at the right moment, was rigged to rise up and let fly a roman candle or two for the general delight of those present. Unfortunately, Mrs. McKinley was so surprised and impressed when the display of fireworks began that she fainted dead away and had to be carried from the room.

Arriving at Wyndhurst 1897

Courtesy of the Providence Library

A dinner did not necessarily end the evening's entertainment. Most of the cottagers had private ballrooms or could, by means of pitching tents or covering verandas, create one. There was generally a dinner first for the select few followed by the dance for hundreds. If you were not quite as select, your invitation would request the honor of your presence at 11:00 P.M. for dancing and a late supper.

Ladies would arrive and repair upstairs to rooms in which they might rest, change, or freshen up. The men had only a "little wash room behind the stairs." The dance might go on all night and end with a breakfast. Bands were often imported from New York City.

"All the fun was imported," one son of a Stockbridge cottager explains. "We also imported the people to have fun with." The estates hosted the events, and on the nineteenth-century social invention "the weekend," also hosted the participants.

"At Highlawn, the winter weekends were great fun," Mr. Morris recalls, "but, one had to pay the bill by curling with Mr. Field." Curling was a team game played on ice with iron elipsoids called curling stones and brooms.

The cottager had the space to entertain, and the rules in place to help avoid awkwardness. Weekend guests arrived on Friday and left Sunday unless otherwise arranged. While there, they followed the schedule.

Weekends at Elm Court were highly ordered affairs with the name of the guests printed neatly on a white card stuck to the bedroom door and a schedule posted downstairs that indicated what diversion who was to take part in at what time. In addition, at Elm Court, a "Stable Order" was posted. Across the top it read, "Carriage or Wagon," "Horses," "Hour," "For Whom." Down the side were listed 28 vehicles: Omnibus, Demarest Rockaway, Brewster Brougham, Victoria, Brewster Surrey, Healey Surrey, Buckboard

Curling at Highlawn House (second from right, Carlos deHeredia)

Courtesy of Mr. William O. Field

(three-seated), Demarest Phaeton, Buckboard (two-seated, new), Buckboard (two-seated, old), Cannon Buckboard (no. 1), Cannon Buckboard (No. 2), Cannon Buckboard (No. 3), Buckboard (single, seat, rumble), Webb Buckboard (M.D.S.), Pony Buckboard, Housekeeper's Wagon, Buckboard (stable), Depot Buckboard (I. & W.), Brewster Roadwagon, Two Wheeler (large), Two

Courtesy of Mr. William O. Field

Tennis at Elm Court, circa 1895

Wheeler (small), Dog Cart, Healey Brake, Skeleton Brake, Baggage Wagon (large), Baggage Wagon (small), and Landau-Brewster. The guest signed up for the vehicle and the hour desired. Across the bottom, one could check "saddle horse" and fill in the name of the horse desired. A man who once weekended at Elm Court recalls, "The choice of horses and carriages was larger than at the average commercial stable in New York City, on the other hand, if Mrs. Sloane's schedule said you rode at one, you rode at one."

Outdoors, there were private tennis courts, ice rinks, golf courses, riding trails and walks, man made lakes, and croquet lawns. Mrs. Emory said that the croquet lawn was so close to the veranda where the adults sat, that quarreling, raised, or angry words were forbidden when the children played. Indoors it was not uncommon to have a private billiard room. Some cottages had squash courts or bowling alleys. The cottages had libraries, writing, music, and card rooms. Bridge and charades were popular. "Opposite was a card table on which there was always a jigsaw puzzle in the making. Our grandfather [W. D. Sloane] was usually seated there before luncheon where we would join him until the gong sounded," Mrs. Emory recalls. Both the things made available to a guest at a cottage and the rules of conduct were ample.

There were social events of a more cultured nature provided at the cottages. Musicales, lectures, recitals by opera singers, Tableaux Vivants, and masques were favorites. One masque, the "Masque of Comus," was presented on a lawn in Stockbridge and set to music using a 1634 manuscript lent by Harvard. The lectures were perhaps less than riveting; a sample of titles include: in 1895, "Do College Women Marry?"; "The Inner Life of Plants or The Soul of Nature" at Sedgwick Hall, September, 1903; "Insects: How to

Courtesy of Mr. William O. Field

Housewarming weekend at Highlawn House, 1910

A Carriage House

Courtesy of the Berkshire Eagle

Know, and to Observe; Some Injurious, Others Beneficial; How to Control Them" at Fernbrook, July, 1904; and "Hard and His Kettle" at Erskine Park, July, 1904. (Hard was a character created by Professor H. M. Penniman for the purpose of telling instructive tales.) Although the titles sound silly, the subject matter was practical and serious. Underlying all entertainments was a seriousness that related to the entertainer's sense of social purpose and place.

In acknowledgement of the responsibility the "permanent summer colony" felt for townspeople, a number of the social events were planned for the whole town. Mrs. Anson Phelps Stokes had an annual Christmas party first at Homestead and later at Shadow Brook. At Highlawn, Mrs. William B. Osgood Field, née Lila Vanderbilt Sloane, gave an annual party with hot chocolate and cider, cakes and cookies.

The Fourth of July was an annual event. Mr. Daley of Lenox remembers going one Fourth to Erskine Park. "It was beautiful. There were colored lanterns everywhere and tents set up on the lawn with food, and music for dancing. The fireworks were extraordinary. Well, it was Mr. Westinghouse doing it, wasn't it?"

Adele Hammond Emory, daughter of Emily Sloane Hammond and granddaughter of Emily Vanderbilt Sloane, recalls, "The Fourth of July to the Hammond family meant a visit to our grandparents. Each year we spent the entire month at Elm Court. The fireworks were a spectacular event. Set up at the end of the lawn on a scaffold, they were varied and brilliant. In the earliest years, we were wakened to watch them from our mother's room... the crowd on the lawn below enjoyed them as much as we did."

Mr. Alex Halpin is animated, "Those fireworks were every year on the 25 acre lawn [at Elm Court], and I bet they cost $30,000. It was a two-hour show."

Mrs. Emory and her sister, Mrs. Breck, also recall the annual reunion held by their mother at "Cozy Cot." Each year, Mrs. Hammond would invite the original Sunday School class she had taught as a girl in Lenox to Cozy Cot for orangeade and cookies and conversation. Cozy Cot, deep in the woods of the Elm Court estate, is remembered both as a cherished playhouse retreat for the Sloane children and grandchildren, and for its "ferocious mosquitoes."

Weekend guests met at the Stockbridge Railroad Station by coachman from Elm Court

Courtesy of Mr. William O. Field

An extension of the responsibility of the leisure class for others, were the many social events organized to raise money for various charities. Some of these were annual events like the Lenox Children's Fair. The beneficiaries were hospitals, libraries, or the Fresh Air Hotel started by John Parsons of Stonover for deprived city children.

Whatever the event, all the newspapers wanted to write about it. In 1891, ***Town Topics*** printed a letter reputed to be genuine. The editor stated that he found it in the aisle of the Madison Square Garden, and because it was such an accurate inside view of the social life at Lenox, he could not resist printing it. Probably it was a total fabrication meant to impart the editor's view of the social life. Cleveland Amory calls the editor of the Gilded Age tattler, "an old blackmailer." Miss Alexandre says, "We were not allowed to read ***Town Topics.*** We certainly would not want to be seen buying it. Mother would dispatch the maid to a street corner in New York City to buy it. Mother would read it when the children were not present. I never saw a copy until I was grown up." Whether the letter is genuine or fabricated, it offers insight into how Society was or was reputed to be at the time.

Lenox, September 15, 1891
My dear Daisy—
*Here we are at Lenox. We arrived in the dark, and drove through the darkness of woods for almost two miles. Mama was tired out and I saw that Victorine was beginning to be cross, and I had visions of her doing my hair in an unbecoming Psyche Knot for my first ball in Lenox. Suddenly we emerged from the woods into the darkest of village streets. **"Mon Dieu,** Mademoiselle," Victorine ventured to say, **"Est ce que c'est Lenox?"** At last we stopped, and I looked out. "Is this the hotel?" I asked... in forlorn accents. I saw a narrow little piazza filled with people. The light streamed from a*

*narrow doorway. A narrow hall was crowded with people. "Come, come" said Mama. "Here we are at Curtis." "Are you sure?" I said. "What a funny place!" I heard a clatter of voices, and stumbled into the hallway feeling cross, dusty and tired, and still uncertain as to whether we really were in the right place, when who should I see in the crowd but [friends]. That settled it. We were in the right place. They all rushed up to speak to us. Everyone said, "Is this your first visit? Where are your rooms? Oh, you have rooms outside. Going to the Stokes' dance? See you later," etc., etc. We had some tea, and then walked half a mile to our rooms. Well, my dear, if you could see our apartment! Such funny stuffy little rooms; low ceilings, floors all uneven; no space for my French trunks. And, then our sitting room! Fortunately, I brought a trunk full of cushions, portieres, photographs and bric-a-brac, and now the room is not half bad. But everyone lives this way here, and it is all right. As soon as we could get our trunks that night, I dressed for the dance at the Stokes.' I wore my latest French triumph in white and gold. It is such a tight fit that I had to struggle to get into it; but then: "**Il faut souffrir pour etre a la mode**, my dear." My hair was in a Psyche Knot, with a ribbon twisted in with a stunning effect. Edith was there, and she was positively green with envy when she put up her lorgnette to look at me. The Stokes have one of the swell places of Lenox, and, let me tell you, they are **the** people of present. Such a ballroom—such a lavish display of expenditure everywhere, as though to say: "See how much we can spend and not feel it." They have one of the biggest houses here and just spend a few weeks in it, just for the season, you know. By the way, the Sloane girls are getting to be really pretty, and they will have millions, my dear.*

Well, the day after the Stokes' dance, everyone was in a turmoil to get ready for the buckboard parade. We had set up our horses in advance, and James had orders to have the decorations done by Thorley. I ordered hydrangeas and ferns and just imagine my rage when I saw half a dozen or more decked out in the same manner. My dear, do you remember those [name deleted], whom we saw at Newport last year? Well they are here in a cottage—at Lenox—the mecca of all social pilgrims. They are in the swim almost, and determined to get there, anyway, and at all hazards. Next season they will probably take a bigger house, and people will forget where they came from and they will be leaders here in a year. On Saturday night I just had time to rush home and dress for the assembly. There were lots of boys there. I had some lovely dances, though, and determined to go in for a good time. My dear, to be in the fashion, you must wear a large white lace veil with embroidery all over your eyes and nose; all the women at Newport and Lenox have them. And don't forget to hold your hand extra high when you shake hands, and just wave it to and fro a little bit.

Next season I intend to make Papa take a cottage here. It is the only way. It is all very well to put up with these queer little houses belonging to the druggist or the furniture man, for a few weeks, but to have a cottage and entertain and have your own men, is the thing to do. Mama says nobody is anybody in Lenox without a cottage. Well, my dear, I am tired out. What with musicales, teas, dances, dinners and lunches and drives, I am about sagged out. Victorine says I shall need a touch of color pretty soon, but I don't want to do that, although some of the girls and women did it at Newport this summer. I expect to be very gay all the week, and dine and lunch and have a bit of tennis at the Stokes, go to another dance there on Friday night, and drive one afternoon. We have to burn candles in our room. Gas is an unknown luxury.
Yours,
Ethel[9]

Costume Party at Highlawn House, 1913

Courtesy of Mr. William O. Field

Olivia Stokes Hatch recalls, "There was a man whose name I can't remember now; the man who used to write a social column in the summer. There would be a column on the society page, one on Newport and one on Bar Harbor and a regular Berkshire column. He [the columnist] would call up and want to know who the house guests were. My family was always against publicity, but we felt so sorry for Mr. X so we'd say occasionally who was there. He'd say, is there any plan? We'd say, 'Oh, we're having a picnic.' That sort of thing. Everyone felt so sorry for him. If we had no news, he'd say, 'Do you have a sandwich?' All the cooks and maids fed him at the back door—sandwiches and what not. He was never a young man as far as I can remember. He was one of those people who always was old. He upped and died. He left plenty of money. Apparently he'd gotten tips on the market from various people. We all burst out laughing. We'd felt so sorry for him and all those sandwiches!"

The public was hungry for every snippet. What news reporters couldn't pick up, they made up, or, they would write things like "Miss Olivia Stokes swam in Lake Mahkeenac today." Mrs. Olivia Stokes Hatch smiles, "As if it were an Olympic event. It was perfectly silly."

Examples of such heart-stopping news coverage include the following:

> The tennis tournament at Lenox which was looked forward to with so much interest has been given up for good reasons, and an inferior contest, confined to members of the Lenox Club, will replace it. It transpired, as the time for the tournament approached, that the attendance of good players would be absurdly small, so there was but one thing to do, and that was—give it up. Last year the tournament was a pleasant success and in one way or another, afforded some good fun, therefore the present failure is greatly regretted.
>
> However, outdoor interest is now centered in the approaching archery tournament, ostensibly in preparation for which the young ladies are devoting a great deal of time to luncheons and dinners, where everyone looks arch and talks archery. They are determined, I understand, that this tournament shall not be a failure.
>
> The first of the subscription dances at Lenox will occur on Saturday evening. If enough available and agreeable men are about—and this is large and important—it will surely be a success, for there will be young ladies in abundance. All of the latter are a little more charming this year than ever before if I am to believe all I read and hear....
>
> Sadly enough, however, I fear Dick and Harry will be sinfully puffing their cigarettes in the Hoffman House Cafe Saturday night instead of doing their duty at Lenox, excusing themselves by promises to be on hand at the next dance, a week hence.
>
> The Lenox Boat Club will parade on Mahkeenac Lake next Tuesday, the boats being trimmed to illustrate historic events and loaded with pretty femininity.
>
> Among those who, during the past week, have wearied of Newport and transferred their affections to Lenox, is Mrs. Anson Phelps Stokes, who... now has the Lenox house in a state of preparation for a number of delightful entertainments already on the books and eagerly anticipated by the entire Lenox contingent. The first of these will occur on Friday evening of this week—a dance. There are three more to follow at short intervals.[10]

Winter Weekend at Bonnie Brae

Courtesy of Mr. J. Graham Parsons

The reporters rarely got more than the guest list and the date of the event unless it was a wedding. Even then, the going was rough. Miss Nathalie Sedgwick married Bainbridge Colby one fine day in Stockbridge in the 90s. "While I pinned the orange blossoms on the tulle veil with a diamond crescent from Bainbridge, Jane Sedgwick was downstairs refusing details to reporters, fresh from the Sloane wedding in Lenox. Refusing on the ground '*we* are not carpet manufacturers,' in the manner of the aristocrats of the 1800s who thought trade beneath them. Which shows what a pocket of tradition a New England village remained."[11] Truly and for whatever reason, reporters fared far better with the Vanderbilts. When Emily Vanderbilt Sloane married John Henry Hammond in New York, the story was on the society pages for weeks and the wedding was on the front page on April 5, 1899.

Two weddings juxtaposed with one another give a glimpse into two different social milieus that operated side by side just before the turn of the century.

When Nathalie Sedgwick was married, the Sedgwicks, although they were poor by Gilded Age standards, led the social life in Stockbridge by viture of lineage. They were the living example of what Choate meant when he said, "In Lenox you are estimated, in Stockbridge you are esteemed."

When Emily Vanderbilt Sloane married, the Vanderbilts were members of The Four Hundred. Although they had promoted themselves into the magic circle rather than demurely waiting for an invitation, they could more than pay their way. The grandfather of a Stockbridge miss reflecting the tension between First Families and The Four Hundred sniffed, "I hope you are not accepting an invitation to those upstart Vanderbilt's." Notwithstanding the delicacy of the grandfather, many sought to be included by the Vanderbilts. "Oh," an old servant said, "if he hadn't been acceptable, he never would have made Elm Court." In the mind of the servant, the invitation to a Vanderbilt home clarified the social position of the man he was discussing.

The night before her wedding, Nathalie Sedgwick danced at the Casino on Main Street in Stockbridge. News coverage of Emily Vanderbilt Sloane's marriage to John Henry Hammond began in earnest in the ***New York Times*** six days prior. The day before the wedding, Miss Sloane had a luncheon, there was a formal showing of the gifts, Mr. and Mrs. William Douglas Sloane hosted a formal dinner, and Mr. John Henry Hammond had a bachelor party at the University Club.

In Stockbridge, Nathalie's gifts lay on a table downstairs watched over by the family dog, Kai. They included glasses and plates, salvers, vases, and a silver box from a rich uncle. In New York, Emily's gifts numbered over two hundred including a diamond necklace and tiara, a ruby and diamond pendant, and a pearl, diamond, and turquoise cluster pin. They were watched over by liveried footmen.

Miss Sedgwick tore an unwanted flounce of lace from her Stockbridge-made wedding gown and stitched it up herself on the morning of the wedding. Miss Sloane's gown was from Paris. Every detail of the cut and fabric was printed in the ***New York Times.*** It had "deep flounces of the rarest quality of lace." Both brides

Courtesy of the Lenox Library

Lawn Tennis Party
at Wheatleigh

fastened orange blossoms onto the tulle veils and went to church.

In New York, the Sloane's carriages lined the street in front of the church. "In order to prevent... the crowding in the streets... a force of ten police officers will be stationed to keep the crowd back from the canopy. Several hundred invitations have been issued..." For a wedding scheduled at noon, "some of the guests arrived at the church at a few minutes after eleven, evidently with the purpose of securing a good seat."[12]

In Stockbridge, Nathalie Sedgwick lived only paces from St. Paul's Church. Still, in accordance with the importance of the occasion, she rode to church in a carriage borrowed from the rector. "In the church at twelve, all the village waited; the grocer, the butcher, and the dressmaker, and some good old Boston names."[13] The church organ struck up the traditional wedding march as the bride holding lilies with satin ribbons appeared in the doorway. Nathalie was preceded down the aisle by one flower girl, a granddaughter of Matthew Arnold.

In New York, an hour-long musical program played by a small orchestra, preceded Emily's arrival. As the great doors at the back of the church swung open, fourteen bridesmaids and groomsmen walked down the aisle ahead of the bride to the accompaniment of three wedding marches, from ***Lohengrin, A Mid-Summer Night's Dream*** and ***Die Meistersinger.*** The bride carried white orchids and lilies.

Nathalie Sedgwick Colby had a wedding breakfast catered by

Delmonico's of New York "as it was a present from a cousin." It was served on the lawn of the Sedgwick House. Emily Sloane Hammond returned to 2 West 52nd Street where the roses were in profusion and greeted her guests under a mammoth bell of lilies and ferns. Guests were served breakfast in the picture gallery. The menu was: Essence de Molissque, Olives, Radishes, Amandes, Oeufs Brouile aux Champignons, Filet de Boeuf a la Creole, Pommes Hollandaise, Les Pouisine Grilles, Jambon a la Diable, Points d'Asperges, Glace, Turban de Fruit, Gateaux, Cafe, Champagne, Apollinaris.

After a Virginia Reel on the lawn, Mr. and Mrs. Bainbridge Colby drove themselves in a horse and surrey to the Lenox train station and then made their way to a honeymoon in Canada. Mr. and Mrs. J. H. Hammond were driven to Grand Central Station, there to take a private railroad car attached to the afternoon train, for Lenox. They honeymooned at Elm Court.

There was a third social set in the Berkshires. The newspapers described the relative social position of one family in that set with

Courtesy of the Berkshire Eagle

At the Gymkhana at Tanglewood (the man on right in the bowler may be Mrs. Hatch's reporter)

the words, "a family extremely well known at Lenox but not especially prominent here." A family on the fringe of Society, they were not excluded or they simply would not have been "known," but they had not achieved social importance. When a wedding occurred in that family, no word, short of the formal announcement, appeared in print. The day before the event, when the announcement placed by the family appeared, it was followed by an editorial comment: "a large attendance is doubtful as Lenox is a distance that only a limited number will care to cover for this event."[14] Only the social events of Society were of interest; those on the fringe, if treated by the press at all, suffered from having their relative place made clear.

Joseph Hodges Choate was a member in good standing, loved and respected by estate owners and the Fourth Estate. The golden wedding anniversary of Mr. and Mrs. Choate was treated by the press as it might have treated a royal occasion.

The invitation was simple. It merely stated: Mr. and Mrs. Joseph Hodges Choate will be at home on Monday, the sixteenth of October, 1911, from three until six at Naumkeag, Stockbridge, Massachusetts. To indicate the import of the event, the card had gold lettering on it.

On October 19, 1911, Mrs. De Gersdorff, a niece of the Choates, wrote the following in a letter: "I will go on and write my account of the Golden Wedding and tell you about the reception before writing of anything else."

Sunday night, there had been a dinner in honor of the event. The reception the following day was much larger. In the morning, Mrs. De Gersdorff went to Naumkeag to make herself "useful arranging flowers. Furniture was being moved to the stable—great boxes of flowers—scene of confusion—our chief work was building a background of golden yellow chrysanthemums and yellow boughs where Uncle Joe and Aunt Carrie were to stand as they received their guests... it was a heavenly sunny afternoon. The reception was a brilliant success.... There was music by a Hungarian band—there were hundreds of visitors—all enthusiasm—there were the presents to interest people and there was a Virginia Reel on the lawn."

Mrs. De Gersdorff wore a new dress of white silk and lace with pearls, white gloves and a white hat with a bit of green velvet and a feather. She acted as escort for guests viewing the gifts, "hobnobbed with all the Stockbridgeites [sic] and acquaintances from Lenox and New York—to say nothing of the relatives... Mr. Spencer of Lenox to whom I showed the presents was anxious to know whether Mr. Morgan's gift—an enormous cup and salver with fruit relief—was solid gold or plated! What makes people so funny?"

Mrs. De Gersdorff wrote that Frank Crowninshield, "seemed to wake up" in the late afternoon and "soon had us dancing through the dining room, library and hall in a chain while the music played on madly."

They danced in a circle around the Choates and "then Frank

called for a Virginia Reel which promptly took place on the terrace. It delighted me to see Carl and George [De Gersdorff] dancing so hard that their coattails were flying in the air."

The dancing was followed by a guest remembering that he had first met Frank Crowninshield when he was fourteen and Frank had stood on his head on the very terrace where they now danced. Apparently knowing Frank less well than the years would indicate, he said, "You couldn't do it now."

"Whereupon Frank arranged his handkerchief upon the turf and then successfully stood upon his head just to show that he was still young."

Frank, still arranging entertainments on the terrace was deserted by Mrs. De Gersdorff who retired to the dining room for tea. No sooner had she settled down than "the hall and drawing room were filled with dancing—waltz and two step and Spanish Boston." They sang a chorus of Auld Land Syne and then a guest went to the piano and played the wedding march. "Uncle Joe and Aunt Carrie impressively marched...slowly in time to the music ... it almost made one cry to see them...." Carrie wore a royal purple brocade with a bridal longette of lilies-of-the-valley and Joe wore a boutonniere of lilies-of-the-valley with ribbons attached. Choate displayed his typical wit replying to a guest who said that the reception was perfect. "Oh, it's only a dress rehearsal for the diamond anniversay."

"It was a never to be forgotten occasion," Mrs. De Gersdorff wrote, "May they live forever. No one can ever fill their places."

5

THE CARETAKERS

My father was paid $41.66 per month. 'Course, I will say we had our fuel supplied—wood and coal, no electricity —and all the produce and poultry that we could eat. No red meat. If they killed a calf up at the house, they sent the liver down to us. They didn't eat the liver in those days, but we loved it.

Mrs. Joseph Franz:
Born 1890, daughter of Mr. Southmayd's superintendent.

Courtesy of the Great Barrington Historic Commission

Groundsmen with handmowers at Brookside

omething woven into the atmosphere of the villages causes some twentieth-century travelers to pause and wonder what it was like to live in Stockbridge or Lenox in the last century. For them, the distance covered over land to reach the Berkshires is not sufficient, they want to travel time as well. If they are lost in reverie about days gone by, it is safe to assume not one such imaginative person is daydreaming about basement kitchens, sub-basement laundries, loading dumbwaiters or running hand mowers over twenty-five acres of lawn. Although the army of servants, by their labors, made the cottages the show places they were, their lot is not the stuff of daydreams.

There are many people in Lenox and Stockbridge today who worked on the grounds and inside the cottages. Many others remember the stories told to them by their parents. They share a keen sense of relationship; the ability to place themselves and their families in the social context, even though that context was forged in the nineteenth century.

One of the children of the estate superintendent at Wheatleigh recalls: "We always quieted down when the season arrived.

Mother would say, 'Now remember, you can't go beyond that tree and no hollering in the yard because the madam is coming.' We were supposed to stay out of sight, we were supposed to quiet down, and we did."

There are differences in diction that seem to coincide with how the speaker identifies his role in the Gilded Age. They are not infallible indicators, but they occur often enough to be noted. Outsiders call the seasonal mansions "estates." Descendants of the owners call the mansions by their names, personifying them. If the descendants are referring to the same house but in the last century, they echo their parents and call it a "cottage." Those who were employed at the mansions call them "places." The differences in word choice are outward manifestations of the more significant difference—position in a social order—that affected life choices, life styles, and attitudes.

"I'll tell you what those places were all about—competition; competition in everything from the flowers they grew to the parties they had," a former gardener recalls.

The average "place" employed eight in the house. That would include, in descending rank, a butler and a cook, a lady's maid, the footman, parlor maid and chambermaid, laundress and kitchen maid. The footman assisted the butler. The kitchen maid assisted the cook. The chambermaid was upstairs, the parlor maid was downstairs, and the lady's maid attended the lady of the house. That was a mandatory skeleton staff "inside." The indoor ranks might swell if the master retained a valet or if, at a formal dinner, extra footmen and waitresses were required, or if a tutor or nanny or nursery maid were necessary. Some of the households also had a seamstress for the production of children's clothes and linens.

The household staff traveled with the family from place to place and lived in the house. They did not travel with the family in the sense of doing so at the same time or with the same travel accommodations, but in the sense that they moved with the family from location to location.

Photograph by Paul Ivory

Servant's Bedroom at Naumkeag

Courtesy of the Lenox Library

Coachman in front of Carriage House at Ventfort Hall

Although he lived above the carriage house, the chauffeur was considered a part of the household staff The chauffeur would drive the car from place to place. If it were so arranged, he might also transport members of the family. Prior to the automobile, the first chauffeur would have been the head coachman. Depending upon the wealth of the family and the number of vehicles, there might also be a second and third chauffeur and an additional number of footmen. A third chauffeur was what in present day we call, inelegantly, a "go-fer." The first chauffeur always drove first; the second chauffeur, under supervision of the head man, was responsible for the upkeep of the cars or carriages, although he might also serve as a driver.

A well-equipped coach had a footman who rode at the back of the carriage or beside the chauffeur in the later days of automobiles. The footman would install the family and learn where they wanted to go, and if they needed a blanket or other comfort. The footman would communicate with the coachman.

"They would never say to me, 'Eugene, get a blanket.' You see, that would be condescending-like. They'd just say something like, 'It's a bit chilly this afternoon.' Then I'd get the blanket and they'd seem pleasantly surprised and thank me for my consideration."

Outside, a cottage employed a superintendent and the number of gardeners dictated by the size of the estate and the extent of the gardens and the greenhouses. The superintendent, at least, was given a house on the grounds. The lesser of the outside workers lived in the town and came to work daily. Some estates had as many as fifty groundsmen under the supervision of the superintendent.

The grounds supplied the household with necessities and niceties. The grounds were certainly ornamental with gardens laid by Frederick Law Olmsted, Guy Lowell, or Ernest Bowditch, but they were also serious business. The gardens supplied the household with fruit and vegetables and flowers, and in some cases, livestock and poultry. This was true not only when the family was in residence but throughout the growing season.

Coachman and liveried footman attending Mr. Giraud Foster at the reins of his four-in-hand (Bellefontaine in background)

Courtesy of the Lenox Library

"I can remember being at the depot every day for the 7:26 A.M. train to New York. Ready to load flowers, fruit, and vegetables for the city house," Eugene Jappron says. "Let's see now, I was a gardener at Elm Court first. I started at about 14 or 16 years old. Then, I got the job as third chauffeur, that was good. Why? Well, because I got a place to live, it was easier work and more money. Then I went to Mrs. deHeredia over at Wheatleigh as footman. That was terrific because I traveled with the family. Went all over. I once went with her to California by private train and of course to the New York house. Then, much later, I went back to Elm Court and worked in the greenhouses. Why did I go into service? Well, what were the choices? There were the mills or service or the General Electric plant—that was later. What do I remember? Well, Mr. and Mrs. White [of Elm Court] would go for a walk almost every day. They always took the same path. We could hear them coming. You'd hear Mr. White calling to the dogs. He had a wonderful deep voice. He was a big man—oh, six feet—and looked very distinguished with his white hair and moustache. She was very petite, and she could wear anything at all and look good in it. Well, we'd hear them coming, see, and we'd all duck behind bushes out of sight. No, they didn't ever want to see us working. And I remember later when I went back to Elm Court, every Sunday, Mrs. White would come down with her guests after Church to show them the greenhouses. The superintendent would be there to lead them through. She was very proud of the greenhouses."

The staff inside and outside the house were likely to have very different attitudes toward and impressions of the owners. "If you were 'outside,' you never got further than the kitchen door of the big house unless it was to arrange flowers in the great hall."

Mrs. Krebs was married in 1916. When her husband returned to Stockbridge after World War I, he was employed as the superintendent at Oronoque. Oronoque had been built in the late 1800s by Birdseye Blakeman. When the Krebs went to live there, it was the cottage of Norman Davis, banker, under secretary of state, diplomat and national chairman of the Red Cross:

"We were given the little cottage at the foot of the property. I lived there for fifty years. My husband just came along at the right time. The old super was fired. Oh, because he liked to go down street and sit around and talk when he was supposed to be working. Well, my husband was born and raised in Boston. I'll never forget the first time he was supposed to kill a chicken. Now killing a chicken isn't so hard if you know how, but, like I say, he was raised in Boston and had never killed a chicken. Anyway, he learned. Outside of the poultry, he took care of the gardens and the lawns. There were acres and acres of lawn and it was many years later that we got a power mower. There were as many as twenty-eight people in the house to feed out of the garden. You should have seen the wheelbarrow loads of vegetables and fruits went up to the house every day. The flowers had to be freshened every day. That to me was unnecessary. There was nothing wrong with those flowers after one day, but that's what they wanted and that's what they got. No, I never went up to the main house when the family was there. No one said anything and I never asked my husband, but I never felt I ought to go. Rosie, my friend, was hired as an extra waitress for parties and she told me that she saw Mrs. Davis come down the great main staircase all dressed in white for

Courtesy of the Great Barrington Historic Commission

Gardener at Brookside

Courtesy of Mrs. Wenzel Krebs

Superintendent Krebs with workers at Oronoque

Courtesy of the Lenox Library

Gardeners at Ventfort Hall

a dinner and Rosie said to her, 'You look just like an angel coming.' But, like I said, I never went up to the main house when they were there. Ah, mercy, I don't know what they did up there, but they kept the people who worked for them busy."

In the well-run household, the servants were not obtrusive. Searles Castle née Barrington House née Kellogg House had a series of narrow staircases running throughout the house cleverly hidden behind false panels and doorways. From the third floor servants' quarters, a retainer could reach the basement kitchen and cellar without going into the main part of the house. It was an odd balance of interdependency that was reflected not only in the manners of everyday life but also in the architecture.

Architectural firms like Peabody and Stearns or McKim, Mead & White discussed construction and placement of the servants quarters in philosophical terms. One such article stated that there was danger of upsetting the balance of the household if the servants quarters are too far removed from the main quarters of the house. A cottage, or a city house of the rich, was actually two intertwined households. There had to be free access between the two without intrusion. The architectural plan had to reflect the interdependence. Although today we look back and see two distinct classes divided by an economic chasm of unthinkable proportions, had you lived then, the subtle intertwining would have been evident. The cross dependence was very personal.

Many descendants of cottagers, when interviewed, tried to explain that the Gilded Age was dead not just because the distribution of wealth changed but because such a life was impossible without servants. They meant not just living without a staff that "did" for one, but without a population that took pride in working for the satisfaction of others. It was a delicate psychological balance achieved along lines unheard of today. The means of achieving personal pride and satisfaction were divided and complementary.

Edith Wharton's chauffeur was named Charles Cook. One day she and her guests made up a driving party. One of the guests who had wanted to try driving had succeeded in getting the party lost. But, it is reported, Cook was along and soon had them back on the right road. It was ego enhancing to the cottager ***not*** to be efficient or adept but in fact, to be ***inept*** and have an efficient retainer. In perfect balance, the servant's ego was enhanced by gratifying the owner's wishes—not his own. Mrs. Franz, daughter of the superintendent at Southmayd's estate, recalls that for thirty years her father packed crates of preserves in glass jars for transport to the city house and never was one jar broken. The complementary division rested on a firm division of labor. A lady or gentleman did not wish to know directions or how to pack crates. Their egos were enhanced by hiring loyal servants adept in specific areas of labor. The owners' egos were enhanced for two reasons: they were able to indulge in conspicuous leisure, a sign of a superior class, and the number of servants testified to their pecuniary strength.

Thorstein Veblen calls the servant class a vicarious leisure class partaking of vicarious consumption. The vicarious leisure proceeded out of the owner's desire to display pecuniary strength and therefore, he would continue to hire servants for more and more specific tasks. The job of one employee at Elm Court was to wind the clocks daily.

Courtesy of Mrs Olivia Stokes Hatch

The men who built Shadow Brook

One of Mrs. Sloane's granddaughters recalls another servant, "She looked like a tea cozy, and she went around with a little feather duster, you know, the kind with a stick on it. Agnes, that was her name and she was there forever and a day. Her only job, so far as I know, was to go around with that little duster."

Putting aside the fact that the clocks were wound and the dust removed, the impact of such a use of manpower was a display of monetary muscle—the ability to assign one servant a single task. The practice served the gentleman and created leisure for the servant.

The "vicarious consumption" of the servants included eating the same food as the household, living within the walls of the opulent houses and wearing uniforms that identified them with "an honorable superior class."[1]

In April, 1981, Mr. Eugene Jappron wrote an article titled, "The Birth of Tanglewood," for the ***Senior Sentry***, The Lenox Council on Aging Newsletter. Although thousands of words were already in print tracing the beginnings of the famous summer music festival, Jappron, former footman to Mrs. deHeredia at Wheatleigh, felt the full story had not been told.

"You're not supposed to reveal anything that happens in private life. You know the reason I wrote that? Revenge. Books have been written on the start of Tanglewood, and my poor lady was never mentioned and she was the one more or less. Without her there'd be no Tanglewood."

In contemplating the article, Jappron was torn between loyalties: protection of his employer's privacy versus the desire to enhance her status. The desire to set the record straight and make sure it included Mrs. deHeredia's contribution won out. The footman's outrage at the slight to her was almost personal. Many of the servants seemed to have taken the family on as a logical extension of their own egos, and the accomplishments of the cottagers seemed to heighten their own status.

Perhaps the "fringe benefit" of raised self-esteem for the servants by association was more appreciated by the majority of servants who were immigrants. One, an Irish girl named Rosie, worked at Edith Wharton's The Mount. When the house was in sad disrepair and threatened with destruction, Rosie was one of the people who wanted it saved and fought to save it. She told people who interviewed her at the time that she remembered every object in the house and where it had been placed. She spoke of The Mount with love and something like possession. Yet after the house was vacated by the Whartons, for the first time in her life, Rosie descended the main staircase of The Mount. It was an exhilarating experience because it had been forbidden and was totally novel. Rosie had lived and worked at The Mount almost her entire adult life without ever using any but the narrow servants' backstairs.

How the psychological balance was achieved between those who lived in the house with seemingly limitless means and those who lived beside them without wide choices did vary from individual to individual and with nationality.

"Our servants are better paid than any other women, well housed and fed, and sheltered from many of the temptations which surround the working girl; they are nursed when they are ill and are not immediately thrown out of employment; and often in old age or prolonged illness, are tenderly cared for by their former employers. Yet many a girl would struggle to keep body and soul together on starvation wages rather than incur the stigma of having been a servant.... The majority of our servants are foreign born and bred."[2]

That was the report of the ***Century Magazine*** in 1899. If servants were necessary to the lifestyle, then the seeds of undoing were always present even as aristocracy tried to establish itself in America. It was true that servants were cared for. Edith Wharton provided the chauffeur, Charles Cook, with a life pension when a stroke prevented him from driving again. Cortlandt Field Bishop, while he disinherited his daughter, he left his valet, William Duport, $5,000 and his private secretary one half his estate. Emily Vanderbilt Sloane White was said to have left her servants one

Courtesy of Mrs. Olivia Stokes Hatch

Nanny at Brook Farm

year's salary each in her will. She went about town before leaving Lenox each season and gave townspeople who had worked at Elm Court a $20 gold piece. She had heard that they had to live through the winter on the money made during the season, and she wanted to assure that they had fuel for heat. Miss Rosamond Sherwood was a friend of Miss Mable Choate of Naumkeag. She recalls going to Miss Choate's for a dinner. There was an aging maid present. She was long past retirement age, but it seems, she enjoyed summers in the Berkshires. Therefore, Miss Choate arranged for her to be part of the household staff that summer. Unable to do much else, Miss Choate had arranged for her to pass the peas. "That, as far as I could tell was her only function in the household." Miss Sherwood noted. "With what pride she came forward that evening and presented the peas to each guest. Wasn't it lovely of Miss Choate to arrange for her to spend the summer in the Berkshires and to find something for her to do, as well?"

A resident of Lenox recalls, "Mrs. White would come to the school before she left each year and ask us what we wanted for Christmas. At Christmas, under the tree in the classroom, we would get just what we'd asked for. It was like a real Santa Claus. One year I asked for skates and I got skates. After she was gone, I hear her daughter Mrs. Field kept it up."

Yet in good Yankee fashion, the desire was for a "small right" over "a large favor." The fierce desire was for independence. So that the psychological balance attained by many American servants was quite different. For all the care and compassion, Americans did not easily assume the role of servant. Mrs. Joseph Franz, born at Southmayd's estate, Stockbridge, in 1890, asked simply, "Why did some people have so much when others had so little?" She went with her husband to see one of the cottages before it was razed by the children in the 1940s. "We just wanted to see it before it was gone. The upstairs was beautiful, large and airy. I'm glad I saw it. But downstairs was the kitchen with a stone floor and little tiny windows just up at the top. No ventilation. Can you imagine standing all day on that stone floor and cooking? Well, that's what some people had to do, and why leave them on a stone floor?"

Another who served in one of the households, in a truly American reformation of ego over reality, condescended to the owners, "I'll tell you what it was all about—each one striving to outdo the other. It was silly to watch, really."

In America, the land of opportunity, the stories about plain folk climbing to dizzying financial heights were accepted in one of two ways. Either the wealthy came to be viewed not as heroes but as role models (every mother's son could become a millionaire), or the stories were seen as pure entertainment.

Those who took the latter view stood back as if the whole thing was spread out before them like a three-ring circus come to town for their pleasure. They watched and with the wonderful objectivity of the critic in the bleachers they reported what they saw and how it stacked up against other diversions.

"Mr. Fahnestock rode a four-in-hand to church up into the forties even. He had to pass my house on the way every Sunday, and I can tell you that he had a fine rig."

"I was very young, but I'll never forget going to Erskine Park for something—maybe the Fourth of July or Halloween. They had torches everywhere along the road; they reflected on the white paths and in the ponds. There were fireworks. It was very beautiful to see."

"Sunday morning everyone gathered at the Post Office after church. Since they were all going to the same place, it was like a parade with beautiful coaches and horses; the footmen dressed just like the ones in England and all the different colors of the ladies dresses."

Courtesy of Berkshire County Historical Society

Estate workers

Others are cynics or perhaps the true reporters of the times. "The cottagers were robbed right and left, but you show me one hundred millionaires in the Berkshires and I'll show you ninety-five thieves, so they robbed the robbers." Those who see the relationship between the servants and the served in this way also explain "how it was done." A butler, a cook, and a superintendent had the power to order goods, pay tradesmen, and pay staff. Some of them kept two sets of books. They would receive a check from the owner for the amount specified in one set of books, pay the grocer the amount owed, and pocket the difference. Or, it was a direct transaction without cumbersome double entries: the grocer or wine merchant or the butcher would simply pay the cook or butler for the privilege of their patronage. The superintendent might also keep two sets of books. A superintendent could send a man home for loafing or otherwise unacceptable behavior. The owner would pay for work days, the superintendent would pay the man for days worked and pocket the difference. However many tricks there were in this unsavory trade, and however many tricksters will never be known for sure.

"Course I'll never forget Stride," Jappron says, "that was Mrs. White's butler. Herbert Stride, that was his name. Well, he had the British accent, you know, and he got up cricket games on the big lawns with other English butlers, I guess. I just tried to stay clear of him, but I couldn't always. I can still see him, over six feet dressed in black, walking around carrying that little white dog, a Pomeranian, I think. You know, he was married to the cook and they built themselves a house at Newport with their own staff. I'll tell you what happened there. The staff is surrounded by all this stuff and they develop a taste for it, and some of them start to think they're as important as the owners of the house. The staff was very often snobbier than the owners who were often very nice."

Perhaps Stride achieved his Newport cottage through graft or by a kind of undeclared pension plan whereby the owners knew what was going on but allowed it if the servants were satisfactory in other ways. Then, too, the unfair practices could go both ways. One of the well-known ladies that traveled to the Berkshires each year stayed at the Curtis Hotel. She traveled with her chauffeur and a footman and a personal maid. An impressive entourage, but she got her nickname for a different reason altogether.

"Promisin' Mary they called her." A man who worked at the Curtis chuckles, "Yup, Promisin' Mary. She'd ask you for this and promise you a tip and ask you for that and promise you a tip She never paid up. So far as I know she never gave anyone a tip Promisin' Mary it was, so that's what they called her."

Everyone knew that the townspeople had to live twelve months on whatever they could make during the two or three months that the cottagers were in residence, so competition was brisk among

Courtesy of the Stockbridge Library

A local businessman

Courtesy of Mr. John Nichols

Caretaker's daughter at Brookside

the suppliers and workers. For some, at least, then, the whole dog and pony show was just business.

For the townspeople, then as now, tourism was good business. Although there was suspicion on both sides, relationships on the surface, at least, were cordial. When Henry David Thoreau was stuck atop Mount Greylock overnight, he found some newspapers left by picnickers. Later he said that the advertisements in the Berkshire press were more interesting than the news. All the ads were addressed to the cottagers. Furthermore, by the Gilded Age, fifty percent of the land in Lenox and thirty-three percent of the land in Stockbridge was owned by cottagers. The combination of their wealth far exceeded the total earnings of the rest of the town's; besides, they were major employers and purchasers.

The Church Street market kept a ledger and daily entries show: "Giraud Foster, six and one half pounds of duck at 35¢ per pound; George Westinghouse, ten and three quarters pounds of ham at $2.69, and W. D. Sloane, four pounds of deer-foot sausage at $1.20 per pound." Those were respectable prices between 1910 and 1924, and not common fare.

Editorials during the period in a paper called ***Lenox Life*** were blatantly supportive of the cottagers' activities. In one editorial about the Lenox Horse Show planned by the cottagers, the editor said that the town was responsible for assuring the success of the social event; to support the cottagers was the first interest of the town. That was one of several similar editorials, and most servants and townspeople took the advice to heart. In response, at least one servant built a cottage, but in a very different way from Stride. Paul Baridon, butler at Clipston Grange, was an excellent flower arranger and wood carver. In 1899, he build a three-story cottage carved from pine. It was a doll's house, fully furnished and carpeted. It had fifteen glass windows with curtains. All the doors were double hung on brass hinges. In true cottage fashion, a piazza surrounded the outside of the house. The project took Baridon months. He built it to be auctioned off at the Lenox Children's Fair at Mrs. Alexandre's Spring Lawn on September 8, 1899. The

Fair was an annual charity event sponsored by the cottagers to benefit the Pittsfield House of Mercy. For weeks before the event, ***Lenox Life*** hummed with speculation about who the lucky bidder would be and how much the doll's house would raise; it was hoped that it would sell for at least $200. Oddly enough, after the event, not one word was written about who did buy it or for how much. The fate of the tiny Berkshire cottage is a mystery.

When Rev. R. DeWitt Mallary's book, ***Lenox and the Berkshire Highlands***, was published in 1902, it demanded another editorial in ***Lenox Life***. The Reverend had been more complimentary of the prior literary tenants of Lenox than the present moneyed tenants. The editorial stated, "Faint praise of the summer dwellers in modern Lenox is not enough. They deserve more than that. The men and women who own these beautiful estates in Lenox today, who have spent vast sums of money in beautifying them, have done much more for Lenox in the aggregate than the ancient generation did, whose names are so constantly heralded to the world."

Living with the assumption of servants was as much a way of life then as it is not now. The houses had to be opened and closed. That meant washing the walls and floors, covering or uncovering all the furniture. Setting the house in order so that the family could arrive and sit down to dinner or leave without a second thought.

"How long did it take me to open a house?" Mrs. Krebs, who worked with her sister opening the cottages at the beginning of the season, ponders, "Well, I had a crew. How long? Well, take for example Oronoque, that took two weeks." But many of the houses were not opened or closed by local crews but by the household staff. That presented a problem in logistics that is unknown in modern times.

"Of course the staff would go ahead to open the New York house so that everything was ready when the family arrived from Lenox."

"But then, who was with the family in Lenox?" his wife asks.

"Oh, I see what you mean, they couldn't stay in the house without staff. Well, that's why they joined clubs in Bar Harbor or Washington D.C. so that they'd have somewhere to go for the couple of weeks."

When the speakers, Mr. and Mrs. Stephen Morris were first married, they wanted to go to Brookhurst, the cottage of Stephen's father, Newbold Morris, but the house was closed. The elder Mrs. Morris thought them mad to go without staff, but they finally convinced her by saying they would "camp out."

When Brookhurst became their summer home, the Stephen Morris' removed the third floor which had been the servants' wing, and maintain the lovely cottage to this day without a staff. "We laugh sometimes to think that we just walk in and set our things down and live here without all the staff and so forth."

Reflecting upon life with servants, Mr. Morris says, "If you were accepted in society, then you couldn't do anything wrong. You could drop your whole plate on the floor at dinner and not be

Courtesy of the Lenox Library

Footman and coach under the porte cochere at Wyndhurst

embarrassed. Oh, well, you might be embarrassed in front of the servants. . . . "

"Exactly," a Berkshire lady said, when she heard what Mr. Morris had said, "You could lose face. At a formal dinner, a footman stood behind every chair and could listen in on all the conversation. The more formality, the poor possibility to embarrass yourself."

The majority of those interviewed seemed to reflect upon the presence of servants both as those who made a gracious style of living possible, and as people with whom one might have a relationship. Although one gentleman who said that he had never thought about the servants at all, just assumed they would be there, added rather apologetically, "but I was a small boy." Others, like Mr. Morris and Mrs. Emory, saw all the possibilities inherent in human relations—love, loyalty, honor and duty, amusement or embarrassment, or jealousy, condescension, resentment and competition.

In America, because of the "American dream" and the democratic ideology, it was possible for the realization of an aristocracy to be in the process of achievement and undoing at the same time. One of the Sedgwick women had a life-long attendant. Toward the end of her days, the companion approached the family and asked to be buried in the "Pie." The matter was discussed at a family meeting after dinner one Thanksgiving. The companion was turned down. She was not a Sedgwick and was forbidden the "Pie." She was buried just outside. As the generations have passed and more and more Sedgwicks have been laid to rest, the circle has widened. She is now within the "Pie." "Illustrating," said the local newspaper editor, "that in America, if enough generations pass, equality is always achieved."

Interestingly enough, only two of the people interviewed said they sorely missed the old days—one man who lived downstairs and a lady decidedly from upstairs. She mourned the loss of gracious living impossible without servants, and he said, "I wish they'd go back to gracious living. What is gracious living? Well, it was a strong sense of family and sit-down dinners."

"I'll tell you what it was, you knew someone else would take care of it." So, with the precision and brevity that was the definition of elegance in another age, Mrs. Morris defines the role of the caretakers and the underpinnings of an age.

6

THE BUILDERS

"My purpose was to have a road the equal of corresponding first class places in Lenox; I ask for nothing better and I shall not willingly accept poorer."

W. D. Sloane:
Letter to Messrs. Olmsted, Olmsted and Eliot, October 2, 1884

Emily Thorn Vanderbilt's grandson muses, "I think, that if you ran a house like that, you didn't have time for anything else." He thinks a moment, trying to express something more about the great houses both in the town and country. In Lenox, he lived at the cottage named Highlawn House and visited his grandmother at Elm Court. In the city, "We lived on Fifth Avenue, and I have always been embarrassed to describe where I grew up." In the Berkshires, standing in one of the cottages, you can learn something of the age and the people from the proportions alone.

The beginning of the estate period in Lenox and Stockbridge is not easily pinpointed. Some mark it as early as the 1840s when Samuel G. Ward bought Highwood, which commanded a spectacular view of Lake Mahkeenac and the mountains, and settled down to gentleman farming and entertaining the literati of the day. Others identify the end of the Civil War, the amassed wealth and lighter spirit, as the time when building began. If it was the end of the Civil War that loosed the pocketbook and the heart to build, and the start of the First World War that changed the attitude and

Photograph by William Tague

Aerial view of Elm Court

Courtesy of The Essex Institute

Highwood,
first cottage of
Samuel G. Ward

ended the period, then the estate period would fit neatly between two wars. However, neatness is not necessarily accuracy. The majority of estates in the villages were built in the 1880s and 1890s spilling over into the twentieth century as late as 1911, and although the Great War changed the mood, it was not until the Depression that the great estates were given away for tax reasons or auctioned off, razed, or deserted.

A local resident muses, "Giraud Foster died in 1945, and Mrs. White died soon after—they were bridge partners, you know—with those two gone, the period was really over, as far as I'm concerned. They were the real generation of builders." They were not only the generation that built, but the generation that understood the reason for the building and believed in it.

If the wealthy had an obligation, it was to amass and spend money; to build for an assured future not just for the sake of show, but to establish an American economic aristocracy. After the Civil War, there was a confluence of events that created the right atmosphere for a display of wealth that was, if nothing else, very entertaining. It was a time when the state of things for the moneyed class seemed stable, and the only conceivable changes seemed destined to be for the better. Perhaps the start of the era was the moment when the idea of an American aristocracy formed and appeared to have mass approval, and the beginning of the end was when there was a rent in the fabric of the mass approval.

Courtesy of the Providence Library

Oakswood,
second cottage of
Samuel G. Ward

Oakswood as the Stable at Shadow Brook

Courtesy of the Stockbridge Library

Max Weber visited the United States in 1903. He wrote, "In its characteristic form, stratification by 'status groups' on the basis of conventional styles of life evolves at the present time in the United States out of the traditional democracy."[1] Although all the elements of Weber's statement were correct, there was an inherent contradiction. The stratification of the status group ***was*** evolving on the basis of conventional style. That is, those who wished to be members of Society limited their behavior and made it conform to what was acceptable. Where they lived, how they dressed, whom they visited and invited, how they spoke, what manner they affected, and whom they married, was decided by what Weber called an "agreed upon communal action." It was the characteristic form by which social stratification took place; the Americans were copying their European counterparts. However, with characteristic American ingenuity and love of speed, the Americans were attempting to accomplish the task in far fewer years and without benefit of titles. There lay the contradiction: trying to evolve an aristocracy in the traditional democracy. The American social elite accumulated all the symbols of aristocracy, but the goal eluded them. They built with purpose, but even as they built, the ground was shifting beneath them.

In 1841, five years before Elias Howe patented the sewing ma-

Grand Staircase at Bellefontaine

Courtesy of Jane Foster Lorber

chine, the invention said to have heralded the rise of industrial capitalism, Samuel Gray Ward bought the first of two pieces of land that would become Highwood. In 1844, Ward bought the second piece to form the first Berkshire cottage. In 1849, William Tappan bought Tanglewood. In the 1850s, as Harriet Beecher Stowe wrote ***Uncle Tom's Cabin,*** the Pacific Railroad surveyed its proposed line, and the Republican Party was formed, Charles Butler created Linwood, in Stockbridge.

In the 1870s, Lewis Carroll wrote ***Through The Looking Glass***; Jules Verne wrote ***Twenty Thousand Leagues Under The Sea*** and ***Around The World in Eighty Days***; and Charles Darwin's ***The Descent of Man*** was published. Charles Dickens died and Marcel Proust was born. In New Jersey, Thomas Alva Edison demonstrated the incandescent lamp; in Boston, Alexander Graham Bell transmitted the first intelligible message by telephone; in New York, John D. Rockefeller founded Standard Oil; the Vanderbilts' Grand Central Station was completed; and Phineas T. Barnum started his circus, "The Greatest Show on Earth"; Solomon introduced his pressure cooker; and E. T. Gerry founded the Society for the Prevention of Cruelty to Children. In Africa, Stanley met Livingston. In Lenox, the old Lenox Courthouse was saved by Mrs. Auchmuty and Mrs. Schermerhorn, and John E. Parsons built Stonover; Colonel Auchmuty built the Dormers: and Samuel G. Ward employed Mr. McKim to build Oakswood almost twenty years after selling Highwood to William and Louisa Bullard.

In the 1880s, Grover Cleveland entered the White House saying, "Honor lies in honest toil," while 1.7 million children under the age of fifteen years toiled honestly for 25¢ per day. At the end of the decade, Benjamin Harrison was elected president and complained that he could not name his own cabinet because party managers "had sold out every place to pay the election expenses." ***Das Capital*** was published in English; The Federation of Labor was founded; Karl Marx died and Franklin Delano Roosevelt, Irving Berlin, T. S. Eliot and Eugene O'Neill were born. George

Courtesy of Robert DeLage

Mr. Edward Searles

Oronoque,
Birdseye Blakeman's cottage,
Stockbridge

Courtesy of the Stockbridge Library

The Trustees of Reservations

Mr. & Mrs. Joseph H. Choate in the gardens at Naumkeag, circa 1900

Westinghouse manufactured Nikola A. Telsa's electric motor and George Eastman perfected the Kodak box camera. The Scottish game of golf was introduced in America, the Football League and the Lawn Tennis Association were founded and Jim Thorpe was born. In London, Henry James wrote ***The Bostonians***; Queen Victoria celebrated her Golden Jubilee; and Jack the Ripper murdered six women. At Mayerling, the Austrian crown prince committed suicide. In New York, the Metropolitan Opera House was built by millionaires led by William K. Vanderbilt because his wife was denied a box at the Academy of Music, and P. T. Barnum put an automobile in the center ring of his circus so the public could get a look at the rarity. In Chicago, Mrs. Potter Palmer told a newspaperman that "People of our position would naturally be expected to have a Corot." In the Berkshires, the Pittsfield newspaper reported that "two American inventors are endeavoring to perfect instruments by which it will be possible to see people at a distance as we now speak to them by telephone." In Great Barrington, William Stanley threw the switch on the first commercial electric system using alternating current thereby lighting twenty-five shops on Main Street as Stanford White began Kellogg Terrace for Mary Frances Sherwood (Mrs. Mark) Hopkins. In Stockbridge, The Casino built by McKim, Mead and White was opened, Birdseye Blakeman built Oronoque, and Joseph Choate hired McKim to build Naumkeag. In Lenox, President Grover Cleveland arrived to dedicate Sedgwick Hall while Charles Lanier built Allen Winden; Captain John S. Barnes built Coldbrooke; W. D. Sloane built Elm Court; Mrs. Robert Winthrop built Ethel Wynde; Mrs. Charles Kneeland renovated an 1837 dwelling and called it Fairlawn; Dr. H. P. Jaques built Home Farm; the Misses Appleton employed Mr. Charles Follen McKim to build Homestead. Within a year, Mr. McKim wrote to Samuel G. Ward at Oakswood: "I want to have the pleasure of writing to you myself, to let you know of an unexpected and great hap-

Naumkeag, Cottage of Joseph Hodges Choate circa 1886

Courtesy of the Providence Library

Courtesy of the Lenox Library

Homestead, built for Miss Julia Appleton by her future husband, Charles F. McKim

piness that has come to me. I am engaged to be married to your neighbor, Miss Appleton." Julia Appleton married Charles McKim at Homestead. She died within the year.

In 1891, Lillian Russell personified '90s glamor. Arthur Conan Doyle published "The Adventures of Sherlock Holmes" in the ***Strand*** Magazine; Rudyard Kipling wrote ***The Just So Stories***, Maxim Gorki wrote ***The Lower Depths*** and Chekhov wrote ***The Three Sisters***. Grover Cleveland was back in the White House. Herman Melville and Oliver Wendell Holmes died, Pearl Buck, Aldous Huxley, James Thurber and John Steinbeck were born. ***The New York Times*** said that Owen Wister, Fanny Kemble's grandson, "has come as close as any man can to writing the American novel" (***The Virginian***). W. L. Judson invented the zipper, but no one used it. Henry Ford built his first car and X-rays, Helium,

Courtesy of Mrs. Olivia Stokes Hatch

Ballroom at Homestead

Morris K. Jesup's Belvoir Terrace

Courtesy of the Essex Institute

North side of Bellefontaine

Courtesy of the Providence Library

radioactivity, and radium were discovered. Gauguin was in Tahiti, Monet was at the Rouen Cathedral, and Toulouse-Lautrec was at the Moulin Rouge. J. E. Alexandre hired a new young architect just out of Harvard to build Spring Lawn, and tore down Catherine Sedgwick's Lenox home to do it; the Aspinwall Hotel was built in Lenox at a cost of $410,000; the Lenox Club voted to offer a reward of $25 "to anyone securing the conviction of autoists who violate the town's speed laws." In Lenox and Stockbridge, Giraud Foster built Bellefontaine; Morris K. Jesup built Belvoir Terrace; George Westinghouse built Erskine Park; Anson Phelps Stokes built Shadow Brook; George Halle Morgan built Ventfort Hall; H. H. Cook built Wheatleigh; Charles Astor Bristed built Lakeside; and John Sloane built Wyndhurst.

Courtesy of the Providence Library

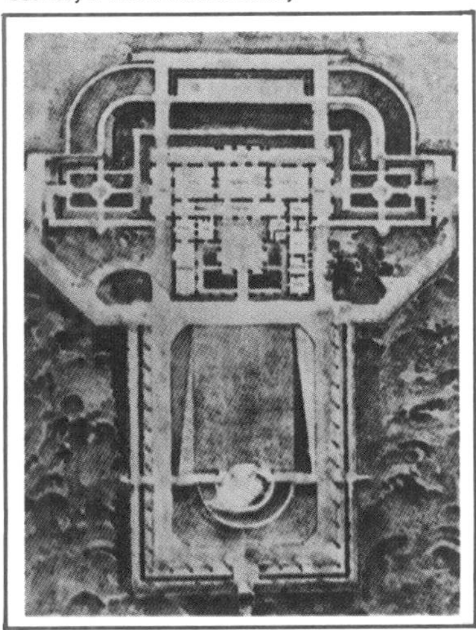

Architect's rendering of Bellefontaine gardens

Between 1900 and 1910, William McKinley and Teddy Roosevelt, the "Trust Buster," were in the White House. Upton Sinclair's ***The Jungle*** resulted in the establishment of the Pure Food and Drugs Act. Henry Clay Frick was shot on the front steps of his New York City palace. With $100,000, Henry Ford founded The Ford Motor Company, and soon after, General Motors and Rolls Royce followed. J. P. Morgan organized The United States Steel Corporation. William James and Julia Ward Howe died. Albert Einstein published a paper on the Theory of Relativity. Less than ten years after Charles Worth, ***"le tyran de la mode,"*** had been quoted as saying, "We live by and for luxury, therefore all the questions we ask ourselves are superfluous, we must assume our roles and that is all," Sigmund Freud published his first paper on theories of human behavior. James Barrie wrote ***Peter Pan***, Henry James wrote ***The Golden Bowl***, and Beatrix Potter wrote ***Peter Rabbit***. The first daily comic ("Mutt and Jeff") and the first neon sign appeared, but certainly not in Lenox or Stockbridge where Dan Hanna, son of

Mark Hanna, bought Bonnie Brier Farm; Robert W. Paterson built Blantyre; Newbold Morris built Brookhurst; the Fahnestocks built Eastover; Grenville Winthrop built Groton Place; William B. Osgood Field built Highlawn House; Edith Jones Wharton built The Mount; Samuel Frothingham built Overleigh; Mrs. Edwards Spencer built Shipton Court and John Alexandre built Spring Lawn. Edith Wharton was in Lenox where she rode as her chauffeur, Charles Cook, drove her Mercedes to the top of Mt. Greylock.

Of thirty-two cottages mentioned, only six are still private homes. Even these thirty-two represent only one third of what was built, not as private residences, but as second seasonal homes. If the ground was shifting elsewhere, it was firm in Lenox and Stockbridge. The cottagers not only owned fifty percent of the land in Lenox and thirty-three percent of Stockbridge, but they were major employers. All in all, their cottages were set down in very sympathetic surroundings. DeWitt Mallary wrote a book about Lenox in 1902, describing the summer colony.

> Nature's inspiring canvas in a frame of art,—this is the Lenox of today. More than half of the area of the township has passed into possession of those who, with large means, have touched the olden picture of scenic charm only to adorn it. An urban class seeking rural retreats has added to the charm of the region by creation of beautiful estates, and one is diverted for the moment from the scenery to the elegance of these extensive properties, whose villas have been built, in recent years, upon an increasing scale of magnificence.... Often during the "season", when handsome equipages are rolling along on every highway and the exploring tourists on foot or wheel are abroad in the land, one hears this question: What is the effect of the incoming of wealth upon Lenox?
>
> The most immediate and perceptible effect of all this change in the outward conditions has been a complete change in the internal life of the village.... Farms that were worth $50 an acre

Courtesy of the Library of Congress

Loggia at Wyndhurst

Courtesy of the Providence Library

The cottage of John Sloane, Wyndhurst

Courtesy of the Providence Library

Architect's rendering of Shadow Brook

Shadow Brook as it was built

Courtesy of the Berkshire Eagle

for potatoes sold for $1,000 an acre for building purposes.... Villas, surrounded by extensive parklike grounds overlooks the landscape at different angles of vision, and dots the hillsides everywhere...[2]

The time had been ripe. All the ingredients necessary had been present. The result of so singular an aim, supported in every quarter, was exceptional. But, however exceptional the results, the problems in building the cottages were often mundane and even comical.

25th August, 1888

Dear Mr. Sloane:

I was sorry not to find you at home when I called some time ago. Your place is very open to criticism because the garden-

ers have been aiming too much to make it bright, gay and splendid, the consequence being a great lack of the quietness and repose of manner which should distinguish a gentleman's country place and a marked disseverance of the locality from the characteristic scenery of the neighboring region. That is what many people like but it is just what in the general plan, the location of the house and its immediate surroundings, it was the purpose to avoid... The advice that I should give you surely would be to eliminate nearly all the shrubs...

Yours truly,
Frederick Law Olmsted
Elm Court
Lenox, Massachusetts
Aug. 26/88

Dear Mr. Olmsted
...as most of the shrubs are those of your selection, I am somewhat at a loss to understand...
Your truly,
WmD Sloane

In Lenox, Mrs. Anson Phelps Stokes had problems of her own. In 1891 work had begun on the Stokes' impressive estate Shadow

Courtesy of the Providence Library

Built by H. H. Cook, Wheatleigh was the cottage of his daughter, Mrs. Carlos deHeredia

Coldbrooke, John S. Barnes' cottage

Courtesy of the Library of Congress

Courtesy of The Berkshire Eagle

Blantyre,
Robert Warden Paterson's
cottage

Brook. It would take two years, five hundred skilled laborers, and one and a half million dollars to build. Ernest W. Bowditch, a landscape architect, was retained after Mrs. Stokes "rejected tentative sketches made by Olmsted."

> In his journal, Mr. Bowditch recalled the circumstances . . . when I met him [Mr. Stokes] he had just purchased the old Ward estate [Oakswood, not Highwood] and adjoining land—in all some 500 acres; had started a gigantic stone house with a Pittsfield architect and had just come to realizing that by no possibility could he drive to his front door in safety, and furthermore, if he succeeded in reaching that point, it was physically impossible to turn a vehicle around unless he had a mechanical turntable. Incidentally, he had no water supply, no sewage disposal and the

(Right) Spring Lawn,
the cottage of
John Alexandre

(Below) Brookhurst,
cottage of
Newbold Morris

Courtesy of the Providence Library

Courtesy of the Providence Library

entrance to his estate was so tangled with his neighbors property that it was cause for anxiety.[3]

To add to whatever mortification Mr. and Mrs. Stokes already felt, after carefully explaining to Mr. Bowditch that, although they had not met him, they understood that the neighbor in question was a difficult, unreasonable man with a bad temper, Mr. Bowditch told the Stokes' that the neighbor was his first cousin.

Mrs. Schuyler Van Rensselaer, an architectural critic writing at the time observed:

> Everyone knows what were the first of all our country dwellings —those old farm houses built by Dutch or English settlers... [next] those colonial dwellings that soon were built for a higher than the farming class... a family likeness claims them all... But there came a time when the traditions of classifying art died out, when our early forms and ideals were abandoned... in general we renounced all attempts at style of any sort... in our country places we see the tendency toward ignorant, reckless originality.[4]

Whatever, the modern reader can make of such criticism, certainly the cottages were unique and different one from another. George William Sheldon, a highly regarded architectural critic writing in the same year as Mrs. Van Rensselaer, was kinder on the same subject, and called the architecture of country dwellings "eclectic."[5] He seemed to rejoice in the variety of the early cottages like Elm Court, Naumkeag and Allen Winden.

Ernest Bowditch, the landscape architect for Shadow Brook, Allen Winden, Belvoir Terrace, and Coldbrooke, came on the scene a little later. He wrote that Charles Lanier's Allen Winden "... designed by Peabody and Stearns was a comfortable country house with little ornamentation located on top of a hill from which the view in every direction was splendid. Next door on the south was a house occupied by Richard Goodman—and old farmhouse that had been altered by Mr. Kim [sic: Charles Follen McKim] of New York with the most charming result and a comparison of the two exteriors was unfavorable for the Lanier mansion."[6]

Courtesy of the Berkshire Eagle

Shipton Court, cottage of Mrs. Edwards Spencer

Jeffrey Platt, architect and grandnephew of Joseph Choate, recalls Naumkeag, "Architecturally, I didn't think much of it to begin with except that it was a very comfortable place inside. Wonderful place to visit. You know it was one thing on one side and one thing on the other, and something else front and back. I don't think it was a shingle style. It was shingle on one side only. Real shingle style was shingle all over. I don't know what happened." It looked as if McKim, Mead and White each had designed a section without consulting one another.

Perhaps the critics such as Mrs. Van Rensselaer were persuasive or perhaps the cottagers needed a more definitive expression of their position, whatever the case, the architecture changed seemingly in answer to her question: "The main question is does it [the architecture of country houses] indeed wholly meet the needs of today practically, expressionally and artistically?"[7] The later cottages were more uniform and were classical. Part of the cottag-

Stonover,
John E. Parsons'
cottage

Courtesy of the Library of Congress

ers' practical need was to follow Weber's notion of "agreed upon communal action." Specifically this meant demonstrating the ability to have a single dress for a single occasion and a single servant for a single task. It was expected that those in Society had the resources to accomplish this single-mindedness. It also extended to their cottages. As the lady of the house had a morning dress, so she had a morning room. As she had a ballgown, so she had a ballroom. The cottages grew as the number of rooms for a single purpose grew.

It may be interesting to the reader and occupant of modern housing that Mrs. Van Rensselaer did not view the country homes "as examples of palatial dignity and richness" as Americans "are a city-loving people and give their country home but a secondary station."[8]

Notwithstanding the "secondary" position that Mrs. Van Rensselaer awards cottages, by today's standards, they were palatial, dignified, and rich beyond imagining. Eugene Jappron, a footman at Wheatleigh recalls: "Over to Mrs. deHeredia's, she had a flower room. I wish you could have seen it. That was a room in the house just for cutting the flowers. Well, in the flower room there was a table all made of tiles—mosaic. It was a beautiful thing. Someone said it was valued at $10,000—just the table."

Ernest Bowditch, having criticized an early cottage, Allen Winden, went on to praise later cottages like Shadow Brook. "When this work was done, I began to realize the truth of the theory that when a man embarks on large enterprises, he is apt to lose interest in the small and even moderated sized... at Lenox, it certainly seems as though comparatively small [cottages] were less interesting and required less time, were perhaps neglected (?), and did not turn out well."[9]

Miss Rosamond Sherwood explains, "You could tell the formality of the house by its size. The bigger the house, the more servants, the more formal the household." So the life inside the houses did differ as the exteriors differed, and so did the amount of respect and service that the cottagers received. The larger the house, the greater the display, and therefore, the greater the respect commanded. But regardless of the differences in the final products, they all had certain things in common.

"The will to grow was everywhere written large and to grow at no matter what or whose expense. I had naturally seen it before... But here, clearly, it was a matter of scale...."[10] They were the cottagers of the Berkshires. They built on the foundation of their personal wealth and they built for permanence. One old-timer summed it up in a single sentence: "Those folks built for forever—for a dollar a day." They expected to be served. They knew they were the new industry of the Berkshires. They took their leisure seriously, and they took a lively and competitive interest in one another. Although they entertained one another with drives and visiting, golf, croquet, squash, horse shows and gymkhanas, picnics, boat parades, bridge, musicales, art shows, dinners and dances, one reporter of the day wrote that the real favorite "indoor sport was comparing views." It was essential to have a charming view from your villa, it was entertaining to establish that you had a superior view.

On October 11, 1892, H. H. Cook wrote Frederick Law Olmsted, "I am thinking of making a purchase of several acres of land near Lenox with a view of improving it. Before doing so I would like to

Courtesy of Providence Library

Ventfort Hall

Ventfort Hall, Architect's rendering

Courtesy of Providence Library

be informed whether or not it has all the requisites for making a fine place."[11] Not only did all the cottagers share with Mr. Cook the desire for a "fine place" but there was no doubt in anyone's mind that their efforts were improving the villages. Except, perhaps, in Stockbridge, while Mr. Cook had to seek permission for the road out of his estate that lay in Stockbridge and had to alter his plans to get it; in Lenox, the town fathers built a new road to the railway station to accommodate the wishes of the cottagers. In Lenox, "superb roads" were "full of gay equestrians and dashing turnouts, handsome women holding the reins of prancing thoroughbreds . . . grooms sitting behind with folded arms . . . while the barefooted boy and girl of the farmhouse look on with covetous eyes."[12] In Stockbridge, a villager was outraged when she saw two people in the street she did not know.

In part, the difference between Lenox and Stockbridge during the estate period was due to the relative sizes of the estates built in each town. Since the estates in Lenox were larger, the logic of the day was dictated, Lenox was the better place to be. Perceptions and judgments were based upon display. The cottagers, the summer people, were inventing and building the world in which they wanted to live. While Lenox gave itself over to the process and lent its assistance, Stockbridge stood back with the sense of an old village bracing for the onslaught, intent upon maintaining its identity. While Lenox seemed dizzy from focusing on the bright birds of passage, Stockbridge seemed to ignore the plumage and demand that if they built their nests there, they had to join the community. Of course, it was easier for Stockbridge. The change there was less abrupt and less encompassing. Not only were the cottages smaller in Stockbridge, but there were fewer of them. The scale was smaller in Stockbridge and therefore easier to manage. All the cottagers desired regard. They sought it by living up as far as they could to the new measure for regard—display. Stockbridge was more comfortable with the old yardstick since by the new one, they were inferior to Lenox. Stockbridge blended Yankee values

Yokun, the Goodman cottage

Courtesy of the Library of Congress

Courtesy of the Stockbridge Library

Allen Winden,
cottage of Charles Lanier

Courtesy of the Providence Library

Thomas Shields-Clark's
Fernbrook

Harris Fahnestock's Eastover
with floor plans

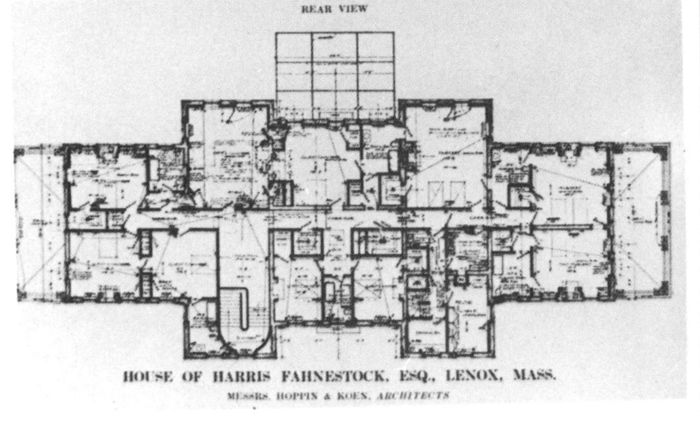

Courtesy of the Prcvidence Library

Overleigh,
cottage of
Samuel Frothingham

Courtesy of the Providence Library

with the ones of the Gilded Age, and fared better by doing so.

Regardless of the differences between the two villages, the cottagers in both had one other thing in common: they were Berkshire cottagers and not Newport cottagers. Newport was as formal as the city. The Berkshires offered the right sort of social intercourse without the stricture of extreme formality. One magazine reporter at the time likened it to the difference between the peaceful silence of the Berkshires and the incessant pounding of the sea at Newport. Quite poetic, but a friend of Edith Wharton's put it more plainly. In 1899, when Edith first came from Newport to the Berkshires, "Walter Berry wrote and congratulated her for getting away from 'all the sogginess' and taking to the hills."[13] ***Town Topics*** simply said that at Lenox one didn't need as many gowns as at Newport. A lady born at the turn of the century, explaining the ***Town Topics*** remark, was quite direct, "I loathed Newport with all its formality and chi-chi. If Elm Court was vast, there was a reason for its vastness—not just show." It is interesting to remember that, compared to life in their city houses, the cottagers felt that they were

Courtesy of Mrs. Adele Emory

The fountain at Elm Court

roughing it when in their thirty-five to ninety-five room Berkshire cottages.

It is not that the same families did not frequent Newport and the Berkshires, Bar Harbor and the Adirondacks. They did. It was a matter of where they chose to build. In common, the Berkshire cottagers held a desire for regard, a love of competition, and a common yardstick for measuring the regard due the winners in the social game. As Mrs. Emory so charmingly explained the yardstick: "Do you know the courtyard [at Elm Court] with the copy of that Roman fountain in the middle? When I went to Rome, I found it, and of course the original was about one third the size of the copy. That gives you the feeling—everything had to be on a large scale. Very magnificent." They also held in common a preference for the lifestyle in the mountains for some months of their social calendar.

A. J. Downing was one of the first American architectural critics. Toward the end of his life, he actually turned his hand to architecture, but died at 37 years of age. During his short life, in articles and books, such as ***The Architecture of Country Dwellings*** and ***A Treatise on the Theory and Practice of Landscape Gardening***, Downing had a profound influence on architecture. In 1865, in ***A Treatise***, Downing wrote that one could "suppose" the proclivities of the cottagers by the style of the cottages they built. A cottager who built a villa in the Grecian or Roman style would be a classical scholar or gentleman with a love of antiquities; the builder of an Italian villa would be one who loved gardens and pictures; the builder of a baronial castle would be a wealthy proprietor, either chivalrous or romantic; one who built a "castellated" dwelling (that is a home with battlements or a tower or other castle-like adornment) would have a desire for display; and the cottager who wanted to achieve the "beau ideal" of an old English country seat would build a Tudor.

Do Downing's definitions tell us anything about the Berkshire cottagers? Mr. and Mrs. Anson Phelps Stokes certainly built a castellated dwelling. The large sweeping stone wall surrounding the terrace on the south side was almost a battlement, except, of course, it had no function for defending the house. Shadow Brook also had a tower. Was Mr. Stokes concerned with display? On September 2, 1893, ***Town Topics*** reported, "The arrival of Mr. and Mrs. Anson Phelps Stokes at Lenox is proof positive that it is now quite the proper thing for the seaside throng to stray toward the mountains.... I understand this mansion [Shadow Brook] is a wonder in its way, and that the only things approaching its mammoth size are some of the buildings on the World's Fair grounds [The Chicago World's Fair, 1893]." Excepting the sometimes exaggerated reporting in the ***Town Topics***, it would appear that, at least, the Stokes' were not immune to display. If at the same time they were credited with trend setting or trend validating, they were probably not interested in display for its own sake, but only as a symbol of their social position. To reduce the builder of Shadow Brook to one who desired only display is unfair, not to mention untrue. It was not so much that they desired display as they desired to show that they were perfectly capable of achieving display. The entry in Mr. Stokes' journal in September, 1894, reads, "At the beginning of the month we moved into our new house, Shadow Brook—September 6th—I was one of a committee of 70 appointed to organize against Tammany." The interesting juxtaposition of the two pieces of information offered in the September journal entry can be interpreted just as the use by the Stockbridge cottage of the Lenox address was: "Father was a political liberal and a social snob."

Downing describes the builder of a baronial castle as a wealthy man who is either chivalrous or romantic. The closest thing to a baronial castle built in the Berkshires is what today is called Searles Castle and was earlier called Barrington House and Kellogg Terrace. In fact, the house was built by a woman, Mary Kellogg Hopkins, widow of Mark Hopkins. But the part played by Mr. Edward F. Searles as Mrs. Hopkins' business manager, decorator, and second husband, is always acknowledged and never underestimated. To describe Mr. Searles as a wealthy man who was either chivalrous or romantic or both is rather amusing. Mrs. Hopkins met Searles when he came to inspect her San Francisco home. Herter Brothers of New York had designed the interiors of that home. Mr. Searles was employed by the firm as an interior designer. When he planned a trip to California for health reasons, Searles agreed to make the obligatory inspection on behalf of Herter Brothers. She was 20 years his senior. She made no secret of her affection and regard for him. After some years, and the completion of the major architectural feat, Barrington House, they were married. It is quite true that he was a successful man in his own right, but his resources in no way approached hers. Certainly he was not the impetuous romantic, her torch burned long without reciprocation. Even if the stories about the trade-offs necessary to land him, including the building of the house, were untrue, he certainly did not act in anything approaching romantic haste. When she died, she left the major part of her fortune to Searles. Joseph Choate, who represented Searles when the will was challenged, wrote to his wife that the ladies in New York society seemed incensed that the money had been left to him. Evidently, Searles' wealth, romantic spirit, and chivalry were all subject to gossip if not question.

It is difficult to say if Wheatleigh is an Italian villa and if Mrs. deHeredia was a lover of gardens and pictures. George Sheldon, writing in the 1890s, described the house as French Chateau style; subsequent writers and the immediate past owner, all described it as Italianate. Although Mr. Cook, Mrs. deHeredia's father and the builder of Wheatleigh, hired Frederick Law Olmsted to do the landscaping, his letters show a greater interest in the roads and farm buildings. In one letter, he calls a halt to further development of the gardens satisfied with the extent of the work accomplished. No one makes mention of Mrs. deHeredia's love of either pictures or gardens, although she did rehire the Olmsted firm to do work creating the terraces. Tapestries covered the walls and the vases were filled with fresh flowers, her footman, Eugene Jappron recalls, but she was primarily remembered as someone who loved people and lively entertainments. "She was a great hostess; many said she was the finest hostess at the time. It was just her personality. Everyone wanted to come to her parties. She started the idea of Sunday service on the lawns. She was almost always 'at home' at tea time and always for Sunday tea."

Giraud Foster, a lover of antiquities, built a copy of the Petite Trianon, not a Roman villa. Grenville Winthrop, an art lover and collector did not build an Italian villa, but Groton Place. John Sloane did entertain the desire to recreate the English country seat with the wide English lawn broken by stately trees, and he did build a Tudor mansion, Wyndhurst. However, Downing can not claim much credit for correctly anticipating Mr. Sloane, as, regardless of what architectural style was chosen, all the cottagers were seeking to recreate the English country seat. Seemingly incorrect in every case, Downing can be forgiven since he wrote ***A Treatise*** at the very beginning of the estate period. He did not foresee how the difference in architecture would belie the life inside the house as often as it would represent it. The architecture of a house is categorical and people are not.

Elm Court was an enormous spreading house in the relatively informal New England shingle style. By its size, one would assume its formality, and true to form, it was formal. There were little white cards placed on the bedroom doors with the name of the guest printed on each. There was a board posted in the hall with the daily schedule. Mr. Morris does assure us that one kept to the posted schedule. Mrs. Wilde, granddaughter of the Sloanes of Elm Court, recalls: "Grandmother was very big on self discipline. Grandmother died at ninety-three, and up until she was ninety, she had certain rituals. She stayed downstairs until 10:00 at night. When she went upstairs, the household closed. Everything was done on the tick of time. She liked to take long walks in the woods." Here another granddaughter picks up the reminiscence, "Each morning, Grandmother would take a long walk. It was a treat to join her, which we could do if we did not 'dawdle.' Breakfast, at which our grandmother was always present in a lovely negligee, was set in English fashion on a marble-topped sideboard." In the afternoon, she rode out in her phaeton with her matched horses, Romulus and Remus. The player piano had rolls of Wagner, Liszt, Beethoven, Chopin and Brahms. There was a formal portrait of Mrs. Sloane seated dressed in pale yellow that "commanded the room." After Mrs. Sloane married Ambassador Henry White, there was a preparatory meeting at Elm Court for the Armistice meeting at Versailles in 1919. Among those who gathered under the giant elm of Elm Court, was General Foch of France. (Years later when one of the chauffeurs from Elm Court traveled to France, he saw the statue of General Foch in Paris. Excited, and thinking to impress the cab driver, he said, "I met him once at Elm Court and had a few words with him." The cab driver responded over his shoulder, "Gee, you must be old." When asked what the few words had been, he said, "Oh, the General and Ambassador White were going out for a drive and they stopped by the garage for an extra blanket.")

Elm Court was the picture of the formal house of a prosperous and powerful family. Yet, the house also included the evidences of a simpler and humorous nature. The grandchildren lived in fear, not of their formal grandmother, but of Mrs. Talbot, "the awful" housekeeper whose formality far outstripped Mrs. Sloane's. "The children ate supper with Mrs. Talbot, separate from the adults and at an earlier hour. When all the grandchildren were visiting Elm Court, we would eat together. Except the Field children, of course, because they lived down the road at Highlawn House. Well, we would be afraid of incurring Mrs. Talbot's wrath, and naturally, that's just when the giggles would start." The granddaughter of Emily Vanderbilt Sloane White seems almost ready to giggle again, seventy years later, at the memory. "Mrs. Talbot did not approve of the giggles. She was more formal than ***anyone***."

There may have been formality, but there was also a sense of humor in the cottage. A prized possession of the woman whose household ran on "the tick of time" was a handless clock. And, Mrs. Emory recalls, "Down the hall, which led to the pantry, the housekeeper's room and a guest room with bath where the ladies left their wraps, there was a sideboard which held a silver pitcher of ice water, a gong, and two seated Chinese figures whose hands you could turn to make their tongues stick out.... If Elm Court was vast, there was reason for its vastness, it was to accommodate a large family comfortably. Grandmother loved to have her family around her."

Regardless of how foreign other aspects of the cottages and the cottagers may be, there is something absolutely accessible and immediately recognizable about a home built for family visits filled with giggling children and a pair of statues constructed to stick out their tongues periodically.

The French chef at Elm Court was in charge of the kitchen with the help of three women. Every morning he would arrive in his buckboard pulled by a white horse to discuss the day's menu. (He had a house of his own on the property midway between Elm Court and Highlawn Farm). Near the greenhouses, there was a peach orchard. One afternoon, a house guest wandered into the greenhouse and smelled the peaches. He told the gardener that they smelled so good, he would like one or two. "Not while I'm here," the gardener said, "The superintendent counts every peach and sends the number up to the house so Mrs. White can plan how many to use or can or send as gifts. But, I'll tell you what I'll do. I'll take off and when I'm out of sight, what you do then is up to you." He doesn't know if the visitor took a peach or not, but he claims the man was Benny Goodman, Mrs. White's grandson-in-law. When asked, Benny Goodman said, "I never visited Elm Court." Wrong about the incident in some of its detail, the gardener knew correctly that produce was counted at Elm Court, and at other neighboring estates.

At Shadow Brook, the "boss gardener" recalled, "Mrs. Stokes was the best manager I have ever known. Many great ladies are so sudden and impervious in their demands on a gardener that he is always nervous and wondering what next. But not Mrs. Stokes. If she was going to have a party she would tell me, a whole month in advance, just exactly what she would want—what flowers and how many, what fruit and vegetables, what herbs for the French chef, how many spring turkeys, how many broilers and ducklings, how much venison. Each morning she sent a list of all the requirements of the big house down to me, and every single radish I sent up to her, I had to keep a record of. It was all in the books and it was known to the penny what the profit and loss of the estate was. It was run like a perfectly organized business."[14] The cottages were not unlike small diversified businesses—part farm, part inn, part caterer.

Many of the grandchildren remember the forbidding servants: "the critical eye of Osborn" (at Naumkeag); the procession of ladies maids at the Bishops' Winter Palace currying favor by tattling to Mrs. Bishop about Miss Bishop, and Mrs. Talbot and Stride (at Elm Court). Yet, the last time Mrs. De Gersdorff remembers the critical eye of Osborn, it was filled with tears at the funeral of Joseph Choate.

Some who worked at the estates remember the imposing natures of the cottagers: "On the place of Mr. Westinghouse in Lenox, I made a hundred acres of lawn. This Mr. Westinghouse was the inventor of the air brakes and the originator of the great company that bears his name. He was a busy man, he never stopped to talk to anyone much. He was one of those geniuses—always working—he had a great workshop on his place, with dynamos and such things in it. When in the country he was always in his workshop." The wife of a superintendent at Oronoque said, "If the lady of the house would have asked my husband to plant the flowers upside down, they would have been put in the ground upside down." Mr. Bowditch ran afoul of Miss Furness when he worked on her landscaping in Lenox. Whatever sharp words passed, Bowditch always feared that a bad word from her had halted further commissions for him in the summer colony. An employee of the Morris K. Jesup's at Belvoir Terrace recalled, "If Mr. Jesup was displeased and wanted something redone, he would always say ***Mrs.*** Jesup does not like it. Well, everyone knew that Mrs. Jesup never minded anything, and never got to say a word when Mr. Jesup was around."

What one image would best symbolize the cottage period? Would it be the deluxe Berkshire trolley with satin appointments and wall coverings? The formidable Stride, six feet tall, dressed in black, strolling the halls of Elm Court with a white Pekingese in the crook of his arm? Is it Mrs. Morse out in her buggy nodding to the gentry the morning after her son, the former poultryman and electrician, eloped with Miss Winthrop of Groton Place? Is it Mrs. Spencer of Shipton Court riding through Lenox with her white pet pig, Rosie, on a Sunday to drop her housemaid at the Catholic church before going to Trinity Church where she would always arrive late, pig in tow? Is it the young people riding out, boys and girls together, unchaperoned for a picnic? Is it an image drawn by a reporter for ***Resort Topics*** in 1904 of a vast park land created by the manicured lawns of one estate after another stretched along Prospect Hill Road? Is it the vision seen through the eyes of Mrs. Daley, as a girl, of the procession of carriages arriving at Trinity Church—a vision of fine horses, polished coaches, liveried servants and ladies in finely made gowns of rich and varied colors? Is it the peacocks on the lawn at Groton Place or the 180 statues at Bellefontaine? Is it the day in May, 1917, when Joe Choate was buried in Stockbridge—"At Stockbridge everything was done according to the Stockbridge tradition and sentiment, that is, there was no hearse—simply a wagon piled with masses of laurel leaves. It was drawn by two of Uncle Joe's horses, not driven, but drawn by Uncle Joe's old coachman on one side and a groom from Naumkeag on the other"?[215] Or, is it the ninety-third birthday party of Giraud Foster at Bellefontaine on November 8, 1943? A buffet was served, and the party gathered around. The festivities took place much as they had for thirty previous birthdays. But on this occasion, just beyond where the guests stood, the Louis XIV ballroom was closed due to the fuel shortage; and beyond the ballroom, throughout the Berkshires, the cottages stood as cold and vacant and closed off from everyday activities as Mr. Foster's ballroom.

Whether that is the image to remember, probably the ***Berkshire Eagle*** reporter was aware on November 8, 1943, that that would be the last report of a social event of the cottage period, or any cottager, that would ever be written.

Courtesy of Jane Foster Lorber

Ninetieth Birthday party of Giraud Foster

Courtesy of Jane Foster Lorber

Table set for the Birthday Party

7

DOES OUR PAST HAVE A FUTURE?

No state once gone can recur and be identical with what it was before.

William James:
The Principles of Psychology

s a people, Americans improve upon the past, rebel against it and romanticize it, but we do not carry it around in our pocket as a common part of our travel kit. Notwithstanding Thomas Jefferson, we are concerned more with where we are going than where we have been. We believe it is our next step, not our last, that demonstrates our national character. Our national posture and vision are focused forward while our past languishes behind unnoticed, gathering dust in inaccessible corners, going up in smoke and down under the wrecker's ball. Like the adolescent trying to effect the appearance of spontaneous generation, we shake loose from the past as if it were impeding forward motion. We want, more than anything else it seems, to be entertained by the past, to view it as if it relates to our everyday lives in the same way (no more and no less) as the theater does. So when we look around to find our roots and traditions, we discover them in sad disarray or various states of destruction.

Just before noon on November 14, 1981, a single event commenced that illustrates life in this corner of the Berkshires better than pages of prose or hours of research. A woman stood at the front door of the house on Main Street, Stockbridge, that has belonged to the Sedgwick family since 1780. She welcomed each guest individually. They came in a steady silent stream. At a few minutes past twelve, the appointed time, the front door closed. It remained closed for thirty minutes. The coral house was silent. The Sedgwick wagon stood in the circular drive in front of the door. It was a plain wooden wagon draped with pine bows and late fall flowers. The brown of the wagon, the green boughs, and the orange and yellow flowers blended and contrasted with the coral house behind it. Even the street was quiet as if out of respect. Few cars travelled this end of the road west of the Red Lion Inn. Old-time townspeople who passed could imagine the scene within: the rector of Saint Paul's Episcopal Church quietly eulogizing as the family members sat quietly. At 12:30, the door opened.

The plain casket was placed upon the wagon by the males in the group. The boughs and flowers covered it. With the pastor at the front of the cortege, the slow walk to the "Pie" began. At a previous Sedgwick funeral, the horse was nervous and there was a disturbance. The man who provided the horse has since died, so the wagon is now pulled by the men in the family. Allowing for the vicissitudes of fashion in dress, the procession could be mistaken for any one from 1781–1981. The pastor in his white surplice, hands folded in front of him, led the way out of the drive and left

A Sedgwick funeral,
November, 1981

Photographs by Carole Owens

onto Main Street. The wagon was surrounded by the surviving members of the Sedgwick family, there was a slight break in the procession and then another group of mourners followed. A woman walking at the head of the second group carried a small bouquet of flowers. No one spoke. At the entrance to the graveyard, the procession turned right and continued straight back to the "Pie." It is said that a Sedgwick child, in the eighteenth century, upon seeing the Sedgwick plot blurted out, "My goodness, it looks like a pie" and was duly punished. However, the name stuck. For generations, the Sedgwicks have been buried in the same spot, in the same manner, with the same procession. All Sedgwick tombstones encircle the larger stones of Theodore and Pamela, the first Sedgwicks to be buried here.

At about 12:40 on November 14, 1981, Mrs. Sedgwick Bond is

laid to rest alongside her father and grandfather and great-grandfather She is laid in a cemetery with ceremony that has continued unchanged. The mourners walk back for a small lunch at the coral house on Main Street.

We cannot expect that every aspect of our history will be preserved as scrupulously as Sedgwick tradition. We have a right, however, to want some part of our heritage preserved and accessible. We have a responsibility too. It is unfortunate that the motivation often comes from mourning what is gone. Across the country, the summer cottages have been abandoned, sacked, demolished, and burned. The palatial homes that the rich built in the suburbs are probably the greatest and most typical of the Gilded Age's contribution to architecture. "By its country estates, the Gilded Age is remembered. The present age will be remembered for tearing them down."[1]

The Field children at Highlawn House, 1913

Courtesy of William O. Field

If we have the opportunity to visit one of the cottages, and if, as we walk through it, we ask, what was it like to build such a place and live in it, the answer to that question is the history of a period. To answer it is to understand the economic growth of a country, the philosophy, the religion, and the values of a country and a time.

The gilt of the Age of Elegance was run out of town by an automobile, tarnished by world war, and put beyond the reach of people by the graduated income tax. In the over half century since it has been safe to say that the Gilded Age is dead and gone, there have been times when Tiffany lamps gathered dust on the back tables of antique shops; the Victorian loveseat was considered ugly and uncomfortable—though cheap; and the architecture of the day impractical, nonfunctional, and peculiar looking at best. During such times, it was thought that:

> McKim, Mead and White...and other classicists, were mere copycats; worse, responsible for stifling and setting back for decades the development of a genuine vernacular, ingenious and, above all, original American architecture...More than five decades after the systematic denigration of McKim, Mead and White...their works have been destroyed, truncated and vandalized.[2]

We were losing the architectural representation of our history and heritage to the fire engine and the bulldozer. Perhaps the architecture was criticized not only for itself, but because it symbolized an age that was being attacked.

William Henry Vanderbilt made $10,300,000 per year. That's $858,333 per month, $190,740 per week, $28,219 per day, $1175.79 per hour. When he left each of his eight children $10,000,000, there was still $17,000,000 left for his wife out of holdings, not including income. The second coachman at Elm Court, William Henry's daughter's estate, made $840 per year, $70 per month, $15 per week, $2 per day, 20-25¢ per hour. Andrew Carnegie said in the ***Gospel of Wealth*** that it was the responsibility of the superior upper class to give to the less fortunate. An assistant gardener left Carnegie's employ at Shadow Brook when he was refused a raise from $60 to $70 per month. A case could probably be made that Carnegie and Vanderbilt had so much ***because*** others had so little. The anonymous Berkshire poet who wrote the lines: "The golf course runs so close by the mill, that the laboring children can see the men at play," would probably have rejoiced had he lived to see the cottages deteriorate.

Courtesy of Jane Foster Lorber

"Boy" Foster
at Bellefontaine,
with his dog, Berry

Perhaps we think we have progressed past a former ignoble economic system. Assume that is true, then why preserve the symbols of a less than glorious past? If we do not, what we lose is the ability to judge where we are and how we got there. Without history, it is possible to believe that things are as they have always been and always will be. You lose the ability to look into a fine old face and catch a glimpse of the girl she was. It becomes impossible to tell if the way things are is progression, regression, or oscillation.

Besides, the history of the Gilded Age is a whale of a story. The scenes are full of the outrageous and splendid, the sordid and the humorous. The dynastic dreams and ferocious deeds, the brilliant accomplishments and the perfectly silly: the scale of the age is easier to grasp standing in a preserved cottage of like dimensions.

The Countess Scherr Thoss said that this generation does not care about history. The granddaughter of Ambassador Henry White, she was a contemporary, a relative, a friend, and one of the social and economic elite. Neither this generation nor that saved history. For the forty years between 1880 and 1920, they struggled to buy history and civilization. But even during that forty-year span, the buying and selling was seen not as a preservation for posterity or the common weal, but a trading back and forth between

American Architect and Building News, Providence Library

Bellefontaine, 1897

individual collections, an intensely private matter reserved for the select. When Mary Jane Morgan died in 1885, the catalogue advertising her collection of 2,628 lots cost Parke-Bernet $40,000 to produce. The collection itself was auctioned off for a record $1,205,153. A record that was not broken until well into the twentieth century. The city of New York, fired by newspaper editorials, was horrified. "Culture was a commendable thing, but what would a woman want of it who never entertained? Furthermore, there were rules about collecting that this Mrs. Nobody had flagrantly ignored."[3] As she was not one of the acknowledged arbiters of taste, how dare she have entered the world of collectors and set a standard at that?

In the 1930s, with the same intensity that the parents had collected, their children rushed to sell. Frederick Field had quite a pedigree. Born in the early 1900s, it may have appeared that the world of Lila Vanderbilt and William B. Osgood Field's son was unshakable. His maternal grandparents were Emily Thorn Vanderbilt and William J. Sloane of New York and Elm Court, Lenox. On his father's side, he was the descendant of Samuel Osgood, the first postmaster of the United States and Cyrus Field, who laid the first transatlantic cable. When in the country, he lived at Highlawn, the elegant cottage set on nine hundred acres. In the city, he lived among his father's collection of armor, crucifixes, sporting prints and manuscripts, not to mention the million dollars worth of wedding presents his parents had reputedly received. Yet, he once said, "We were underprivileged. Even then we knew that our way of living was going out, and that some day we would have to change our lives and revolt against the tradition."[4] And revolt they did. Frederick became a member of the Communist party, and after contemplating it since 1959, published his memoirs in 1983 under the descriptive title, ***My Life From Right to Left.*** One of the Stokes'sons married Rose Pastor, a vocal and well-known Socialist and a Jew, and the Winthrop girls married servants, and Susan Frelinghuysen (Mrs. George) Morris registered her dog, "Miss Rosie Morris," in The Social Register. Some of them may have sold the symbols of their parents' status, because of the economic realities of the 1930s. Others may have done so out of rebellion.

In the 1940s, "the house wreckers proceeded up Fifth Avenue. One by one, the palaces that had been built to last forever have been dismantled, their treasures scattered by the Parke-Bernet."[5] It does not seem to be as much a matter of date, as the Countess suggested, as of place. Americans do not seem to preserve.

Still, there are always notable exceptions. Although all seven of the Vanderbilt city mansions are gone, the two houses Emily Thorn Vanderbilt and W. J. Sloane built for their daughters, Mrs. Burden and Mrs. Hammond, still stand next to one another on 91st Street. The Waldorf-Astoria is gone, but W.E.D. Stokes' Ansonia is not. Mrs. Astor's "last word" in city palaces is gone, but Grenville Winthrop's, Cortlandt Field Bishop's, and Mrs. deHeredia's city houses are there. So are their country addresses: Mrs. deHeredia's Wheatleigh, Mr. Winthrop's Groton Place, Mr. Bishop's Winter Palace and the Sloane's Elm Court.

There are also individual exceptions; people who provided, during their lifetimes and through their estates, for the establish-

Bellefontaine, 1949

ment and enrichment of museums. When Grenville Lindall Winthrop of Groton Place, died in 1943, he left his art collection to the Fogg Museum of Art, Harvard University. It was estimated that the 4,800 items had cost Mr. Winthrop $6,000,000 to amass. The introduction to the seventy-two page catalogue says, "Who else among the most distinguished collectors of his generation has had comparable powers of discrimination in so many contrasting categories?" The collection included Chinese and French art, Egyptian, Persian, and Mayan sculpture, Wedgewood pottery, Italian, Flemish, French, and American paintings including works by Degas, Renoir, Whistler, and Copley Stuart. What could only have been seen at No. 15 East 81st Street, New York, Mr. Winthrop's city address, or at Groton Place, Lenox, was now on display for the benefit of the public.

Morris Ketchum Jesup of Belvoir Terrace, Lenox, provided two million dollars, half during his lifetime and the other half after his death, for the establishment and continuance of the American Museum of Natural History, New York. The philanthropies of Andrew Carnegie of Shadow Brook are legend. Anson Phelps Stokes, the builder and original owner of Shadow Brook, was a philanthropist during his lifetime. When he died on June 23, 1913, the first headlines estimated his fortune to be in the neighborhood of $25,000,000. The directors of a number of worthy causes, including art museums, who had benefited from Mr. Stokes' kindnesses during his life, must have held their respective breaths. But by August 2, it was reported that Mr. Stokes had left an estate of less than $1,000,000 divided between his wife, nine children, and fourteen grandchildren.

Perhaps because they had depleted their fortunes, or perhaps because they subscribed to the attitude that history and civilization were the private collectibles of the elite, many estates were auctioned, "the treasures scattered by the Parke-Bernet" or other auction houses.

On July 24, 25, and 26, 1946, what was "formerly the property of Giraud Foster of the estate known as Bellefontaine" was auctioned by Tobias, Fischer and Company, New York City. The illustrated catalogue was 101 pages and listed 1,044 items. The fine furniture, carpets, tapestries, art, china and books had ornamented the thirty-five room cottage. The 106 bronze and marble statues listed were in gardens that dotted the 180 acre estate.

Mrs. Georgie deHeredia's cottage, Wheatleigh, was auctioned as were the furnishings "in situ." When Cortlandt Field Bishop's collection was auctioned by the American Art Association in 1935, there were 331 rare etchings and engravings including Rembrandt's. His collection of furniture and art objects from every country and almost every century numbered 724 items. That did not include what his wife, Amy Bend Bishop, had decided to keep, nor his collection of rare books, which had cost $1,000,000 in 1922. The latter was auctioned by the Parke-Bernet.

In the 1960s, the word "environmentalists" achieved a prominent place in the American language. We became a country of sav-

Two views of Ananda Hall being razed

Courtesy of the Berkshire Eagle

ers, conservers, protectors, and recyclers. One was either for trees and conservation or against God and the betterment of mankind. We went back to nature and back to basics. We did not build if we could restore, repair, or add on. The Berkshires got a second wind. Not only did people want to go to the country, they wanted to see old things when they got there. The question today is not so much should we protect the remnants of our past as what is left to save and how can we do it?

By and large, Americans express their value system by how they spend their money. Given the law of finite resources, the more money spent on a service, project, or function, the more the decision makers valued it. The problem of restoration and retention of the Berkshire Cottages is a problem of dollars and cents. The Historic Preservation Agent for Berkshire County hopes to educate citizens to the value of preservation in order to influence legislation that will result in the necessary funding. In the meantime, he works with the municipalities to create alternative uses. The problem is more severe in Lenox than Stockbridge, he explains, partly because there were simply more and larger houses in Lenox. The

Courtesy of the Providence Library

Elm Court,
1880s to 1980s

Photograph by Mimi MacDonald

Courtesy of Berkshire Historical Society

Lenox railway station, 1890's

Photograph by Robert Owens

Lenox railway station, 1980's

larger the house, the harder it is to adapt to modern uses. That is part of the reason, but the other part is that in Stockbridge there is a tradition of preservation and beautification that goes back to 1853.

In that year, Mrs. Goodrich started the Laurel Hill Association. She involved every man, woman, and child in the village of Stockbridge in beautification. Stockbridge, population 1,900, created the model for town improvement. It was a model copied by Boston and London. A hundred and thirty years of practice has helped Stockbridge meet the challenge of the estates—the marvelous pink elephants, part dream and part intrusion into twentieth century reality.

Courtesy of the Providence Library

Shadow Brook, 1893

In 1939, for a song, you could have bought the home of Mrs. Alfred Gwynne Vanderbilt Baker on property developed by George Westinghouse with his generator and his playhouse, set among the system of ponds and trails he developed. You could have had the home of Grenville Winthrop, endower of the Harvard University art museum, and descendant of John Winthrop, the first governor of Massachusetts and bringer of the fork to the American dinner table. Having turned down $300,000 earlier, Mrs. Robert W. Paterson sold Blantyre for $35,000. Today, the Berkshires is restoring itself. In Lenox, they are contemplating an Estate Law that would encourage developers who want to buy the large tracts of land for modern uses to preserve the main house and the integrity of the estate by offering them a tax incentive. It is hard to

Photographs by Sherman E. Hall (Courtesy of Stockbridge Library)

Shadow Brook, 1956

forget, however, that we are almost too late at our new-found appreciation of the past. Of the ninety-three cottages built during the Gilded Age, many are gone and many others are in disrepair.

The Berkshire cottages were conceived as exclusive. Today, they have a new kind of exclusivity—extinction. They are disappearing one by one, never to be duplicated. Perhaps the uniqueness and the scarcity of such dwellings will heighten their value and motivate us to protect and maintain what we have. It is ironic that a thing so carefully conceived and constructed at such cost, not only in dollars but in human ingenuity, craft, labor, and imagination, has been so carelessly destroyed.

The cottages stand silent at the mercy of their next owner. That is, if they are standing at all.

PART II: TOURING THE BERKSHIRE COTTAGES

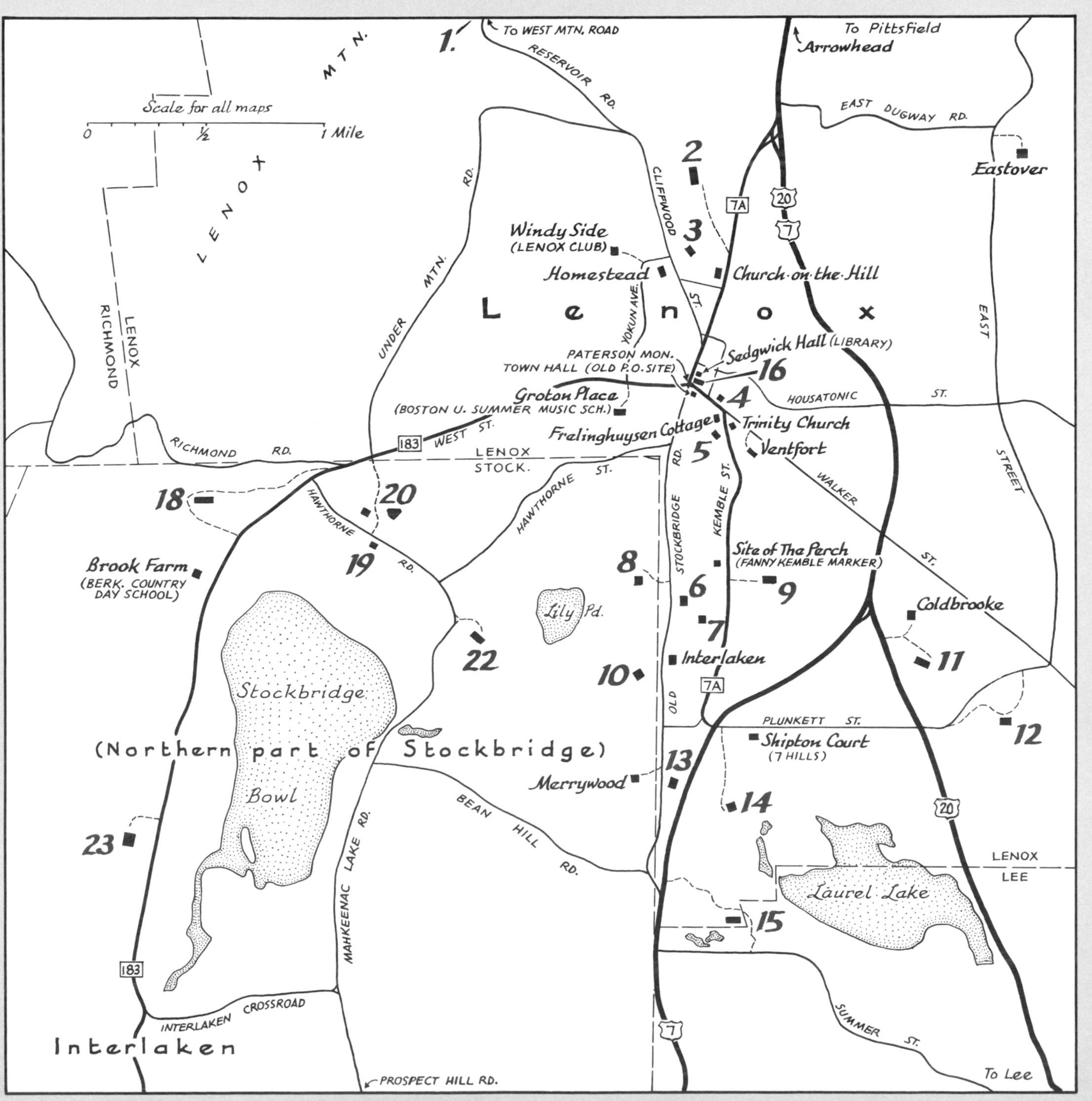
To WEST MTN. ROAD
To Pittsfield
Arrowhead
MTN.
RESERVOIR RD.
EAST DUGWAY RD.
Scale for all maps
0
½
1 Mile
Eastover
LENOX
CLIFFWOOD ST.
Windy Side (LENOX CLUB)
Homestead
Church-on-the-Hill
Lenox
LENOX
RICHMOND
UNDER MTN. RD.
YOKUN AVE.
EAST STREET
PATERSON MON.
TOWN HALL (OLD P.O. SITE)
Sedgwick Hall (LIBRARY)
Groton Place (BOSTON U. SUMMER MUSIC SCH.)
HOUSATONIC ST.
Frelinghuysen Cottage
Trinity Church
Ventfort
RICHMOND RD.
WEST ST.
LENOX
STOCK.
HAWTHORNE ST.
WALKER ST.
HAWTHORNE RD.
STOCKBRIDGE RD.
KEMBLE ST.
Site of The Perch (FANNY KEMBLE MARKER)
Brook Farm (BERK. COUNTRY DAY SCHOOL)
Lily Pd.
Coldbrooke
Interlaken
OLD
PLUNKETT ST.
Stockbridge
(Northern part of Stockbridge)
Bowl
Shipton Court (7 HILLS)
Merrywood
BEAN HILL RD.
MAHKEENAC LAKE RD.
LENOX
LEE
Laurel Lake
INTERLAKEN CROSSROAD
Interlaken
SUMMER ST.
PROSPECT HILL RD.
To Lee
1 2 3 4 5 6 7 8 9 10 11 12 13 14 15 16 18 19 20 22 23
7A 20 7 183

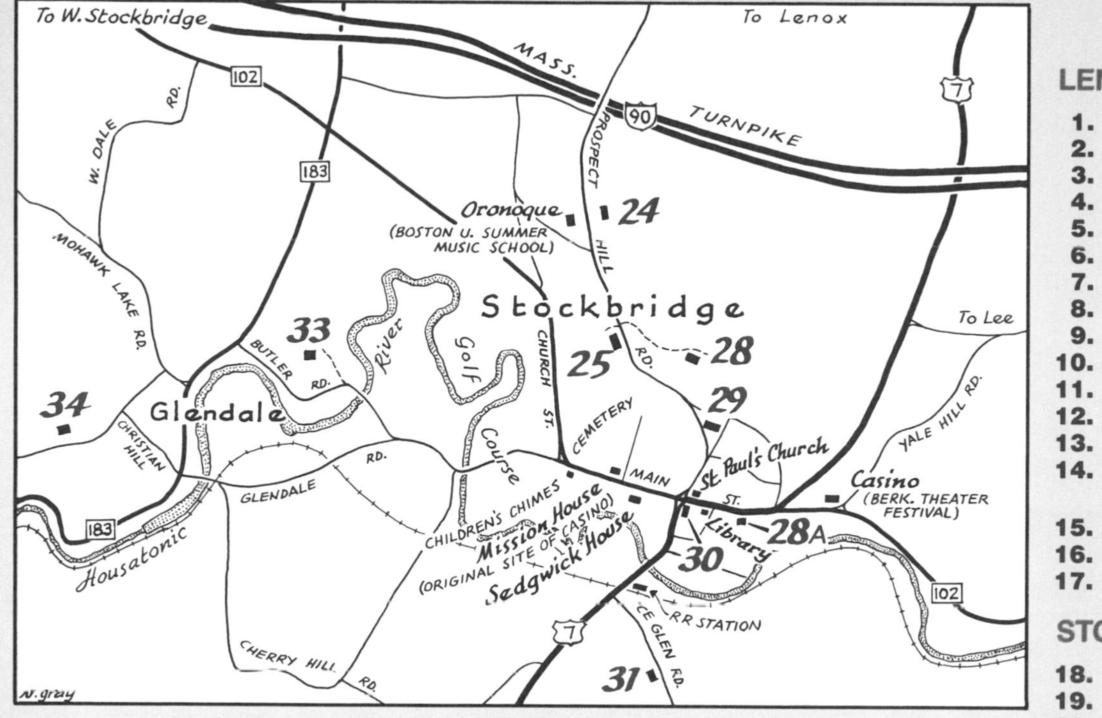

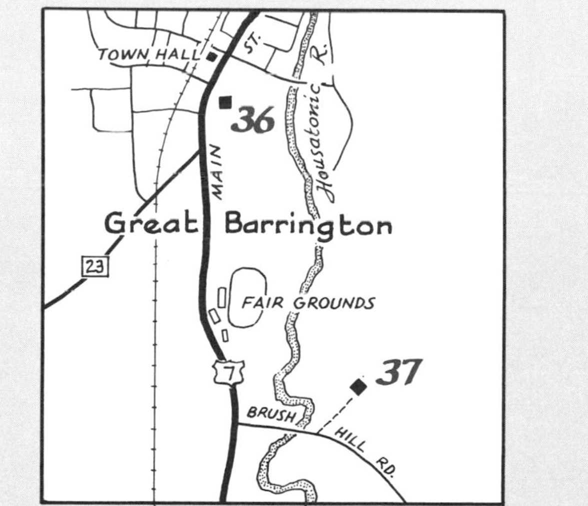

LENOX

1. **FERNBROOK**/*Avalon School*
2. **ASPINWALL HOTEL**
3. **BELVOIR TERRACE**
4. **ORLETON**/*The Gateways Inn*
5. **SPRING LAWN**/*Bible Speaks*
6. **ANANDA HALL**
7. **WINTER PALACE**
8. **ALLEN WINDEN**/*Berkshire Christian College*
9. **BELLEFONTAINE**
10. **ELM COURT**
11. **WYNDHURST**/*'Cranwell'*
12. **BLANTYRE**
13. **OVERLEIGH**/*Avalon School*
14. **THE MOUNT**/*Edith Wharton Restoration and Shakespeare & Co.*
15. **ERSKINE PARK**/*The Ponds at Fox Hollow*
16. **THE CURTIS**
17. **BROOKHURST**/*Private Home*

STOCKBRIDGE

18. **SHADOW BROOK**/*Kripalu Center*
19. **THE LITTLE RED HOUSE**
20. **TANGLEWOOD**
21. **HIGHWOOD**/*Private Home*
22. **WHEATLEIGH**
23. **BONNIE BRIER FARM**/*The Desisto School*
24. **CLOVER CROFT**
25. **NAUMKEAG**
26. **BONNIE BRAE**/*Private Home*
27. **WINDERMERE**/*Private Home*
28. **EDEN HILL**/*Congregation of Marians of the Immaculate Conception*

28A. **LAUREL COTTAGE**/*Tennis Courts*

29. **HEATON HALL**
30. **RED LION**
31. **KONKAPUT BROOK**/*Riverbrook School*
32. **STRAWBERRY HILL**/*Private Home*
33. **LINWOOD**/*Norman Rockwell Museum*
34. **CHESTERWOOD**
35. **SOUTHMAYDS**/*Private Home*

GREAT BARRINGTON

36. **SEARLES CASTLE**/*Barrington House/Kellogg Terrace*
37. **BROOKSIDE**/*Eisner Camp*

THE COTTAGES

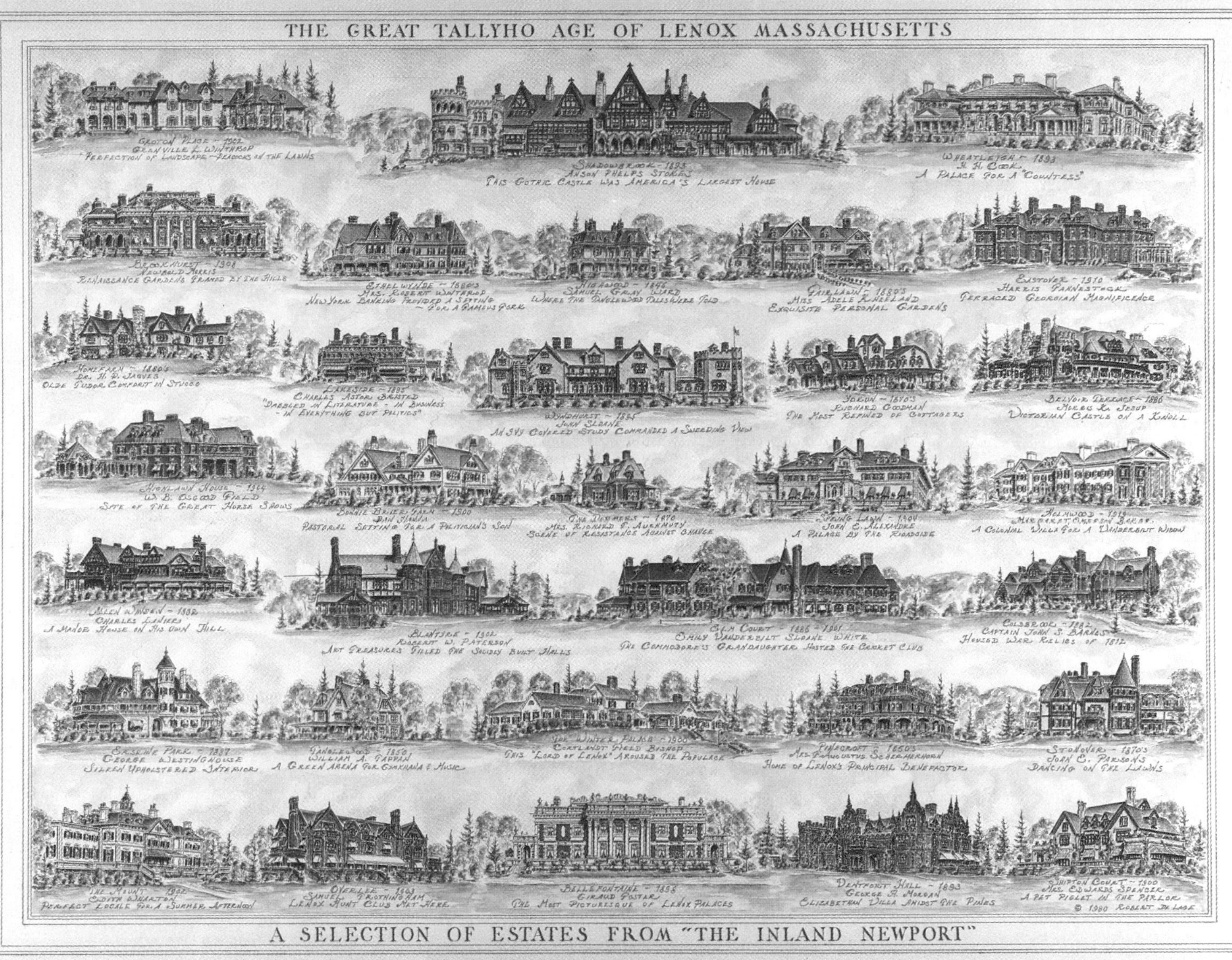

The cover of this book is
"The Great TallyHo Age" by Robert DeLage.
Copyright: © 1980, Robert DeLage

Stockbridge Railroad Station

Photograph by David Frank

1

WALKING THROUGH THE VILLAGES

"Tourists always come here to find something. They used to come looking for Arlo Guthrie and Alice's Restaurant. Then they were looking for Norman Rockwell and his studio. Now they ask me for the 'Pie'— they're looking for Edie Sedgwick."

A Stockbridge Police Officer

As you approach Stockbridge and Lenox from the south, you gradually ascend. You move up and away, leaving behind the bright and common symbols of our present day including the revolving plastic signs of fast-food stands and discount electronic stores. You will not see another "chain store"; you will not see a movie-house; you will not be able to eat a cut-rate burger or a "franchised" slice of pizza again without leaving the two villages. The predominant color around you will be green, or white, or orange depending upon the season.

As the road turns and dips into Stockbridge, you pass the Stockbridge railroad station on the right. Today there is no train; it is a restaurant, but it appears as it did in 1891, the third and last station to be built on the spot since the railroad came all the way up to Stockbridge.

You may sit in a white wicker chair in the afternoon on the front porch of the Red Lion Inn; an inn that has been in continuous use since 1773. As you look up and down Main Street you may think, as many others have before you, that this is perhaps the prettiest town you have ever visited. You may try mentally to block out the automobiles from the picture before you and imagine it as it was, feeling confident that if the cars would disappear, the town would be as it was. A woman may buy a beaded bag in an antique store and as she picks it up, she may imagine the previous owner. She holds it and wonders where, by what owner, in what time past, it has been carried. For that evening out, opening and closing the clasp of the bag or staring at it a moment as the light catches the beads and fires them, the woman feels she touches and carries with her a piece of another time. On that porch in Stockbridge, you feel the past all around you as if you have entered it.

"Everyone that visits here has a feeling that there is a lot going on behind those trees. There is, but a stranger doesn't know what," a real estate agent tells you. Just as the trees screen the estates from the passersby on the road, so you feel that you have entered the past and are, at the same time, screened from it and cannot quite see it.

What accounts for this pretty little town? Who built it and lived in it? Why do locals call the Red Lion the inn of presidents? Why do you think you have heard of the Berkshires as if it were a period of history ***and*** a place, like Newport or Gettysburg, long before you remember hearing of it? What were the names you heard or saw since entering the town and why do they all seem to strike a chord of recognition?

The peace that settled around you when you drove up into the hills, the feeling of well-being that came from leaving the hum of the

Photograph by David Frank

The Sedgwick Pie

everyday world, now alters slightly. It is not enough to sit quietly on a summer afternoon passively enjoying the street scene. You are energized. It is not the energy of the adult workworld—businesslike, focused, and directed. It is the energy of memory—your memory—of you as a child. Whether you associate it with finding the berry patch or searching Granny's attic or digging in the vacant lot. You recognize the exhilaration of the treasure hunt. You will not be disappointed.

For some, history has value merely because it is removed in time. Old is "good" because it is fun and different. They are the romantics. Others judge the past as harshly as the present by personal standards. The casual observer of history glances back now and then without much concentration. The historians are content to catalogue it all without judgment—"lest we forget." Not one, the romantic, the judge, the casual observer, or the historian, will be disappointed in the Berkshires. The romantic will be soul-satisfied by the sheer display of the past tucked into the hills, behind the hedges, and up the winding roads of the villages. The judge will find much to shake his head over in the discrepancy of blinding, sense-numbing wealth and poverty. The casual observer will find his attention riveted by the gilt of the last century. No historian dare pass over the Berkshires without the comment that Lenox and Stockbridge were country seats of the rich and powerful. Then their money and power shaped the world, and whether by our adherence or our rebellion or both, shaped ours.

So with the smug warmth of a child buttoned up and sent off by a loving parent with a tin cup and the promise of berries over the next hillock, you go forth on foot down Main Street. You go left, away from the shops knowing, as the child in each of us does, that the best treasure is found off beaten paths.

On the left, less than a city block down from the Red Lion, is a coral house. It looks like the picture postcard of the "American Home" past or present. The ideal and the vision are timeless. It is the home built by Theodore Sedgwick in the 1700s, and it is a Sedgwick home even today.

You walk the broad avenues with the trees overhanging the roads. It reminds you of something, perhaps a poem with the words like "dappled sunlight" and "a bower of trees." You feel you're discovering the truth of something. How the times shaped the art perhaps, because all around you is a canvas, and the light and shadows and images are the ones

St. Paul's Church, Stockbridge

The Children's Chimes

Photograph by David Frank

Photograph by David Frank

of American art in word and on canvas. No one has to tell you that American writers and artists walked these streets because you recognize it, as surely as an old friend, in the flavor of their works. That Melville sat not ten miles from you writing of oceans and whales makes eminent good sense. That a not-exhaustive search would yield the house at Tanglewood of Hawthorne's ***Wonder Book*** and his writing desk is as much as you would now expect. That Norman Rockwell painted the street you walk, and people like those you pass, and called it Americana goes without saying, as it does that it was on the piazza of Edith Wharton's cottage a few miles away that Henry James said, "Summer afternoon; to me those have always been the two most beautiful words in the English language." It all seems quite simple and right. And if Pope or Gray never saw the country graveyard to the right (that you now cross the street to enter), what of that? They wrote of ones like it.

As you swing the low gate open and enter the graveyard, you may not be able to hear Joseph Choate laughing as he explains, "I have just decided to become a permanent resident of Stockbridge. Today I have bought a plot in the town cemetery." Here in Stockbridge cemetery you will find the final resting place of Choates and Fields and Astors and Henriette Deluzy–Desporte The trees overhang the stone markers which, in turn, lean in different directions at odd angles as if to patiently explain by the antisymmetry that each was placed by imperfect man and has withstood many a high wind and change in temperature. No neat rows with duplicate markers; no precision here at all. The narrow road leads back to what appears to be a yard within a yard. It is called the "Pie." In a town where (folks tease outsiders) even the crickets say "sedg-wick, sedg-wick," you have stumbled upon the Sedgwick burial plot.

In the "Pie," all Sedgwicks are laid to rest. The mute stones respectfully face the center where the monuments to the first Sedgwicks rise higher than the others. It looks like a silent classroom with the rows of children circling the teachers, waiting expectantly. Some of the names are rubbed almost smooth, but they are there from Theodore Sedgwick, delegate to the Continental Congress and friend of George Washington, to Catherine Sedgwick, author, to Ellery Sedgwick, editor of ***The Atlantic***. On Judgment Day, the legend goes, all the Sedgwicks will rise up, and will be required to see and greet only one another.

As you leave the graveyard and

The Tiffany Windows of St. Paul's

Photograph by David Frank

Photograph by Mimi MacDonald

Poodle Tower at Wheatleigh

walk back toward town, chimes sound behind you. It is 6:00 P.M. The carillon in the Children's Tower, a memorial to David Dudley Field's grandchildren, have sounded on summer evenings since 1878.

You continue your walk back down Main Street past the Red Lion, the shops, the library, the Old Corner House to the intersection of Main Street and Yale Hill. There on your left is the Casino. You have missed five o'clock tea at the Casino by one hour and ninety-five years. But in an hour or two, you could see a performance there. The sign reads The Berkshire Theater Festival. It looks the same as it did in 1887 except that it is now white and not yellow and has an enclosure around the upper porch. Of course it has been moved from the spot on which Stanford White, at the instruction of Joseph Choate and David Dudley Field, built it. It once stood further up Main Street on the spot where the Mission House is now.

History stretches along the road you have just walked, from the Indian Monument up beyond the graveyard to the Casino you stand before now. There are places, as there are moments, in which a bulk of information you have been struggling with seems to clarify and you can say, "Oh, now I understand." On the streets of Stockbridge, you may experience that phenomenon. The great bulk of American history seems to become quite clear. You sense that some of the key players in American history crisscrossed along the road you have just walked. Theodore Sedgwick smiles at Catherine across the years and across the yard as he dashes for the train to Philadelphia. Catherine Sedgwick then moves back into her formidable nineteenth-century salon to chat with Mrs. Fanny Kemble Butler. They drive out together to tease and yet stand off in awe of the morose Hawthorne who, in turn, waits for Melville in his front yard. Hawthorne could wave to Samuel Ward showing Longfellow and others from his Boston dining club, The Saturday Club, around the Berkshire Hills. While Joseph Choate, hustling up into those same hills on his way home, balances cases that fended off income tax and toppled Tammany Hall. He tips his hat to the boy, Ellery Sedgwick, and the girl, Rachel

Photograph by David Frank

The Casino

Field. As Joe leaves for England, Frederic Crowninshield swings into town, and could see Hawthorne and Melville and Dr. Holmes leaving the Laurel Cottage at midnight. Across the years and across the street he could watch his son Frank grow to a man, "the last true gentleman," and leave the Casino with Daniel Chester French and family. The editor and the sculptor would tip their hat to Mrs. Sherwood coming down Yale Hill to collect her mail at the Stockbridge post office. Included among the mail is a book from Henry James: "For Cousin Rosina." Outside the post office again, she receives a smile from the man off to collect a letter from the ***Saturday Evening Post***. Norman Rockwell who smiles from under his hat as he leaves the post office on his way to paint a child who, as a man, walks past you now on Main Street, Stockbridge. So from Indians to eighteenth-century political America, to early nineteenth-century literary America, to later nineteenth-century Society and twentieth-century artistic commentary, America crisscrosses your path and becomes Americana. The idea of the thing, not the linear facts to memorize, but the concept flows down Main Street into your grasp. So you too tip your hat to the Indians and the Sedgwicks and the Fields and the Messrs. Choate, Crowninshield, French, and Rockwell, in short, to your heritage. Of course at no one time could all of these people have walked the streets of Stockbridge together. Their residencies span the years. It is simply the magic of Stockbridge that you are able to sense their presence all at once.

Leaving Stockbridge for Lenox, you have a choice. You could travel Route 7 or, beginning on Main Street, you can turn onto Pine Street and then left onto Prospect Hill. If you choose the latter, you will pass on the left: Joseph Choate's Naumkeag, Henry Field's house, Sunset, and Birdseye Blakeman's Oronoque. On your right are: David Dudley Field's cottage, Eden Hill, Henry Field's first cottage, Windermere, Bonnie Brae and the site of Clover Croft. Much further down on your right there is a sign for Wheatleigh, and on the left, across from the Lion's Gate at Tanglewood, Hawthorne's Little Red House.

Past the Little Red House, look out across Stockbridge Bowl and up into the hills, there, where a large red brick structure stands today, is the original site of Shadow Brook. At the intersection, turn right onto West Street. Just before you reach town, on your right, is Groton Place, the former estate of Grenville L. Winthrop. It is the cottage from which both his daughters left on their much-publicized elopement.

As you approach the center of town, you sense a difference between Stockbridge and Lenox. Lenox seems quieter, more formal, as if this Yankee town wore a shirt with more starch in it.

Entering from West Street, your first view is of the Curtis Hotel rising behind the Paterson Monument. It looks more institutional than romantic. It was an "institution" during a now romanticized period of history. From the mid-eighteen hundreds, the days of Fanny Kemble when it was called the Berkshire Coffee House, to the Gilded Age, it was the hotel at the center of Lenox life.

Stand facing the hotel and turn ninety degrees to the right, and you are looking at the spot where the old post office stood. To the left

Sedgwick Hall
(The Lenox Library)

Photograph by Mimi MacDonald

is the courthouse of the shiretown turned Sedgwick Hall and now the Lenox Library. Behind the Curtis are houses that the Curtis Hotel once rented during The Season and called cottages.

The stretch of Main Street within your view holds the signs of the periods of Lenox history. At the highest point is the Church on the Hill where the first white man to settle in Lenox, Jonathan Hinsdale, is buried. When Fanny Kemble came to town to visit Catherine Sedgwick, the famous actress is said to have fallen in love with the town. She offered to give a reading to benefit the poor. She was told, "Lenox has no poor." Undaunted, Fanny Kemble gave her reading and donated the proceeds to buy the bell for the church. Down from the church stands the old court house, and then the site of the old post office where all the cottagers gathered "twice or thrice a day." A local woman has a different view of Main Street. She doesn't see it as a visual explication of history, but as a testament to the city fathers.

"Don't say we in Lenox don't know city planning. Along Main Street, you have the old ladies' home followed by the church and then the funeral home. That's planning."

As you stand at the Curtis, you are at a nexus. Three roads stretch in front of you—Old Stockbridge Road, Kemble Street, and Walker Street. Along Walker Street are the Candle Light Inn and The Gateways, formerly the Proctor cottage, Orleton. Down Kemble street is the Trinity Church across from the Alexandre cottage, Spring Lawn and Frelinghuysen cottage. Down Old Stockbridge Road is the Berkshire Christian College built on the site of Charles Lanier's Allen Winden. All three roads intersect Route 7 at different junctions downhill. Traveling any of these roads, the estates are visible.

2

TOURING THE COTTAGES

"I suppose it's a mile from your gate to the front door?"
"Just about."
"And do you keep deer in the park?"
"We do."
"And peacocks on the terrace?"
"I'm afraid so. All the storybook things."

Dorothy L. Sayers:
Busman's Honeymoon

he cottages are listed by number that corresponds to the numbers on the map. Their specific location can be found by consulting the map. If the home is a private residence today, the location is not marked on the map out of respect for the privacy of the present owners. Strange cars coming unbidden up private drives can be disconcerting.

Information about the original owners and construction of the houses is followed by a description of their present day use. If the cottage exists today, its use can be placed in one of ten categories. The smallest category is "private homes"; the other nine categories are museums, inns, restaurants, condominiums, time-sharing resorts, religious orders, theaters, schools, and those destroyed.

This list is compiled for the convenience of those travelers who wish to find the estates today. It is compiled with no great hope that the list will remain accurate very long after publication. Alternative uses for the estates are not so much difficult to find as seemingly too easy. The men and women who built them did so out of a whole fabric of philosophy and economic conditions—an ***idée fixe***. The latter part of this century has had no fixed idea about how to retain them. Inns, restaurants, schools come and go, leaving their mark but not the ability to sustain both the massive old structure and the modern economic plan. The houses, like family heirlooms, are passed from hand to hand, used at times and left at other times to gather dust. Unless they are finally and completely destroyed by razing or fire, their future is uncertain.

They are somehow optimistic in line and size, outrageous, overwhelming to the psychology of modern man, meant as symbols of a landed American aristocracy brought down by the progress, the ideals, and the businesses they thought would sustain them. They were an appropriate symbol of ideas that prevailed in our past. And like those ideas, they are left behind without certain application in today's fast and streamlined world.

FERNBROOK

(Lenox)

Courtesy of the Providence Library

Fernbrook

Fernbrook was the cottage of Thomas Shields Clarke. The estate comprised more than three-hundred acres of farm and forest land on Yokun Mountain. The house was built between 1902 when the land was purchased and 1904. The name was taken from a brook that ran through the property. The house was designed by Wilson Eyre. As with so many of the cottages regardless of the architect, the local contractor, Joseph Clifford's Sons carried out the plan. the plan.

According to Mr. Clarke's wishes, Fernbrook was rustic. Steps were rough hewn stone leading from patio to terrace, the grounds were left wild rather than cleared for parks and formal gardens. Inside the walls were of oak and the hardwood floors were stained dark. Walls were covered with tapestries and a collection of ancient arms. Where more conventional cottages were divided into rooms, at Fernbrook, an informal central hall doubled as the main living room in the old English style.

Mr. Clarke was a sculptor and painter. Among his works is the statue, "To Alma Mater" done for Princeton University. His studio occupied the whole northwest wing of the house. It was 30 by 42 feet. It was designed as a replica of a room in an ancient Sicilian monastery. The studio was dominated by a large fireplace and surrounded by a balcony built to allow visitors to watch Mr. Clarke work. Plaster casts and clay models of works-in-progress lay all around.

Today Fernbrook is part of the Avalon School as is Overleigh.

Fernbrook

Courtesy of the Providence Library

2 THE ASPINWALL

(Lenox)

The Aspinwall began its first season as an inn in 1902 with a bang. Mr. Seavey, the manager being a literal man in the fashion of his day, used a cannon.

The Aspinwall was built on the old Aspinwall Woolsey estate by the Aspinwall Hotel Company, O. D. Seavey, president. It was one of the largest hotels built in the Berkshires with four-hundred rooms. It was run like a cottage or like the finest of European hotels featuring every convenience: steam heat, telegraph office, long distance telephone, resident physician, modern fire equipment, elevators built into brick shafts. In addition, the Aspinwall offered more "Old World" charms: an orchestra in residence, an extensive stable, fireplaces in each room, piazzas, and promenades plus walking and bridal paths on the two-hundred acre grounds. A carriage and uniformed attendant met all trains in Lenox to transport guests.

Like the Curtis, the Aspinwall continued the custom of "house guests" and "cottagers." It housed a hundred or more guests under the hotel roof and also offered cottages for renting.

The hotel was 1,460 feet above sea level and therefore commanded a spectacular view. That view was another "must" for a proper Berkshire cottage or Berkshire inn.

In 1904, under Mr. Seavey's direction, there was a dinner for a party of railroad men in the Aspinwall's private dining room. It was done true to the spirit of the times:

> On Monday evening, Mr. Seavey was given another opportunity to display his taste in table decorations . . . the decorations were of the old time cinnamon roses and mountain laurel, the flowers being so arranged as to convert the round table into a locomotive wheel.

Like Heaton Hall, another large wooden hotel, the Aspinwall heavily advertised its fire prevention attributes—hoses, pumps, fire escapes, and the separation of furnace and kitchen facilities from the main hotel. Unlike Heaton Hall, the Aspinwall burned to the ground in 1931.

Today, the site of the Aspinwall is called Kennedy Park. You can still see the old stone gates that marked the entrance. After a respectable hike, you can find the famed view from the Aspinwall.

Hand-colored postcard of the Aspinwall Hotel

Courtesy of Mrs. Edward Daley

Belvoir Terrace

3 BELVOIR TERRACE

(Lenox)

Morris Ketchum Jesup created this estate. His father died when he was seven years old. By twelve, Jesup had left school and was working in the New York office of Rogers Locomotive Works. In 1854, at the age of twenty-four, he started a small business handling railway supplies. His business thrived and he branched out into banking, solidifying his fortune so that at fifty-four years of age, Morris K. Jesup retired. For the next twenty-four years, until his death in 1908, his contributions were widespread. The American Museum of Natural History received $2,000,000; $1,000,000 during his lifetime and an equal amount at his death. He supported a number of expeditions: the Carl Lumholtz expedition to Northern Mexico; the Jesup North Pacific Expedition; and Peary's North Pole Expedition. He was president of the Peary Arctic Club, but did not live to see Peary succeed. He was also a staunch supporter of educational and theological institutions including Harvard, Yale (his father's alma mater), Princeton, and the New York City

Photograph by David Frank

Union Theological Seminary.

His retirement coincided with the building of Belvoir Terrace. The completion of Belvoir Terrace is commonly dated 1886, it is probable that the work began in 1884 and took two years to build as it did with many of the cottages. The house is soul-satisfying to the collector of historically illuminating minutiae. The flower room is connected to the study by a short passage. In the passage is a pulley device that raises a trap door fit into the wood flooring. Below is the wine cellar. In the study, the paneling is a deep lustrous wood finely engraved. The ceilings are 10 feet and the paneling 6½ feet high. At six points the paneling opens and exposes secret compartments of various sizes.

Between 1905 and 1955, there were two owners. One was a Mr. Shepard. A woman of wealth and bearing said,

"Of course no one went to Belvoir Terrace during that period."

"No?"

"Well, no. Mr. Shepard wasn't ***known***, you see." She looks up to determine if it ***is*** seen. Unsure, she clarifies, "It doesn't matter how many oodles of money one had if one was not attractive."

"Oh."

"He did something. Was it chain stores?" She asks her husband.

He shrugs. He doesn't know. After all, Mr. Shepard wasn't known.

Mr. Shepard was blackballed by the Lenox Club. Apparently undaunted, he joined the Stockbridge Golf Club, and paid off their mortgage—a generosity the Lenox Club could have used at that moment.

In 1955, Belvoir Terrace was purchased by Mrs. Edna Schwartz for use as a summer arts school for girls. It offers professional instruction in fine arts, dance, theater, music, gymnastics, tennis, and swimming. The school offers individualized programming for each participant and offers the girls the opportunity to live in a magnificent home that has been well maintained by the present owner, Mrs. Schwartz. It is traditional to close each season with a game of hide-and-seek. The instructors hide from the students. The successful instructor is usually the one who hides him/herself in one of the secret compartments in the paneling of Morris K. Jesup's study.

Two views of the Library at Belvoir Terrace

Courtesy of Mrs. Nancy Goldberg

ORLETON

(Lenox)

By the "more-than" formula, Orleton was never properly a "cottage," but it was a Lenox summer residence. It was built in 1912 by Harley Proctor of Proctor and Gamble. There is a popular notion that this was a Stanford White house. A story made the more interesting by the need for Mr. White to have designed it posthumously. The visual "proof" sited in support of the tale is the exceptional entrance hall staircase. Regardless of who the architect was in fact, the staircase is the house's most charming feature. Furthermore, the house is interesting both because of the owner and because of its present day use.

One of the favorite tales in the Berkshires is that when Mr. Proctor built the house, he requested that it "look like a bar of Ivory soap." Although the tale tells you a great deal about the way in which Mr. Proctor earned his living, it tells you nothing about the house.

"Oh, no. Not true at all. Absolutely no," says Mr. Proctor's granddaughter. After a moment's thought, she adds that she doesn't think it looks the least bit like a bar of Ivory soap, and asks, do you? There is the problem, it does look the least bit like a bar of Ivory soap.

Today Orleton is called The Gateways. It is a four-star restaurant, chef-owned and chef-run. When Queen Elizabeth visited Boston during the Bicentennial, it was The Gateways' own, Chef Gerhard Schmid, who cooked for her.

The Gateways is also a small inn with rooms on the second floor. If you request the suite, you will find your bed in the second floor sunporch where her grandchildren remember Mrs. Proctor sitting. It is the suite in which Arthur Fiedler stayed when he conducted at Tanglewood.

Photograph by Mimi MacDonald

Orleton

Photograph by David Frank

The staircase at Spring Lawn

5

SPRING LAWN

(Lenox)

Spring Lawn was built in 1904 by J. E. Alexandre. The architect was the young and then unknown architect from Boston, Guy Lowell. Miss Anna Alexandre who still lives in Lenox just down the road from her father's cottage recalls, "Guy Lowell had practically just finished his training at Harvard, so when Father wrote him, he took the next train. That was just what Father wanted. He didn't want to wait for one of the well-known architects." It was named Spring Lawn because there was a spring at the bottom of the property. Each morning, the gardener would bring up a pail of spring water for Anna.

On June 6, 1903, a news article reported that in order to build Spring Lawn, Mr. Alexandre was tearing down the home where Catherine Sedgwick had lived with her brother. As the house was being built, the Alexandre family lived next door at Frelinghuysen Cottage and oversaw the work. Mr. Alexandre died in 1910, only six years after the cottage was completed.

Many of the interior architectural details of the cottages, if not entire exteriors, were copied from Europe's notable houses. In the entrance hall of Spring Lawn, the staircase may remind you of Henry the VIII's Hampton Court.

Today Spring Lawn is part of The Bible Speaks College.

ANANDA HALL

THE WINTER PALACE

(Lenox)

Both were in Lenox. Ananda Hall was built by Cortlandt Field Bishop. Construction began in 1922 and was completed in 1924.

In all, the Bishops owned five cottages. The first was the Winter Palace. Mr. Bishop inherited Interlaken from his mother, and bought the Goodman cottage that stood on property next door to Ananda Hall. Ananda Hall was by far the fanciest. It took two years and four hundred men to build. The plumber who installed Mrs. Bishop's private bathroom tells the following story:

"Oh, honestly, it was beautiful—tub, toilet, all beautiful pale green. The side walls went right to the ceiling, all marble, walls, floor, honestly it was something. We kept her [Mrs. Amy Bend Bishop] away until it was all done, until it was absolutely finished; then we said, 'Well, now we want you to come in and see your bathroom.' She walked into the bathroom and she slipped—the first foot she put in the bathroom. She stepped right back out and said, 'Take that floor out of there.' The two tile setters looked at her and said, 'Do you mean that?' She said, 'I mean it. I will not set another foot in that bathroom with that tile like that.' And in them days, you know, they used to set tile in concrete, but they took it out."

Ananda Hall was razed by the Bishop family in the 1940s. Mr. Bishop enjoyed a "reputation" in a time when privacy and anonymity were respected. Not unnaturally then, the stories surrounding the razing of Ananda Hall are in descending order of infamy. The first is that after having improved the value of the land by erecting a home on it, the property tax went up, and this so infuriated the volatile Mr. Bishop that he had the home razed to maintain the lower tax assessment. The second story is that his will specified that the home be razed upon his death since he was indisposed to the idea that others enjoy it after he was gone. The third is that his will specified that his wife and his "friend," Miss Edith Nixon, live together in order that any other part of his will be executed.

Drawing by Robert DeLage

It is quite true that Cortlandt Field Bishop and other of the cottagers were angry about the rise in land taxes after World War I, and in response, Bishop did raze something, but it was not his house but his barn. Mr. Bishop was not a simple man. He razed his barn to save taxes, and yet he bought October

The Winter Palace

Mountain, 14,000 acres that had belonged to Harry Payne Whitney, and gave it to the town to preserve. There is no reason to believe that Mr. Bishop wanted to stop Edith Nixon or Amy Bend from enjoying the houses or any of his property. The last of the rumors is the true one, the women lived together in Winter Palace, so Ananda Hall was superfluous and was razed.

Since the women lived there together, a whole new set of stories sprang up to explain the situation. Some say Miss Nixon was his lover. Others say Mrs. Bishop's emotional problems rendered her unable to care for herself, and to assure his wife a companion, Mr. Bishop provided both for the living arrangements and the payment of that companion in his will. Perhaps both explanations are true, but whichever it was, the name of the house, Winter Palace, became appropriate for another reason. The Bishops had named it the Winter Palace to indicate their love of winter sport, and their intention to use the cottage even during the winter months. After his death, some said that the name was suitable because the two women living together in the house "was rather like a Russian novel." No one visited them. Amy Bend Bishop, beauty and one of The Four Hundred, and Edith Nixon, Irish housekeeper who became private secretary, confidant, beneficiary, and mistress or nurse, were locked into one another's company, alone in the cold winter—a unique couple.

"There must have been," the former resident of Lenox goes on, "a miasma about the place as not many yards away there was another estate where two sisters and a brother lived. The sisters, for reasons long forgotten, never spoke to one another and communicated through the brother."

ALLEN WINDEN
(Lenox)

Situated in Lenox Allen Winden was built by Charles Lanier in 1881. The architects were Peabody and Stearns. The landscape architect was Ernest Bowditch. The Peabody and Stearns records are in the Boston Library along with blueprints and elevations. A card index holds, in many cases, the original records of costs related to the building of these homes. The Lanier cards are marked "composite" which means that only the year, the structure to be built or altered, and the total expenditure survive. Even so scant a record is revealing of the times. Mr. Lanier was a constant builder as were many of his class in his day. Chronologically his dealings with Peabody and Stearns were:

Courtesy of Mr. & Mrs. Edward Daley

1881	$29,931.04[1]	House, Lenox
1886	21,733.20	
1887-88	22,521.26	
1888	6,781.77	Cow Barn
1889	11,032.14	
1893	2,824.50	Old Stable alteration
1895	1,384.67	Alteration
1896	25,334.86	N.Y.C. House alterations
1899	6,960.00	Choir Room, Trinity Church (built in
	145.00	memory of his wife[2])
1903	14,202.17	House alteration, Lenox
1906	1,879.50	Tea room alteration
1914	18,963.00	Cow Barn changes
1914	18,803.00	Stable

Eleven years and a total of $182,496.11 were dedicated to building. It was part of a way of life provided you were a New York City banker and a gentlemen.

Mr. Lanier was an intimate of J. P. Morgan through his banking interest. Although Mr. Morgan's sister and her husband, George Halle Morgan, owned Ventfort in Lenox, contemporary accounts say he stayed with Mr. Lanier. According

Hand-colored postcard of Allen Winden

to Mr. Bowditch who kept a journal, Morgan had at one time "bailed out" Mr. Lanier and his bank. Mr. Lanier was distantly related to the poet, Sidney Lanier, and Mrs. Lanier was both an Egleston and granddaughter of General Paterson. The monument in the center of Lenox commemorates his war deeds. Such family connections back to the Revolutionary War were highly valued during the estate period. Money was sufficient to pay for a place in the upper class structure, but lineage represented another rationale for American aristocracy. Money and power were certainly craved and revered but were not sufficient.

Today, Allen Winden is the Berkshire Christian College. Lanier's house was demolished in the 1920s. In the 1930s, the present brick house was built in its place. In the 1950s, the property was sold to the Berkshire Christian College. "Allen Winden" sits on a rise; hence the Gaelic name meaning windy. The land descended from the house east and west to Laurel Lake and Lake Mahkeenac (Stockbridge Bowl) respectively. During the estate period, the cottages were carefully placed for "views." A contemporary account says, "Allen Winden occupies a commanding view on a high hillside. Its grounds are considered by many to be as beautiful as any in Lenox. The great lawn contains almost every variety of flower that can flourish there and the conservatory is another evidence of Mr. Lanier's love for horticulture."[3] The description affords the twentieth-century visitor an opportunity to mark the changes in topography both on individual estates and the general landscape. For example, neither lake is visible today from Allen Winden.

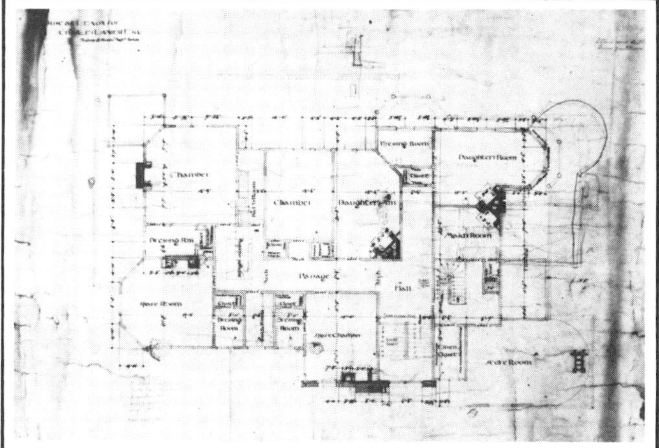

Floor plans of Allen Winden by Peabody and Stearns

Courtesy of Boston Public Library Print Dept. Peabody & Stearns Collection

BELLEFONTAINE

(Lenox)

Bellefontaine was built by Giraud Foster in 1897 who hired the architectural firm of Carrere and Hastings. They were the same architects who designed the New York City Public Library for the Astor family and Brookside for Mr. William Stanley of Great Barrington. Although the date of the house is commonly listed as 1899, the July 3, 1897 issue of ***American Architects & Building News*** pictures Bellefontaine. The house was built of white marble and pale brick. The marble was from the quarries at Lee, Massachusetts, four miles away.

The house was approached by a long drive through the woods, and the only hint of what splendor awaited the visitor, was a glimpse of statues placed along the drive. The house was built around an inner court with a waterway, a long narrow pool, and surrounding it were examples of Mr. Foster's collection of statuary. They took all forms from Adonis to gargoyles, from Hercules to goats. They were imported or copied from statues in France and Italy.

Mr. Foster died in 1945 shortly before his ninety-fifth birthday. In 1947, Bellefontaine was sold to the Fathers of Mercy. One of the cottagers noted in his diary alongside "get hair cut"—"Bellefontaine sold today for $1.3 million dollars including the 1,800 statues." For many years, the statues formed the centerpiece of one of the great mysteries of Lenox. Shortly after Bellefontaine was purchased by the seminarians, locals say, all the statues disappeared. Some thought the good fathers had sold them. Others said that they were offensive to the religious occupants of Bellefontaine, and that they decapitated the statues and buried them in the waterway.

Bellefontaine

The auction catalogue printed shortly after Mr. Foster's death, and before the property became a seminary, lists hundreds of statues. Hundreds were sold at auction, but not eighteen-hundred. Unfortunately the keeper of the diary is gone, and we cannot ask him what he meant. It is not clear that Bellefontaine sold for anything close to 1.3 million dollars. The New York Times reported that the estate was appraised at one hundred and twenty three thousand dollars. The stamps affixed to the deed of sale appear to represent a sale price of forty thousand dollars. The truth lies between those two figures, not beyond them. So, the number of statues is also questionable. Whatever the number, what happened to the rest?

In February, 1949, the interior of the house was totally destroyed by fire. It was then rebuilt by the new

Courtesy of Jane Foster Lorber

occupants and became the Immaculate Heart of Mary Seminary. The devastating fire of 1949 left only one room, the library, unscathed. The outer walls were not destroyed by fire but were altered by the seminarians. Sadly, then, most of what exists at Bellefontaine today is only an echo of what once was. But pictures taken after the fire show some statues still in place. The last owners solved the old mystery. In their digging, they found the rest of the statues. They had, after all, been buried, and like Bellefontaine, they are much altered. They were found piece by piece, head by arm by torso.

A favorite story told about Foster by Cleveland Amory and many local residents is: A tour guide was discouraged from bringing paying sightseers up the elm-lined drive to view Bellefontaine. Angry, he decided to make one more trip. Mr. Foster was entertaining on his terrace. The guide spoke loud enough to be heard, "Ladies and Gentlemen, this is the home of Mr. Foster who made all his money in one day. He married it."

Notwithstanding the story, Giraud Foster and Jane Van Nest were on an equal footing when they married. Andrew Foster, Giraud's grandfather, arrived in America from Scotland in the early 1800s. He carried with him letters of introduction to the best houses and ample funds. He had sailed across the ocean in what was apparently his own ship. The Van Nests also arrived in America in the early 1800s. They were from Holland where, as the "Van" indicates, they were land owners. Both families established their American social and financial standing in New York. Jane and Giraud were each grandchildren of the original emigres.

The couple was childless until 1904. Parents for the first time,

Courtesy of Jane Foster Lorber

The Reflecting Pond at Bellefontaine

Dining room mantle, and a corner of the salon at Bellefontaine

Courtesy of Jane Foster Lorber

Giraud Foster was fifty-four years old and Jane Van Nest was in her late forties. So late in life was it, that Mrs. Foster was diagnosed as having a tumor. Contrary to the diagnosis, their son, Giraud Van Nest Foster, was born at the Waldorf Astoria in New York City and was, from the day he was born, called simply "Boy."

When Boy was ten years old, a friend of Mrs. Foster's asked, "To which school will you send Boy?"

The answer was, "Groton, of course."

"But," the friend asked, "can Boy read or write?"

The son had spent his early years at Lenox, New York, Palm Beach and on the Continent traveling with his parents, not in school. An experiment was conducted and it was discovered that Boy could do neither—read nor write. Tutors were hired. Among them was George Livermore who would later marry one of the daughters of Charles Astor Bristed of Lakeside.

Boy did attend Groton. He arrived "in state" with chauffeur, footman and nanny in two cars to transport them. Even at Groton, his manner of arrival was noted and occasioned a response. As soon as the entourage departed, Boy was beaten up.

Called Boy Foster all his life, he told a family member that the fact of his father's death really struck him when he returned to Bellefontaine for the funeral service and the butler, Paul Roth, opened the door and said, "Good afternoon, Mr. Foster."

Giraud Foster was the builder of Bellefontaine, collector of art, antique furniture and statues, a man of taste and a man about Lenox, president of his club and supporter of good works. Perhaps not the only things we laud today, then they marked him a gentleman. Like a gentleman he lived, among marble columns, French antiques, art and, of course, the statues of Bellefontaine.

ELM COURT

(Lenox)

Elm Court was built by Mr. and Mrs. William Douglas Sloane, to be accurate, from 1886-1900. Although the completion date is accepted as 1887, the Peabody and Stearns records show "additions," "alterations," and "changes" in 1889 ("addition — $40,158.64"); 1893 ("addition — $32,352"); 1899-1900 ("changes — $62,297.48") The card is headed "House and Additions, Lenox." It may be that some of the additions and alterations were outbuildings of which there were many. But a grandson of Mrs. Sloane recalls: "As a child, I would go up and down the halls and staircases of Elm Court and sometimes arrive at a wall. The halls or staircases led nowhere because of the way the additions were put on."

eleven bedrooms upstairs and a guest bedroom downstairs. Elm Court, at different times, housed four children, twelve grandchildren and the thirty-six great grandchildren of the Sloanes. They agree on the ultimate size of Elm Court. They also agree that the size reflected Mrs. Sloane's desire to have her family visit often.

At any rate, $180,967.19 plus a reported $50,000 for the original one acre, or $230,967.19 was expended on Elm Court over fourteen years ***not*** including the initial cost of construction nor necessarily including any interior furnishings or alterations. To put that in perspective, not in 1980 dollars but in 1886 dollars, one only has to consult George William Sheldon. Mr. Sheldon published ***Artistic Country Seats*** in 1886-87. He included ninety-seven buildings, ninety-three homes and four casinos in his book. "The cost of sixty two — fifty eight houses and four casinos — are known . . . thirty three are $30,000 and under; eighteen are between $30-100,00; only six are over $100,000, of which two

Courtesy of the Stockbridge Library

Elm Court, 1886

A granddaughter, however, says, "That's perfectly silly. I don't remember that. I think the house was always the same size."

Whether the entries in the Peabody and Stearns file reflect additions to the external structure or internal alterations, the result was a ninety-four room house with

Ccurtesy of the Lenox Library

Solarium of Elm Court (looking into Salon)

are over $200,000."[4]

In 1904, ***Berkshire Resort Topics*** reported, "It was in 1887 [sic] that Mr. and Mrs. Sloane began the creation of Elm Court and the intervening years have seen so many acquisitions of contiguous lands, so many improvements and enlargements to the original buildings and the erection of so many new structures, that the place has become famous, not only in Lenox but throughout the country, as an example of what the progressive modern spirit, backed up by abundant captial can accomplish."

Emily's father, William Henry, was credited with nearly doubling the Vanderbilt fortune during the nine years that he had sole control over the Vanderbilt interests. He died suddenly of cerebral hemorrhage in his home in New York in 1885. It was Emily who was called urgently by the servants when they found him. She lived in a connecting mansion. William H. left each of his eight children $10,000,000—half outright and half in trust. These eight children were builders: Cornelius built the Breakers, Newport, Rhode Island, 1893-95; George W. Vanderbilt built Biltmore, Asheville, North Carolina, 1895; Frederick built a mansion in Hyde Park, New York in 1898; William K. built Marblehouse in Newport, Rhode Island in 1892; Mrs. Hamilton McK. (Florence) Twombly built Florham Park in Madison, New Jersey; Mrs. Lila Vanderbilt Webb built Shelburne Farm in Vermont; Mrs. Elliot (Margaret) Shepard built in Scarsborough, New York and Emily built Elm Court in 1886 in Lenox.

William Douglas Sloane, with his brother John, ran the firm of W & J Sloane Co. which their father had started in New York City. It was an upholstery and carpet firm. W. D. married Emily Thorn Vanderbilt, the daughter of William H., in 1872. It may have been of the

Fireplace, Elm Court

Courtesy of the Lenox Library

Sloanes that Mrs. Astor (***the*** Mrs. Astor née Caroline Schermerhorn) was thinking when she said, "I buy my carpets from them but is that any reason why I should invite them to walk on them?" Or, perhaps the mention of carpet was accidental, and Mrs. Astor meant only to be understood as commenting on persons "in trade."

William Douglas Sloane died in 1913. In 1916, Mrs. Margaret Stuyvesant White died at The Poplars, the cottage in Lenox the Whites often rented. Mrs. White was the wife of Henry White, former ambassador to Italy and France, and the mother of two children, John C. White, secretary of the American Embassy in Athens and the Countess Scherr Thoss of Berlin. She was also a sister-in-law of Mrs. William K. Vanderbilt as was Emily Sloane. Emily and Henry White were married, and spent summers at Elm Court. A servant recalls, "Both her husbands were lovely men, but very different. Mr. Sloane was a small man, dark and quick. Mr. White had white hair and must have been six feet." Mr. White died at Elm Court in his seventy-seventh year, July 15, 1927. An assistant gardener was present when Mrs. White arrived at Elm Court in the summer of 1946. She was attended by a nurse who asked her to go upstairs and rest. Mrs. White declined, saying, "No, I'm going out to the solarium; I have never seen the gardens look so beautiful." Emily Thorn Vanderbilt Sloane White died at Elm Court on July 29, 1946 at the age of ninety-four.

Reflecting both Mrs. White's longevity and her love for the game of bridge, a wag commented: "She survived two husbands by many years, but she only survived her bridge partner by ten months." (Her bridge partner was Giraud Foster of Bellefontaine who died September 23, 1945.)

After Mrs. White's death in 1946, the family attempted to run Elm Court as an inn. "For nine dollars a night, you can stay at Elm Court," Colonel Wilde, son-in-law and owner/manager told Cleveland Amory in ***The Last Resorts***. "For twenty-five dollars, you can stay in Mrs. White's bedroom. But if we find someone wants to stay in that room for that reason, we don't let them." Today, although Elm Court is still owned by the family, it is deserted and boarded shut.

Elm Court, 1902

Courtesy of the Providence Library

WYNDHURST

(Lenox)

Wyndhurst
The house John Sloane tore down to build his cottage

Courtesy of the Stockbridge Library

Wyndhurst was begun in 1892 by John Sloane, six years after his brother had built Elm Court. It was designed by the architectural firm of Peabody and Stearns, the firm William Douglas Sloane had used, but the results were strikingly different. Six years had made the difference in the concept of cottages. While Elm Court is shingle style, Wyndhurst is a Tudor and far more formal in appearance.

Wyndhurst, sited on two hundred and fifty acres, was completed in 1894. The landscape architect was Frederick Law Olmsted. Notwithstanding Mr. Stokes' Welsh gardener at Shadow Brook, who went about mumbling at the stupidity of American techniques, Mr. Sloane paid Olmsted $15,500 to remove all the top soil before laying the forty-acre English lawn and the gardens.

The land was originally known as Blossom Farm. It belonged to Reverend John Hotchkin of the Lenox Academy. Dr. Hotchkin counted Mark Hopkins among his students at the well-known academy.

The first house on the property was a simple farm house built by Reverend Henry Ward Beecher in 1853. Reverend Beecher was so widely known in his day that at one point he contemplated running for the presidency of the United States. He was the brother of Harriet Beecher Stowe, and the son of a man who had questioned the respectability of fishing, Dr. Lyman Beecher. Henry Ward Beecher had to lay aside his presidential ambitions because he had appetites for diversions far more stimulating than fishing. Neither a total hypocrite nor entirely unself-aware, the reverend preached that love was the

Wyndhurst

basis of religious experience and that God would forgive all. Regardless of his transgressions, Beecher had constant supporters. At Blossom Farm, he wrote his "Star Papers," a well-known, widely read and quoted tract in the 1800s. Blossom Farm was soon being called Beecher Hill by the locals, and to this day, the high point on the property is called that.

Beecher sold the property to General John F. Rathbone in 1869. Rathbone moved Beecher's house from the crown of the hill, and built another. He wrote Beecher that he intended to name his new home Beecher Hill. Beecher wrote back to Rathbone: "If you call it by the name indicated in your letter, I shall esteem it a greater compliment than if I had received a title from an English university." For whatever reason, Rathbone named his cottage, not Beecher Hill, but Wyndhurst.

Courtesy of Arrowhead

John Sloane razed both Blossom Farm and Rathbone's Wyndhurst, but retained the second name. The Sloane house was built of Perth Amboy brick. At the south end of the house a tower was built where guests enjoyed a view of the mountains and lakes. The tower was attached to the house by a loggia, but could be reached from inside the house by climbing stairs in the billiard room. The east side of the house was dominated by a piazza that ran the length of the house. On the west side was a porte cochere that, according to the Peabody and Stearns records, had to be repaired several times before it was certain that it would not fall. Parts of the cottage were covered with ivy, and the area around the porte cochere was filled with greenery.

The entrance to the house from either side led into the great hall. The ceiling was covered in leather, dyed and stamped with fleur-de-lis. In the staircase, there is a stained glass window. Worked into the glass are the words, "Follow me to Heaven." The window was probably installed by the Jesuit order that occupied Wyndhurst after the Sloane family; it does not show on the Peabody and Stearns sketches. Nevertheless, a woman who played at Wyndhurst as a child said, "That window is perfect for I am sure that the next stop after Wyndhurst is heaven."

The estate included stables and farm buildings. On the estate, the Sloanes raised Jersey cows.

Today Wyndhurst is for sale again. The cottage passed from the Sloanes to their children, the Griswolds. It then became, along with Blantyre, Pinecroft and Coldbrooke, the Berkshire Hunt and Country Club. In 1939, it became the Cranwell School run by the Society of Jesus. After the school closed, the golf course when it was a club, remained open for use by townspeople and visitors. Recently there have been plans for Wyndhurst to become a condominium or a conference center or something else. It will not be resolved until it is sold and the plans approved by Lenox.

Photograph by David Frank

Detail of fireplace at Wyndhurst

The grand staircase at Wyndhurst

Photograph by David Frank

BLANTYRE

(Lenox)

Blantyre was formally opened by Mr. and Mrs. Robert Warden Paterson in September, 1904 with a large garden party. Mrs. Paterson received in the corner of the library/music room, and guests were then passed across the width of the house on the terrace and were served tea and chocolate in the conservatory. Sherry's orchestra played seated in a palm bower constructed for the fete in the south corner of the terrace. All the ground floor rooms, containing the Paterson art and antiques collection, were opened for the inspection. The guest list numbered seventy including every cottager name from Alexandre, Barnes and Bristed, Foster, Frothingham and Jesup to Sloane, Westinghouse, Wharton and Winthrop. According to the newspaper account in 1904, the house had been started in 1901 and was actually completed August, 1903, but September 12, 1904 was the official opening.

The architect was Robert W. Robertson of New York City. The story goes that he was summoned to Lenox to see Mr. Paterson's tract of land, drew a rough sketch on the back of an envelope which Mr. Paterson approved and the house was built just like the sketch without further ado. The house was 165 by 50 feet with a 30 by 75 foot extension for servants quarters. The locals have always called it a "Scottish castle." In fact, the cottage is Elizabethan. The misconception probably arose from the name rather than the look of the house. Blantyre was the name of Robert's father, James Paterson's estate. In turn, James had taken the name from the town Blantyre, Scotland, birthplace of David Livingston ("Dr. Livingston, I presume?") who was Mrs. James Paterson's cousin.

Photograph by David Frank

Perhaps no one room in any of the cottages has more of the feeling of an English manor hall than Blantyre's entrance hall. Typically it runs the width of the house (28 by 34 feet) from porte cochere to tiled terrace. At either end of the hall are two plant rooms that Mrs. Paterson always filled with palms. Among the fronds were strings of miniature lights. The doors from the hall to the dining room and salon were hung with tapestries. Pieces of the furniture were copies of that found in Hatfield House,

The entrance hall, Blantyre

The Paterson Suite, Blantyre

Photograph by David Frank

and the walls sported mounted heads of moose, elk, caribou, sheep, and deer.

Over the next two or three years, Mr. Paterson acquired adjoining land until the original fifty-acre tract grew to 230 acres; twenty-five acres of which were lawn. The estate also contained 175 square feet of greenhouse space heated by hot water pipes and lit by electricity.

The Paterson's New York home was described by the press as a "veritable museum." They were

Photograph by David Frank

The Salon at Blantyre

The dining room, Blantyre

Photograph by David Frank

later to add an art gallery to Blantyre. In addition to the Lenox estate, the Patersons had a New York home, a Canadian fishing lodge, and a winter retreat in Georgia.

Today, Blantyre looks much as it did in the Paterson's day except that the gallery has been removed from the building. The cottage is a charming inn affording its guests the opportunity to step back into the Gilded Age. Nothing has been spared in providing graciousness, attentiveness, and setting for the guest of the inn. In order for the management to create such an atmosphere, the inn is for the exclusive use of its guests, and the proprietress can not allow any sightseeing. There was a time when the house first opened that people could come in and look around, but like Mr. Searles, who closed his house after curious visitors arrived with scissors to snip a souvenir tassel from the curtains, the staff at Blantyre found the enthusiasm of the sightseers interfered with the smooth running of the house.

OVERLEIGH

(Lenox)

Situated in Lenox, Overleigh[5] was built by Samuel Frothingham. The landscape architect was E. Maitland Armstrong. The architects were Adams and Warren of New York City. Mr. Adams was the son-in-law of Dr. Greenleaf, a long time Lenox cottager. The general contractor was Joseph Clifford's Sons, a firm that was also hired to do the Bullard alterations on Highwood in 1899; to oversee the elevator installation at Wheatleigh in 1901; to build the Choir Room at Trinity Church for Mr. Lanier in 1899; to build the stable at The Elms for Mrs. Robeson in 1901; and to execute Mr. Weeks' architectural plans for Heaton Hall in 1904. Regardless of the architectural firm retained, local workers, and very often the same ones, executed the plans.

Work on Overleigh was begun in April, 1902 and completed in December of 1903—not an unusual time span for the building of a cottage.[5] The "just New England cottage style" of Mrs. Iasigi's Clover Croft was no more. The new idea was classical, what a young boy once called "mini-castle style." The main hall still ran the width of the house, no longer from porch to porch, but from porte cochere to piazza. The piazza was a wide-tiled terrace that ran the entire length of the building.

The library furniture was upholstered in pigskin. The living room was built to convert into a ballroom. In order to accomplish the dual role, the living room was sunken by three steps which correspondingly raised the ceiling two feet; with the furniture removed, the proportions were adequate for a ball. The room was oak paneled and hung with tapestries; the marble fireplace was imported from Rome. Under the ground-floor conservatory was a squash court.

The Frothinghams had been frequent visitors to the Berkshires prior to building Overleigh, residing at the Poplars. It was at the Poplars that Mrs. Henry White had died. When Overleigh was com-

Courtesy of Mrs. Edward Daley

Overleigh hand-painted postcard

Photograph by David Frank

Overleigh, drawing room/ballroom

Overleigh

Courtesy of the Providence Library

pleted, Miss Meyers, Mrs. Frothingham's sister, stayed at the Poplars.

Mr. Frothingham was a partner in the New York City real estate firm of Frothingham & Moore. He was "horsey" and Overleigh became the site of the Berkshire Hunt.

Today, Overleigh is part of the Avalon School. Fernbrook is another of the residential centers of the school. Between thirty and sixty students live at each campus. The young people are learning-impaired for any of a variety of reasons. The program, therefore, combines special education, counseling, physio-, speech, recreational, occupational, dance, music, and art therapies. The Poplars was demolished.

THE MOUNT

(Lenox)

The Mount was built by Edith Wharton in 1902 on a 130 acre tract bordering Laurel Lake for which she paid $40,600. The house was, in large part, a copy of an English country seat in Lincolnshire designed by Sir Christopher Wren and called Belton House. Mrs. Wharton's architect was Francis V. L. Hoppin, not Mrs. Wharton's friend and co-author, Ogden Codman. Although Codman is said to have begun the work of planning the house with Mrs. Wharton, she replaced him with Hoppin because Codman had gotten too expensive. For The Mount, she paid $50,000. She should receive as much credit for the final appearance of the house as the architectural firm of Hoppin and Koen as they were said to have followed her instructions exactly.

The Mount is truly a cottage—formal and elegant. Mrs. Wharton's dedication was to proportions rather than size, and she carried that idea forward in The Mount. Although it is a very large house by today's standards, it was not so then. The second decorating idea that Mrs. Wharton held dear was to create privacy and communication simultaneously. At The Mount each room was both self-contained and yet connected. If the doors between rooms were closed, one had complete privacy, and if the doors were open, all the rooms flowed into one another and ran the length of the house as did the galleries.

The two stories used by the family were built along galleries. The ground-floor gallery with stucco walls and tile floor served as the entrance hall. True to her treatise on houses, the main stairs did not dominate the entrance but lay off to the right. The staircase was dominated by painted panels. Upstairs the gallery was more formal. It had a marble floor and long windows. It was decorated with marble statuary and furniture.

The library had oak book cases

Photograph by Mimi MacDonald

The Mount

Photograph by Mimi MacDonald

Edith Wharton's library

running from ceiling to floor on three walls. Between two book shelves, was a large fireplace flanked by chairs. A decorative screen hid the doorway. The ceiling was white and the floor was oak covered by rugs. The room afforded a view of the terrace and the gardens and lake beyond.

Outside on the second floor was a tiled terrace that overlooked both the formal gardens and Laurel Lake. It was enclosed with a marble balustrade and covered by a striped awning. On that terrace, under that awning, the "literary rough and tumbles," as Edith Wharton called them, took place. The group often included poet and editor Richard Watson Gilder, lawyer and author Robert Grant (author of ***Unleavened Bread***), Howard Sturgis, Walter Terry, "Bay" Lodge (poet son of the Senator), playwright Clyde Fitch, and, in 1904, 1905 and 1911, Henry James.

Mrs. Wharton was a writer, and they say, it was in Lenox that she felt she could do her best work. It was unusual for a woman to have a profession, but more so for a woman in Edith Wharton's social sphere. She worked every morning propped up in bed. She finished her work before leaving her room as it was her intention that her writing not interfere with her other obligations. Edith Wharton left The Mount in 1912, as her marriage was ending, never to return again.

Today, The Mount is home to "Shakespeare and Co." and is a historic site operated by Edith Wharton Restoration. The tours through the houses are very special in that they are dramatizations. The actors from "Shakespeare and Co." assume the roles of occupants of the house — owners and staff — and recreate the life above and below stairs. Many of the tours, which more properly might be called one act plays, are followed by tea in the dining room and discussion. Proceeds go toward the major restoration effort underway at The Mount. When the drawing room ceiling was water damaged, the elaborate rosettes and garlands had to be recreated; not only is the house being saved, but vanishing crafts are being revived at The Mount.

ERSKINE PARK

HOLMWOOD

(Lenox)

Erskine Park was the cottage of George Westinghouse. Built in 1893, it was quite an amazing white Victorian building with a red roof. It was set among interconnecting crushed white marble roadways that passed over white marble bridges. The ponds beneath the bridges were man-made. On the property, Mr. Westinghouse built a power plant to light the cottage and grounds, and he generated enough power to light the streets of Lenox. At the back of the property, he built guest cottages and a playhouse for his children. The playhouse was so substantial that today it is used for real performances staged for the owners and guests at Fox Hollow.

Inside the house, the walls and ceilings of the rooms were covered with tufted fabric creating an unusual appearance of either exceptional luxury or a unique padded cell depending upon one's personal taste.

The cottage Westinghouse built for his wife was razed by Margaret Emerson McKim Vanderbilt. She was the widow of Alfred Gwynne Vanderbilt who died on the Lusitania on May 7, 1915. In 1919, she built her country estate, and called it Holmwood. It was at Holmwood that plans for the first Berkshire Summer Musical Festival took place.

The distinctly twentieth-century use of the distinctly nineteenth-century cottage is in evidence at Holmwood. Today it is called The Ponds at Fox Hollow and is a time-sharing resort. Holmwood is a clubhouse for the owners of the condominiums. The units are built around a series of ponds that were originally envisioned and executed by George Westinghouse.

Erskine Park

Courtesy of the Lenox Library

16

THE CURTIS

(Lenox)

If you were not invited to a house party, and you wanted to put yourself in the way of an invitation, if you had an invitation, but there was no room to accommodate you at the cottage; if you were an ordinary traveler, that is, not an intimate of a "cottager," or if you wanted to stay in the Berkshires beyond the customary country weekend—Friday night to Monday morning—you had a choice of hotels.

The first hotel in Lenox was the Curtis, or what Fanny Kemble had called "the Old Red Inn." Fanny Kemble Butler was a well-known actress in her day. She came from England and fell in love with the Berkshires. Known for the appeal of her voice on stage, she was equally known for her tongue off stage. Mrs. Samuel G. Ward confided to her diary, "Mrs. Butler (Fanny Kemble)—what wonderful variety of expression! She is full of genius. I like to be in the room with her, I like to look at her and hear her talk, but I do not care to converse with her."

Fanny took complete responsibility for putting the inn on the map. Through her efforts alone, she contended, the Curtis was not only filled, but filled with the best and most interesting people. In 1902, one author wrote, "The register books of the Berkshire Coffee House, Fanny Kemble's 'Old Red Inn,' and its successors of today, are classic in autographs and become historical, sociological or genealogical to the reader according to his penchant."

Mr. William O. Curtis, himself, took Fanny on a ride one afternoon in one of the Curtis carriages. During the ride, Fanny explained her position on the reason for the success of the Curtis. At the end of the ride, there was an overcharge, in

Photograph by Mimi MacDonald

Mrs. Kemble's opinion, of fifty cents. "The five dollars is for the ride," replied Mr. Curtis, "the fifty cents is for the sarce."

By the Gilded Age, The Berkshire Coffee House had become The Curtis Hotel. It was no longer the hostelry of those who came to Lenox for legal reasons, the court having moved to Pittsfield in 1868. The new clientele came for pleasure not business. In 1904, ***Berkshire Resort Topics*** reminded its readers that Mr. Curtis had been proprietor since the 1850s and the Curtis had been the "stopping place of Presidents, statesmen, literateurs [sic] and men of note in the commercial and scientific world, until no resort in the country is better or more favorably known."

The Curtis was four stories high. On the main floor were an office,

The Curtis

assembly room, reading rooms, parlors, and dining room. The furnishings were home-like with floral arrangements everywhere. On the upper floors were the guest rooms. It was advertised that every guest room was an "outside room" and had a "scene of mountain or valley . . . solid mahogany furniture, pictures and carpets of the highest grade." However, not all had a private bath. The hotel had sixty-eight fireplaces, "window balconies" in almost every room and three roof balconies affording expansive views of Bear, Rattlesnake, and Monument Mountains, the Taconics to the south, Tyringham Valley to the southeast, and October Mountain to the north.

In May, 1904, the Curtis had a "full house" of seventy-five guests. The guest could enjoy the billiard room, pool room, or card rooms during his stay. Outside, the privileges of the Lenox Club were offered Curtis guests in addition to tennis courts, boating, and driving. The guests may have stayed inside the hotel or in one of the two cottages owned by Mr. Curtis on Church Street.

Mr. Curtis was assisted by eleven key employees: head clerk, desk clerk, steward of the house, bookkeeper, head waiter, assistant steward, chef, baker, pastry cook, head porter, and night watchman plus a complete indoor and outdoor staff.

Unlike other Berkshire hotels which closed in November, the Curtis was open year-round. The winter guests, interestingly, were predominently the cottagers.

Today, the Curtis has been completely renovated. It is senior citizen housing. The main floor will be rented for shops.

BROOKHURST

(Lenox)

Brookhurst was built in 1905 by Newbold Morris. The architect was Francis V. L. Hoppin of Hoppin and Koen, New York, who also did Edith Wharton's Mount (1902), and Eastover (1910) for Harris Fahnestock. Hoppin was also the landscape artist, so the gardens are an integral part of the overall design of the house.

Newbold Morris purchased the estate from William B. Shattuck and retained the name Brookhurst, although the original house burned and Morris built the present brick home. He retained the barn, superintendent's cottage and other outbuildings, all of which had been designed by the same architect for Mr. Shattuck. It wasn't until many years later that Mr. Morris' son, the present owner of Brookhurst, learned that Mr. Shattuck's architect had been James Renwick. So while the "lord of the manor" resided in a "Hoppin" his superintendent lived in a "Renwick."

The Morris family dates their American heritage back to Louis Morris, the first governor of New Jersey. Newbold was sometimes mayor of New York and a staunch opponent of Tammany Hall. When Mr. and Mrs. Newbold Morris died, the property passed to their sons, Augustus Newbold[6], George L. K., the artist and Stephen, a diplomat. They divided the property into three parts. Newbold took the east section including the "Renwick cottage." He later gave part of this property for the Morris School. George took the west parcel and erected so modern a home that the magazine article written at the time was titled, "Mutiny in the Berkshires." Mr. and Mrs. Stephen Morris took the center section with the main house.

Photograph by David Frank

Although it is still a lovely home and setting, the Morris' have marked the changes—some planned and some not. There is a one-third mile drive to the front door that was lined by elms; Dutch elm disease claimed most of the trees. The old main gates were removed to allow a school bus to pass into the grounds of the Morris School. Many of the estates that remain private homes today, the Morris' have had to scale down, renovate, and otherwise dedicate

Brookhurst,
architect Francis V. L. Hoppin

Photograph by David Frank

From the Loggia, Brookhurst

themselves to making the house livable in the twentieth century. Brookhurst retains the original charm and feeling although it has been altered. The third stories on either side of the main house (which were the servants quarters) have been removed. "It's odd," Mr. Morris says, "to think that my mother could not imagine living here without eight in staff, and we come in each summer, just the two of us, and live here alone."

The original Brookhurst,
architect James Renwick

Courtesy of The Stockbridge Library

SHADOW BROOK
(Stockbridge/Lenox)

Photograph by William Tague

Aerial view of Shadow Brook

Built by Anson Phelps Stokes, Shadow Brook has been called the largest house in America. Completed in 1893 and consisting of a reported one hundred rooms, it may have been the largest house in America for two years until George Washington Vanderbilt completed his 250-room mansion, Biltmore, in Asheville, North Carolina.

The Stokes chose a local architect, H. Neill Wilson, of the Wilson firm, Pittsfield, Massachusetts. The landscape architect was Ernest Bowditch. Mr. Wilson certainly designed one of the largest homes of a non-classical style in America. Although parts of Shadow Brook (the tower, for example) were reminiscent of a castle, the overall impression of Shadow Brook was of a country house. Regardless of its size, it retained that air of hunting lodge or country dwelling that blends rather than contrasts with the landscape. Like Elm Court's, Shadow Brook's foundation and first floor were of marble. Since it was quarried locally, it was almost an economy. The second and third stories were of stucco and wood in a style reminiscent of Tudor. The tower was completely marble.

The 738 acres included a working farm, Brook Farm, gardens and riding trails. The stable was a converted Charles Follen McKim house, Oakswood, built for Samuel G. Ward in 1878. Anson Phelps Stokes' son, Isaac Newton Phelps Stokes wrote his mother February 5, 1893: "It does seem a pity not to use the Ward house or to convert it into stables. Mrs. (Dorr) of Macao says Mr. McKim always regarded the house as one of his best creations."

Shadow Brook rested on a slope above Lake Mahkeenac. In ***The Wonder Book***, Nathaniel Hawthorne had named that slope Shadow Brook: "In the summertime, the shadow of so many clustering branches, meeting and intermingling across the rivulet,

Hand-colored post card, Shadow Brook

Courtesy of Mrs. Edward Daley

was deep enough to produce a noon-tide twilight. Hence came the name of Shadow Brook."[7]

Anson Phelps Stokes' financial interests were broad—merchant, banker, clock manufacturer, and real estate investor. His avocations were as varied as his financial interests. He helped to found the Metropolitan Museum of Art. He amassed a fine collection of Americana. He was an inventor and received two patents, both in 1903 and both related to "marine architecture," for a centerboard and a globular floating battery. He was a photographer and writer.

There was a strong charitable and religious characteristic in the family through the generations. Anson's interest in philanthropy was shared by his family. His grandfather, Thomas, founded the London Mission Society. His father, James Boulten Stokes, was a founder of the Association to Improve the Condition of the Poor. His sisters, Caroline and Olivia, were noted philanthropists. Anson's son, Isaac Newton Phelps Stokes, was an architect dedicated to better housing. He was part of the New York Commission that passed a better housing law, and he designed a number of new and improved tenements. Anson Phelps Stokes' brother, William Earl Dodge, builder of the Hotel Ansonia, seemed to have inherited the same concerns—along with $11,000,000 at his father's death—but with a bent of his own. In 1917, he wrote a book, ***The Right to be Well Born***, in which he set forth the idea that human beings had the right to a better start in life through application of stock-breeding techniques which he had perfected on his horse farm in Lexington, Kentucky. W. E. D. also advocated the registration of human pedigrees.

Another of Anson's sons, James Graham Phelps Stokes, lived at the University Settlement House on New York's East Side and developed an interest in Socialism.

Shadow Brook

Courtesy of Mrs. Olivia Stokes Hatch

Courtesy of the Lenox Library

Morning room, Shadow Brook

There, he met Rose Pastor, a reporter for the ***Jewish Daily News*** and a socialist. They were married from 1905-1925 during which time, in 1918, Rose was sentenced to ten years in jail under the Espionage Act. The sentence was reversed upon appeal. During the appeal, she made a statement which has become famous:

> For ten years, I have worked and produced things necessary and useful for the people of this country and for all those years, I have half starved... but the moment I left the useful producing class—the moment I became part of the capitalistic class, which did not have to do any productive work to exist—I had all the vacations I wanted, all the clothes I wanted. I had all the leisure I wanted—everything I wanted was mine without my having to do any labor in return for all I had received.[8]

Rose accepted no alimony after the divorce in 1925 and lived and died in poverty in 1933.

In 1898, Anson Phelps Stokes lost a leg as a result of a riding accident at Shadow Brook. He had enjoyed the house that took two years, four hundred workers and close to $1,000,000 to build and furnish, for only five years. The house that covered an acre of ground space lost its charm. By 1904, ***Berkshire Resort Topics*** reported that Shadow Brook would be run as an inn. The 738 acres, with a quarter-mile frontage on the lake, the house and even the furnishings remained as the Stokes' had left it "in a paradise which few men of wealth have attempted to attain." A room was to be had for thirty-five dollars per week, "Truly this is not beyond the reach of the ordinary Lenox resorter, and there seems no reason why the house should not be filled."

However, like Elm Court forty years later, Shadow Brook did not succeed as an inn. It was sold again as a private cottage in 1906 to Spencer Shotter ("something in turpentine, I think") who sold it to perhaps, its most famous owner, Andrew Carnegie in 1917. Mr.

Carnegie bought it both because it reminded him of his native Scotland, and because he liked to fish. He fished with a local man far less wealthy than he, but who enjoyed Mr. Carnegie's respect as "a good fisherman who knows the spots."

Obviously, a grand spot for fishing, Anson Phelps Stokes' head gardener had gone down to the water's edge to inspect the damage after a storm, and came upon a man fishing on Shadow Brook property.

"Who are you?" he asked.

"Who are you?" the man countered.

Angry at not getting a direct reply, he countered hotly, "*I* am the caretaker of this whole estate. Now, who are you?"

"I am the caretaker of the whole United States," replied Grover Cleveland.

Carnegie summered there ("I still remember him riding in his carriage in the summer heat—all in black. It must have been uncomfortable, but he wore black because he was very old and therefore, very formal.") He died at Shadow Brook in 1919.

In 1922, Mrs. Carnegie gave (or sold) the estate to the Jesuit Society of Jesus. It burned to the ground in March, 1956, and was rebuilt. The present structure is not aesthetically gratifying to view, but it is edifying in that it is positioned just to one side and covers approximately the same land space as the original house. The Shadow Brook sign is still next to the drive, but it is a holistic health center called Kripalu Center, and in Mr. Stokes' rock garden is a picture of a guru. Mr. Stokes probably wouldn't mind. A man who understood small ironies inherent in a changing world, he once declared the gold is his teeth at customs to indicate his position on the gold/silver standard debate. "Thereafter," his granddaughter says, "he and grandmother were always passed through the customs without a word."

Salon, Shadow Brook

Courtesy of the Lenox Library

19 THE LITTLE RED HOUSE *(Stockbridge)*

The Little Red House

The Little Red House is a cottage in the literal sense of the word. Perhaps it has no place in a story of the Gilded Age, but the elite may well not have found the Berkshires and claimed it as one of their summer colonies, if not for the literati that predated them. Then too, the Little Red House is inexorably bound to two other houses, Tanglewood and Highwood, called the first Berkshire cottages.

They are bound together by the little house's most famous tenant, Nathaniel Hawthorne. To separate the three is a little like trying to follow the Abbot and Costello routine, "Who's on first?"

The Tanglewood of the Hawthorne books, ***The Wonder Book*** and ***Tanglewood Tales***, is not Tanglewood but Highwood. Samuel G. Ward, the owner of Highwood was not responsible for bringing Sophie and Nathaniel Hawthorne to the Little Red House; it was Caroline Sturgis Tappan, who owned Tanglewood, but was renting Highwood. Only later, after Hawthorne had finished ***Tanglewood Tales*** and left Stockbridge,

Photograph by Robert Owens

would Mrs. Tappan build a house and call it Tanglewood. When Hawthorne used the name Tanglewood for Highwood, it was sheer invention. Nor did Hawthorne ever call his little house Tanglewood or, for that matter, the Little Red House. The Tappans and the Wards called it the little farm house. Mrs. Nathaniel (Sophie) Hawthorne called it "The Little Red Shanty." Hawthorne only commented that "the house is as red as a scarlet letter." Finally, although all three have Lenox postal addresses, Highwood, the Red House, and Tanglewood, are actually in Stockbridge. But, that's fine because, as Fanny Kemble, actress and friend of all three families, once explained, "Poor Hawthorne never knew where he was at all. He didn't even know he lived in Stockbridge sending all his letters to me addressed Lenox." Then of course, what is the Little Red House today, is not. The present building is more a rendition than a replica. Knowing all this, it becomes easier to remember where the author lived when writing ***The Wonder Book*** and ***Tanglewood Tales***: when he wrote ***The Wonder Book***, he lived on the grounds of Tanglewood; when he wrote ***Tanglewood Tales***, he did not.

Hawthorne, Sophie, their children, Una and Julian, came to the Red House in June, 1850. Their third child was born there. Hawthorne had been ousted from his job at the Custom House in Salem, Massachusetts in 1849. By May 1850, although the ***Scarlet Letter*** was just published and well received, money was an issue. The house was let to the Hawthornes for seventy-five dollars for four years.[9] The very reasonable cost of the house was a persuasive factor, and the result of Sophie's longtime friendship with Caroline Tappan. That friendship was an additional inducement to move to Stockbridge. Furthermore, Samuel G. Ward was sympathetic and involved with the literati of the day. It was he who showed Nathaniel Hawthorne around the neighborhood and left Hawthorne with the feeling that the house on the Stockbridge Bowl would be comfortable and stimulating physically and socially. Something Salem had not been since Hawthorne's ouster from the Custom house.

Hawthorne stayed in the Little Red Shanty only eighteen months. It is interesting that Hawthorne's reasons for coming to and leaving Stockbridge are identical and offer an insight into his personality. He first raved about the beautiful scenery. Eighteen months later, he grumbled that the scenery kept him from his work and that so much beauty was oppressive. (Although he wrote both the ***House of Seven Gables*** and ***The Wonder Book*** and formed ideas for ***Blithesdale Romance*** during his stay.) His high hopes of society after his rejection in Salem were altered within eighteen months, and he said he looked forward to resuming a quieter life-style this time in West Newton. By October 30, 1851, his friend, Ellery Channing wrote: "He (Hawthorne) always, I believe, finds fault with the people among whom he settles." The most persuasive reason for coming, to a man who had worried all his life about money, was probably the low rent. That first fall, perhaps when the ardor was mutual, Hawthorne collected the apples from the orchard in front of the farm house without problem. By the second fall, the very thing that had so attracted Hawthorne became the final determiner in the decision to leave. Caroline told Sophie that for so low a consideration, the apples were not included in the rent. Hawthorne wrote to Caroline Tappan:

> In the first place permit me to notice the question which you put to Sophie, whether she would not prefer to receive kindness rather than assume rights. I do not know what would be her reply; but for myself in view of the infirmities of human nature in general . . . I infinitely prefer a small right to great favor.

Hawthorne had raised the issue of apples to a lofty plain. Largess had brought him and largess now undermined his pleasure in the little house and pointed up a deteriorating relationship with the people who had urged him to come. However, some biographers suggest that apples and vistas and social demands did not do as much to drive Hawthorne out as did one man—Herman Melville.

Here again, something in Hawthorne's nature turned what he seemed most to desire into something that repelled him. In June, 1850, as Sophie readied the little house, Hawthorne lay in bed at Highwood with the flu. He was offered a loan by Lewis W. Mansfield, a well-to-do writer. Hawthorne refused, and Mansfield sent a case of champagne instead. Hawthorne wrote to thank Mansfield, saying "I will not drink it now but reserve it for some especially bright and festive occasion. If a man of genius, as has not and then happened by, should sit at our humble board, I shall let loose a cork."[20]

It was two months later, after the August 5th dinner at David Dudley Field's, that Hawthorne uncorked the champagne and served it to Herman Melville. All biographies of both man mention the relationship between the two. Melville made any such oversight an impossibility by dedicating his greatest book, ***Moby Dick***, to Hawthorne. The fact that ***Moby Dick*** was completed during the time (1850-51) when they were both in the Berkshires has made the dimensions of the friendship of even more interest. There is a secondary cause of interest, their relationship illuminates attitudes towards love and friendship that we do not hold generally today.

Melville's letters survive and leave little doubt of the feeling he had for Hawthorne. So does his essay "Hawthorne and Mosses." Mellow, in his biography of Hawthorne, is quite forthright: "What was astonishing in Melville's essay were the unmistakeable sexual implications of the imagery." Melville loved Hawthorne in a way that was more common in the 1850s and less understood today. Did Hawthorne return the love? We can't know without his letters. In the 1880s when Nathaniel's son, Julian, approached Melville for his father's letters to include in a biography, Melville said they were destroyed. We can not be sure they were destroyed, but we can be certain that Melville did not want them read by the public at large. Perhaps Melville destroyed them because they did not evince a return of the love Melville felt.

Did Hawthorne, as he did with scenery, society, and even special friends like the Tappans, begin by returning the affection and end by fleeing from the Little Red Shanty and Melville's neighborhood? A possible answer is in some lines of poetry Melville wrote as an old man entitled "After the Pleasure Party."

> Nature, is no shallow surge
> Against thee either sex may urge.
> Why hast thou made us but
> in halves—
> Co-relatives? This makes us
> slaves.
> If these co-relatives never meet
> Selfhood itself seems
> incomplete.
> And such the dicing of blind
> fate
> Few matching halves here
> meet and mate.[11]

Was Melville thinking of Hawthorne? Perhaps, as he had been in 1850, when he wrote from Arrowhead: "My dear Hawthorne... By what right do you drink from my flagon of life? And when I put it to my lips—lo, they are yours not mine. I feel that the Godhead is broken up like the bread at supper and that we are the pieces. Hence this infinite fraternity of feeling."[12]

Moby Dick would cap Melville's career, and he would live on forgotten, publishing his own work. Hawthorne would go on to new heights—every new book anticipated by an adoring public. Perhaps some of what determined that outcome happened in two houses in the Berkshire hills: Arrowhead and the Little Red Shanty. Hawthorne was by nature both a solitary man and a man who had found contentment within his intimate family circle. For both these reasons he turned inward and distanced himself from people. By November, 1851, family, bag, and baggage piled onto a farm wagon, he left the "Little Red Shanty."

Today, the Little Red House—as it is now called—is maintained by the Tanglewood Festival, an activity of the Boston Symphony Orchestra. It is used as a facility of the Berkshire Music Center where music students attend classes. There are volunteer tour guides during Tanglewood season—July and August. The original cottage burned to the ground in 1890s. In 1947, it was reconstructed using the old foundation. The external house was constructed true to old photographs. Inside, the house is divided into music rooms for the students. The house contains period furniture and Hawthorne first editions a gift from Bowdoin College where Hawthorne graduated along with Henry Wadsworth Longfellow and Franklin Pierce.

20

TANGLEWOOD
(Stockbridge)

Probably every visitor to the Berkshires today knows where Tanglewood is. They may not know that when they park their car to attend a concert at Tanglewood, they are leaving their car in Lenox and walking to Stockbridge.

William Aspinwall Tappan bought property from Mr. Daniel Barnes in 1849 to be known later as the estate, Tanglewood. It is reasonable to assume that from May 5, 1849 when William and Caroline Tappan purchased twenty-eight acres and sixty-one rods from Daniel Barnes for $4,310.94, to July 15, 1851, there was no house on the Tappan grounds except the Little Red Shanty rented to the Hawthornes. It is a reasonable assumption because after renting the red house to the Hawthornes, the Tappans rented Highwood from the Wards. If they had another house on their estate, presumably the Tappans would have lived in it. Further, the 1850 Stockbridge Census shows Mr. Tappan listed as "a farmer, land value $4,000." Since the land itself cost $4,310.94, there is no indication of an "improvement" such as a house.

In 1850, Sophie Hawthorne wrote to her mother, "Mr. Ward was kind enough to give a sketch of the porch of Highwood for the ***Wonder Book***." We know by this letter and the rest of the information, that Hawthorne used Highwood as the model for the house he named Tanglewood in ***The Wonder Book*** and ***Tanglewood Tales***. ***The Wonder Book*** was finished July 15, 1851. Since the Tappans built their house after Hawthorne wrote ***The Wonder Book***, they took the name from the book as the Anson Phelps Stokes would do forty-two years later with Shadow Brook.

Although visitors may know where Tanglewood is, they may not realize that it is next-door to Highwood. Throughout the biographies of Hawthorne, it is assumed that the Wards owned all the surrounding property, and that when the Tappans let Highwood, they sublet the Little Red Shanty to Hawthorne. Were that true, Mr. Ward would have been Mr. Hawthorne's landlord. That, however, is not the case. Horatio Bridge, a classmate of Hawthorne's, helped the Hawthornes set up their new household and

wrote to his wife:

> ***July 18, 1850 La Maison Rouge Cara Mia, Be it known, then, that Hawthorne occupies a house painted red, like some old-fashioned farm houses you have seen. It is owned by Mr. Tappan, who lived in it a while, but he is now at Highwood, the beautiful place of Mr. Ward.***[13]

It is far easier to understand the argument between the Tappans and the Hawthornes over the yield from the apple orchard if the Tappans were the owners of the property rather than tenants arguing over what would then have been Mr. Ward's apples.

Today Tanglewood is the site of the Berkshire Music Festival. It is as an outdoor music center that Tanglewood has achieved its most widespread fame. Tanglewood was the gift of William and Caroline Tappan's granddaughter, Mrs. Andrea Hepburn, to the Berkshire Music Festival in the 1930s. The Music Festival at Tanglewood is visited during its annual eight-week season by hundreds of thousands of people.

Tanglewood

Photograph by Mimi MacDonald

21

HIGHWOOD
(Stockbridge)

In 1841, Samuel Gray Ward bought land from the widow of Cyrus Huwlitt, and from Daniel Barnes in 1844 to form Highwood. Samuel G. Ward was from Boston. He was a representative of the London firm of Baring Brothers as his father, Thomas Wren Ward, had been before him. Ward started the well-known Saturday Club, a literary gathering that included Henry Wadsworth Longfellow.

Samuel Gray Ward is often confused with Sam Ward, Julia Ward Howe's brother and husband of Emily Astor. Even contemporaries confused the two Sams. Henry Wadsworth Longfellow separated them by calling Samuel G. Ward of Highwood and Boston: Good Sam. "The 'G' stands for good," he said. It seems Samuel G. was the more conventional of the two. To further complicate the identities of the men, they almost became brothers-in-law. However, Henry Ward died after becoming engaged but before marrying Samuel G.'s sister Mary. In fact, one of Jenny Lind's biographers, Gladys Denny Schulz, makes the mistake in ***Jenny Lind: The Swedish Nightingale***. She writes that Jenny married Otto Goldschmidt at Sam G. Ward's house and then goes on to describe Sam Ward. Sam and Emily Astor Ward lived in New York City, Jenny was married at No. 20 Louisberg Square, Boston, the home of Samuel G.

As a wedding present, Sam gave her a locket containing two likenesses: one of Daniel Webster and one of George Washington. She called it her "good luck locket," and thereafter, wore it at all her concerts. Others have reported that she was married at Highwood, confusing not the two Sams, but Sam's two houses.

Highwood

We know from his wife's diary that when Sam first purchased the land, he had intended it as a year-round residence. After his father died, Sam was persuaded to take his place at Baring Brothers, and Highwood became a summer residence. He has always been distinguished as the "First of the Lenox Cottagers." Never mind that his property was in Stockbridge, locals date the start of the Cottage period at 1846—the year Mr. Ward built Highwood. Yet it is not at all clear that Mr. Ward actually built Highwood or when.

In 1841 when Samuel G. Ward purchased the first piece of land, the deed marks the property line "beginning at the Southeast corner of the house." Mr. Ward purchased land five and two years before the 1846 date, and we know, from Mrs.

Photograph by David Frank

Ward's letters to her father-in-law in Boston, that they occupied what she called "Highwood" as early as 1845. We also know that Ward had construction work done from letters to his architect, Richard Upjohn.[14] The letters are dated 1846 from Pittsfield. The fact is that the letters were dated ***after*** Mrs. Ward's letters to her father-in-law postmarked Highwood. That coupled with mention of an existing house in the Huwlitt deed, causes one to ask if Mr. Ward built Highwood at all, or was he, with the help of architect, Richard Upjohn, renovating the widow Huwlitt's house? Perhaps there is no way now to be certain about the genesis of the "first cottage," however, there is one piece of evidence supporting the notion that Highwood was not built but renovated. It has to do with the architect, Richard Upjohn.

Richard Upjohn was born in England in 1802. His first commission as an architect came after he emigrated to America. Although he made his reputation designing churches, that first commission in 1833, was for a house. Since he was the first president of the American Institute of Architecture from 1857-76, his work has been documented. Not only was his work distinctive, but he was credited with favoring the gothic style and

Photograph by David Frank

Highwood today

Courtesy of Boston Public Library Print Dept. Peabody & Stearns Collection

Highwood, architect's rendering

legitimatizing it in America. The simple fact is, Highwood does not look like an Upjohn. It is in fact more easily explained if the architect were working within the constraint of an existing house. It is harder to believe that during the very years that he was establishing his style, he changed that style to build one house, Highwood. Those who believe Upjohn did build a house for Ward, say the difference in style is the result of subsequent alterations. Although the house was altered by the next owners, those who still believe Upjohn built, not renovated it, would have to decide why it does not look like other houses Upjohn built, but does look almost exactly like Bonnie Brae built by local craftsmen for Henry Ivison less than six miles down the road.

Ward sold the house to Dr. and Mrs. William Bullard in 1855. The Bullards altered it at least twice since Sam Ward wrote to Upjohn complaining that the workmen were too slow. In 1899, records from the architectural firm of Peabody and Stearns show:

Bullard, William & Mrs.	**Lenox**	**Alterations**
General Contractor	Joseph Clifford's Sons[2]	2,540.49
Plumber	William A. Johnson	1,075.00
New Plumbing		1,297.00
Comm.		180.79
Transportation expense		19.23

Another entry, undated, shows "Mrs. William S. (Louisa N.) Bullard building a stable for a cost of $6,040.00, [with a] $302 Commission and $38.68 Transportation" paid to Peabody and Stearns. The present owner believes there was a second major renovation after William N. Bullard, Jr.'s marriage during the period 1917-20. Although the architect of the second renovation is not known, the landscaping was done by Copland and Cleveland, the firm that lost the contract for Central Park to Frederick Law Olmsted.

William's sister Kate Bullard lived with her brother summers at Highwood. In 1920, probably as a result of her brother's marriage, she built an "Italian Villa at a cost of $300,000" on the Highwood property to the left of the main house. She died that winter in Boston. Never occupied, the villa was torn down in 1923 by William. He didn't want to live in it, and he didn't want to sell it and have strangers live so close. ***The Berkshire Eagle*** reported that the Bullards preferred the history and charm of Highwood to a $300,000 villa. The newspaper commended them for sound values and something like "Yankee" good sense.

Today Highwood is a private residence. It has had only three owner-families in 137 years, if one begins, by tradition or force of habit, with Mr. and Mrs. Samuel Ward. From 1846-1855, the Wards occupied the house. Bullards occupied the house 1855-1961—Mr. and Mrs. William S. Bullard, Louisa N. after her husband's death, her son William H., and his wife after his death. Since 1961, the present owner has lived at Highwood. If Highwood is the renovated farm house of Cyrus Huwlitt, then only four families occupied it in almost 150 years.

WHEATLEIGH

(Stockbridge/Lenox)

The Tiffany windows in the main staircase at Wheatleigh

Photograph by David Frank

Wheatleigh was built in 1892-1893 by H. H. Cook, Esquire. The architects were Peabody and Stearns. Wheatleigh is a gracious Italianate villa with an entrance courtyard dominated by a fountain. The entrance hall is enhanced by two matched Tiffany windows. It is one of the few places in the Berkshires where the windows themselves rival the beauty of the view seen through them. There is an enormous fireplace in the hall. The original drawings submitted to Mr. Cook include dozens of sketches of fireplaces as the fireplace was a gathering place and central focus. As in many of the cottages, the entrance hall cuts straight through the width of the house to doors that let one out onto a wide piazza. The view is of the mountains in the far distance, Stockbridge Bowl in the middle distance, and the Frederick Law Olmsted gardens close-at-hand.

It is said that Mr. Cook built Wheatleigh to give to his daughter as a wedding present when she married Carlos deHeredia on February 4, 1891. It would not have been an unusual gesture. Mr. Sloane gave Highlawn to his daughter Lila when she married W. B. Osgood Field, a city house to Adele when she married J. Burden, and a city house next door when her sister, Emily, married John Hammond. There is nothing in the formal correspondence between Mr. Cook and Messers Olmsted, Peabody or Stearns to indicate his intention, but perhaps there wouldn't have been. Regardless of the intent, Mrs. deHeredia was mistress of Wheatleigh far longer than her father was master.

In response to the question—"How did Mr. Cook make his money?"—a former servant shifts a bit in his chair and smiles, "Oh, well, he owned Fifth Avenue, you know." Echoing the stories of "the countess," he adds, "Mr. Cook had so much money, he was delighted to add a title to the family. See he didn't need any money, nor did his daughter, but a title was welcome." From the first moment you enter the circular drive of Wheatleigh, you have no doubt, that countess or no, Mrs. deHeredia lived like a queen.

Henry H. Cook was, in fact, a banker and director of railroads. If he owned Fifth Avenue, others shared in his good fortune. However, as the descendant of Captain Thomas Cook who came to America in 1635 and founded Portsmouth, Rhode Island, and a grandson of Judge Constant Cook who built part of the Erie Railroad, H. H. Cook did not lack real estate.

Today Wheatleigh is an inn.

Photograph by David Frank

Entrance hall, Wheatleigh

Over the years, the cottage has been altered. Walls have been moved to create bedrooms. The tapestries that dominated the front hall have been removed. Still the house maintains its charm. There is a trick when looking at old houses: look at detail that would have remained untouched even if the house were redecorated or renovated. Unless it was "gutted," the ceiling moldings, staircases, fireplace mantles, and doors were probably left unaltered. They are the glimpse of the past.

The property is greatly diminished in size. Wheatleigh, like Shadow Brook and Elm Court, among others, was also a farm. The farming aspect was taken seriously by the cottagers as were their stables and greenhouses. At one time Wheatleigh included all of these. Today the lower part of the estate, the part in Stockbridge, has been purchased to build condominiums. The gatehouse at the front of the drive is separately owned and is a private house. The symbol of Wheatleigh today are the ornate gate posts, wrought iron forced into soft and imaginative shapes atop the solid, outsized brick posts. They bespeak the privacy and gracious living that was Wheatleigh; and to the degree that twentieth-century realities will allow, is the inn today.

BONNIE BRIER FARM

SHAUGHLIN

BECKWITHSAW

(Stockbridge)

There are three names for one estate in Stockbridge. Ordinarily, the new owner retained the housename even if he razed the house and rebuilt. For whatever reason, the three owners from 1892-1916, each selected a different name for the same house.

The builder was Leonard Forbes Beckwith, chief engineer of the New York City Telephone Company, also credited as the architect. In 1892, he built his summer house in Stockbridge and placed the inscription, "Manor of Beckwithsaw" on the hall fireplace. For all the talk of titles and coats of arms in the Berkshire hills, Mr. Beckwith actually possessed one. The arms of Beckwith consisted of three hinds' heads around a silver and red fret below, and two roses above.

In 1904, negotiations to sell Beckwithsaw to Mr. and Mrs. Sam Hill began. The thirty-room cottage was situated on eight-hundred acres and the sale price included furniture, rugs, and a billiard table. After a year of negotiating, the Hills bought it for $90,000 in 1905. Mrs. Hill renamed the cottage Shaughlin after moving the inscription and coat of arms from over the fireplace.

Mr. Hill was never happy in New England. Almost as soon as he purchased, he wrote a letter stating with some sarcasm that he had bought the place "actually with the desire to help out the tax gatherer in that part of the country." Ironically, in the same letter, Mr. Hill said, "I regard real estate as a liability and not an asset." It was ironic because, less than eleven years later, in 1916, the home was sold to H. R. (Dan) Hanna for $500,000.

The much-married son of Mark

Photograph by David Frank

Bonnie Brier Farm

Photograph by David Frank

Bonnie Brier Farm

Hanna bought the summer place as a wedding present for his fourth wife. She called it Bonnie Brier.

Mr. Hanna added a barn. Known as the largest barn in the United States, it covered twenty-thousand square feet in floor space and housed one hundred horses. It burned to the ground in 1955.

However, the real fame of Bonnie Brier is not attached to the house or barn or even to Dan Hanna's famous name. (In 1900, Joseph Choate wrote his daughter, Mabel: "...***Life*** has a cartoon of 'Mark Hanna's Dream' of Imperialism. It represents him with the Queen prostrate before him, Lord Salisbury and myself holding up her train, while he is putting her crown on his own head with all the magnates of both realms looking on in admiration. Jo [a child of Joseph Choate] is so captivated with it that he won't let me send it to you.") The enduring fame of Bonnie Brier is that it was the first site of the Berkshire Music Festival. The festival did not move to its permanent home at Tanglewood until 1937. On August 21, 1934, ***The Berkshire Eagle*** headline read, "Horse Show Ring Made Amphitheater for Festival Opening at Hanna Farm." It was held at Bonnie Brier the first two years of its existence, 1934 and 1935. The uplifting quality of transferring events to the out-of-doors seems to have had a special impetus at Bonnie Brier. In 1938, a new owner had twelve elms and sixty maples transplanted to form Gothic arches and create an outdoor cathedral.

Today, Bonnie Brier is the DeSisto School. The present owners have taken an interest in the house and its history. Restoration efforts have begun. Paint was stripped off the paneling restoring the wood to its original state; chairs that were original to the house were hunted down and repurchased. In keeping with the Bonnie Brier Farm tradition of outdoor events, in 1983, the director of the school was married on the lawn and mingled with guests from atop an elephant.

24

CLOVER CROFT

(Stockbridge)

It was built in 1890 by Amy Gore (Mrs. Oscar) Iasigi. She purchased the land in 1889 from David Dudley Field—five acres for $10,000. In 1891, when Mrs. Iasigi purchased a second parcel of land from David Dudley's brother, Henry Martyn Field, inflation had set in. For $10,000, she was able to purchase only three acres. In 1900, Mrs. Iasigi again added to her estate, purchasing three-tenths of an acre for one dollar from Henry I. and James Graham Parsons.[15] In 1905, the price having been right five years previously, Mrs. Iasigi purchased eight acres from the Parsons for eleven dollars. In 1911, she added eleven acres to the property purchased from Franklin A. Palmer for $2,472. At that point, the estate contained approximately twenty-eight acres.

The architect was A. W. Longfellow and the landscape architect was Guy Lowell. Guy Lowell, like Amy Gore, was from an old Boston family. A July 6, 1904 article in ***Berkshire Resort Topics*** describes the house and gardens in this way: "There may be more pretentious places in the Berkshires than Clover Croft, but there are none more charming."

The house was wood shingle style as were Naumkeag and Elm Court. The three-storied structure was approximately 80 feet long by 40 feet wide. The dining room was paneled in California redwood. The living room and front hall were oak. Like most cottages, the front hall ran the width of the house between two outside porches. From the eastern porch, Mrs. Iasigi could step almost directly onto one of the paths of her formal garden. When asked about the architectural style of her Stockbridge home, she replied, in proper Bostonian fashion, "just the New England cottage style."

Today, eighty years of perspective, shows Mrs. Iasigi to be half right. New England cottage style divided into two periods. The shingle period of which Clover Croft was an example, and the classic styles typified by Bellefontaine and Wyndhurst. The former intending to blend with the New England landscape, and the latter meant to replicate European grandeur.

The house burned to the ground. The formal gardens grew untended to abnormal heights, and parts toppled in the wind. The property was divided into five building lots. The center lot, including the foundation of the old house and the formal garden, is owned by the author.

When Mrs. Iasigi died in 1927, her assets were listed in excess of $1,000,000. Her Boston home was valued at $200,000 and her Stockbridge home and property was valued at $45,000.

Clover Croft

Courtesy of the Stockbridge Library

25

NAUMKEAG
(Stockbridge)

Photograph by David Frank

Naumkeag was built by Joseph Hodges Choate in 1885-6. Interestingly, Mr. Choate did not want to build in Stockbridge at all. He had told his family over the years that, when he retired, he wanted to return to his boyhood home of Salem. His family felt otherwise. In a compromise of sorts, the Choate family built in Stockbridge, and named the house Naumkeag, the Indian name for Salem.

The architest was originally Choate's friend, Charles F. McKim, however, the work was turned over to "his promising young partner," Stanford White. Naumkeag has been called one of the last of the great shingle-style cottages. It was designed in a year that marked a turning point for the firm of McKim, Mead and White. Soon after 1886, their architectural designs clearly reflected the classical style. Naumkeag was a last attempt at shingle style, but it reflects not only the end of one idea, but the beginning of another, and actually, the result is more whimsy-style. Parts of Naumkeag are shingle, parts are classical, and parts are Naumkeag's own. So while the style of architecture has been called New England shingle style, in fact, the style, like the man, was unique.

"Naumkeag was always fun," a local who was a frequent guest says. When asked what made it so much fun, she replies, "The people, of course; isn't that what always does it?" Joseph Choate was, like his house, an enviable blend. He had status and distinction as a lawyer and ambassador; audacity and humor as a man; and that which we all secretly hope for, to be sought after because we are entertaining.

The gardens were initially designed by Frederick Law Olmsted. After a dispute, however, the landscaping was completed by Nathaniel Barrett of Boston. Part of the intention of the shingle style was to make the cottage fit harmoniously with the natural surroundings. Olmsted seems to have had a similar plan for the gardens. In the Olmsted records there is a note "To trim the hedges to follow the contours of the mountains on the horizon." The flower gardens were carefully planned and yet retained a wild country feeling.

When Miss Mabel Choate became mistress of Naumkeag, she altered the gardens. It is said that the family was unnerved by the ex-

Naumkeag

Staircase at Naumkeag decorated for Christmas

Photograph by Mimi MacDonald

tent and expense of the project. However, it is also reported that her landscape architect, Fletcher Steele, and her accountant were so adept, that the project was paid for out of profits, and her capital was not touched. When she died she left, not only the house, but funds to maintain it as a historic site.

Like Naumkeag in Choate's day, Naumkeag today is fun to visit. It is run by the Trustees of Reservations, and guides tell stories and have a grand time showing everyone around. Possibly no other present day use of the cottages is more satisfying than the historic sites like Naumkeag, The Mount, and Chesterwood.

Garden at Naumkeag

Photograph by David Frank

Courtesy of Mr. J. Graham Parsons

Bonnie Brae

26

BONNIE BRAE

(Stockbridge)

It was built in 1873 by Henry Ivison, the great-grandfather of the present owner. The guest book, beginning August 11, 1873 and continuing to the summer of 1983, rests in the library. The portrait of Henry's daughter, Catherine, hangs in the dining room. The house is a living testament to the dream all the cottage builders had and few achieved—continuity: the dream that generation after generation would summer at the country seat as the European aristocracy did and, therefore, help establish the American counterpart. It was not to be.

One of the first entertainments noted in the guest book is a tea on September 18, 1873. The ten guests included Henriette Field, the Ivisons' neighbor.

Across the street, in the late 1800s, Birdseye Blakeman built Oronoque. Ivison and Blakeman were partners in a publishing firm in New York. The Ivison house passed to Catherine. Catherine Ivison and James Anson Parsons had two sons, Henry Ivison and J. Graham, father of the present owner.

The guest book reads: "May 13, 1884. Opened our house in Stockbridge for the season. Found everything in excellent order, both in the house and about the grounds"; "December 13, 1903... with two maids, came up from New York and then to sail for Naples"; "June 23, 1910—arrived with two maids. More maids will follow tomorrow with baby and a nurse." The short entries described the age, however, it was not the bliss we imagine. The house "had a poor little inadequate furnace and only one bath," Mrs. J. Graham Parsons recalled. In addition to summers, the family often spent Christmas at Stockbridge. They "imported their own fun" which meant inviting friends to house parties. Mrs. Parsons told her son about one winter house party, "You can imagine what it was like lining up in the cold hall waiting your turn. At other times of the day there would be little oases of heat, the spots by the fireplaces; all of us running through cold hallways, running from oasis of heat to oasis of heat."

About the same time that Stephen Morris' father at Brookhurst announced the death of society to his sons because white tie was no longer required at dinner, Mrs. Henry Parsons, born in 1861, and Mrs. J. Graham Parsons, born after, divided on what was proper socializing.

"Aunt Hattie was a very Victorian lady and liked to have tea in the manner of the Victorian age and all the formalities and social etiquette of those times," said Mrs. J. Graham Parsons' son. "My mother was social in the modern sense." Small changes in the social fabric were noted sorrowfully or argued over long before the crushing blows of inheritance tax, income tax, war, and political reform were to wipe out an age, not modify it.

Today, Bonnie Brae is a permanent residence for what the townfolk call "year-round summer people." The house was "de-Victorianized" in the 1920s when Aunt Hattie built "Wee Haus" across the valley in Stockbridge leaving Bonnie Brae to the more modern Mrs. J. Graham Parsons.

The house went out of the family in 1945 and became the summer cottage of Mr. Walter Hoving of Tiffany and Company. It was repurchased by the Parsons family in 1963. Today, in order for Henry Ivison's great grandson to live there without spending uncounted dollars on heat, he has insulated with polyurethane—quite a twentieth century intrusion into the old walls.

Walking out onto his front lawn, Mr. Parsons says, echoing the sentiments of the original cottage builders, "I wish more of the homes were still in the hands of original families."

WINDERMERE

(Stockbridge)

Architects and landscape architects were brave fellows forging a new field at the time Windermere was built. This house predated their assent. So that, possibly the most interesting of all the cottages in the Berkshires is neither very large nor is it breathtaking. Its architect is unknown and probably was not an architect at all but a local builder. Even the exact year it was built can only be guessed at as no one made note of it. Some even argue that it was not a cottage at all. They say it was built too early, the 1860s, but Highwood, reputed to be the first cottage, predated Windermere. They say it is too unimposing; however, given the definition of a cottage, it almost conforms: it was not a primary residence, the builders had a home in

Windermere

Courtesy of the Stockbridge Library

New York, and it was situated on more than thirty acres. However, in fairness to those who do not call it a cottage, it probably did not have twenty rooms, and its name reflects the literary period in Stockbridge, not the estate period. Windermere is a lake in Northwest England's "lake district" and Stockbridge was called the "American Lake District" during the literary period. But there is even equivocation there, the name also has been spelled Windemere and Windymore. Yet, to its mistress, it was everything a cottage should be, a retreat, a dream come true, and a symbol of her hard-won social position. Windermere, regardless of how you classify it, and like no other of the houses, does what we will all the cottages to do: it tells a story. That is really what we ask of a house whether it's a log cabin or a marble palace.

The stories of the Berkshire cottages begin in 1841, the year Samuel G. Ward bought the first parcel of land to form Highwood, but this story begins in Paris, before the lady of the house and the gentlemen had even met. In that year, Henriette Deluzy-Desportes was hired as governess by the Praslin family. The events leading up to her dismissal in 1847 and the subsequent murder of the Duchess of Praslin by her husband the Duke, have been told and retold in fact and fiction for more than a century.[16]

Within hours of Madame Praslin's death, the Surete Nationale had determined that the Duke of Praslin was the murderer. He escaped justice by taking arsenic and died without confessing. Then the action was taken that was to make Henriette an international woman of intrigue, a femme fatale, an object of curiosity or pity or enmity: the Surete Nationale arrested her for complicity. It is difficult now to imagine the furor caused by this murder almost 140 years ago. With the Duke dead and Mademoiselle Deluzy imprisoned, all public interest focused on her. There were headlines in Europe and America, and the press had no difficulty condemning her in advance of her judges. As she was allowed one hour of exercise each day in the prison courtyard, thousands lined the walls and windows to watch. She was released after three months in prison, from August 17 to November 19, 1847. She had endured numerous interrogations. The public statement given upon her release condemned her and set her free equally:

> Did Henrietta Deluzy herself ever consider the possibility of this crime?. . . There is not the slightest doubt that she wished to encourage M. de. Praslin to rebel against those who had separated them [but] at no point have we been able to discover anything that presents the character of legal complicity. Henrietta Deluzy is nonetheless very culpable. She violated the sacred trust that her position of governess imposed upon her and which introduced her into the bosom of the Praslin family. Her faults may be numbered among the causes that led to an appalling catastrophe. She will be punished by the memory of blood and grief that henceforth will be inseparable from her name, but it does not belong to human justice to inflict upon her any other expiation.[17]

Why was there any question of her complicity? When the murder occurred, she had already been dismissed by the Duchess and was not even part of the household. In

All This & Heaven Too, Rachel Field builds her plot around a triangle of mutual affection between two kindly people, Henriette and the Duke, and a mad Duchess who refused a letter of recommendation leaving the girl destitute and driving the Duke to a mad act. The King's prosecutors in 1847 hypothesized an adulteress affair between Duke and governess in which the governess, wishing to become a duchess, actively plotted the murder that he executed. It was to the King of France's advantage to have the guilt of the Duke mitigated. It was inconceivable to allow a family so close to the throne to be publicly denounced. So at thirty-fours years of age, Henriette became the eye of a hurricane which assisted the downfall of the "July Monarchy"—the last monarchy in French history. King Louis Philippe was deposed, and Louis Napoleon Bonaparte was elected President of France. Although by 1858 he had dictatorial powers and called himself Emperor Napoleon III, his legal title was always President of France.

Henriette had spent three months in a French prison in the late summer and early fall of 1847. By so doing, she had helped to topple a monarchy. She was as unaware of that as she was of a young American traveling in Europe and visiting Paris. Perhaps Henry Martyn Field was part of the curious crowd that came each day to watch Henriette pace the prison yard.

Henry Field was the son of a minister, David Dudley Field of Stockbridge, Massachusetts, and a minister himself. His brothers were quite incredible in their accomplishments. Stephen was the last Supreme Court Justice to be appointed by Abraham Lincoln. David Dudley Jr. was a distinguished New York City lawyer who represented Samuel Tilden in the contested Tilden/Hayes presidential election among other notable cases. Cyrus West succeeded in laying the transatlantic cable. (Stockbridge had one of the first cable offices in brother Jonathan's law office which still stands today on the corner of Main and Pine Streets, Stockbridge.) Henry, like his family, was religious and a distinguished part of the "Fabulous Fields" who were representative and a sterling example of the American ideal. Henry was literate, educated, well-traveled, moral, and upstanding. In 1851 when he was twenty-eight and she was thirty-eight, Henriette Deluzy-Desporte and Henry Martyn Field were married.

Henriette had spent the month after her dismissal as governess and before her arrest, in poverty-stricken conditions in Paris. Trying to adjust and absorb the wrenching shock of her dismissal, she wrote: "I could heal body and soul if only I could spend a few weeks in the country working and thinking, breathing that clean air of which I dream and which I know to be essential to me."[18] As Mrs. Henry Field, she occupied Windermere on "The Hill," Stockbridge, Massachusetts. She had gotten her dream of healing and happiness. She wrote from Stockbridge on July 24, 1873: "We live a life of complete calm and repose . . . the weather is delicious and I indulge in dolce far niente, in contemplating the landscape always varied."[19] When she wrote that, she was sixty years old and ill. She died within two years. Her obituary in the ***New York Times*** is striking and unusual in that her name does not appear; she is referred to only as Mrs. Henry M. Field. Henriette Deluzy-Desporte,

July, 1813—March, 1875, is buried in Stockbridge, Massachusetts.

Henry outlived Henriette by twenty-eight years. He was married again to Fanny Dwight. The second Mrs. Field did not wish to live in Henriette's house, and they built Sunset directly across the street for a reported $25,000. Henry dedicated a good part of his life to writing the biographies of his more famous relatives: ***The Record of the Family of the Late Reverend David Dudley Field***, and biographies of David Dudley and Cyrus Field. He had planned to write a biography of Stephen Johnson Field, but it was never completed.

> When in the evening of his life he contemplated the past, his melancholy was tinged with regret that his brothers had been born to great deeds and he but to celebrate them.

On September 30, 1906, a year before Field's death, Joseph Hodges Choate wrote a letter regarding a deed to water rights held by Henry Martyn Field and the eleven others who made up The Hill Water Company:

> *Dear Mr. Schley:*
> ***I send the deed of water rights signed by all the parties personally except that Mrs. Field has signed for her husband, Dr. Field, who from old age has absolutely lost his mind, so as to be incapable of doing anything...***

Henry Martyn Field, a quiet, gentle, perhaps disappointed man, brother of three famous men, husband of a notorious French woman, enthusiastic biographer of the Fields, silent for a lifetime about his first wife, is buried in the Stockbridge cemetery to the side of the square that encloses the other Field graves. He is buried between Henriette Deluzy-Desportes, illegitimate child, woman of intrigue, "the French Mrs. Field," and Fanny Dwight who could trace her descendants back to the roots of Americana and the Puritan ethic, the two Mrs. Henry Martyn Fields.

Photograph by Robert Owens

Eden Hill

28

EDEN HILL LAUREL COTTAGE

(Stockbridge)

David Dudley Field, older brother of Henry, also had two houses in Stockbridge: Eden Hill, also referred to as Eden Hall, and Laurel Cottage. David Dudley Field was a lawyer in New York City in his day much the way Babe Ruth was a baseball player in his day. Rachel Field, his grandniece, describes him in ***All This and Heaven Too***, the story of Henriette Field, as a large man with clean-cut features and a manner both easy and authoritative. His most active period as lawyer and law reformer were the ten years following the Civil War. Many of the cases involved Constitutional questions so that his activities in court were precedent setting in a profession where precedent is the bedrock. At seventy-seven, he was still active as a lawyer. As distinguished a lawyer as David Dudley was, he was most widely known as a law reformer. He was largely responsible for New York having a Penal Code and a Code of Civil Procedures. They were called the "Field Codes," and he the "Father of the Code."

Brother Stephen had been appointed to the U.S. Supreme Court by Abraham Lincoln in 1863. By August 1858, Cyrus West had successfully sent the first transatlantic cable. In 1857, David Dudley was named chairman of the commission to codify New York law, and by 1867, the state of New York had adopted David Dudley's civil and criminal codes. He was stirred by familial association to imagine an International Code of Nations, and he turned his attention to international law. The three brothers each sparked the imagination of the other, and of their nephew Stephen Dudley, son of brother Jonathan. Stephen Dudley had been in his father's Stockbridge law office to receive the first cable, and was moved to turn his attention to electricity and communications, inventing the electric train and improving the ticker tape.

David Dudley's city residence was on Fifth Avenue and Stuyvesant Place in New York, and the first of his summer cottages was Laurel Cottage, Stockbridge. Laurel Cottage was on Main Street just down from his father, the Congregational minister. Reverend Field had been minister in Stockbridge from 1819 to 1837 at a salary of six hundred dollars per annum. In 1851, he returned to Stockbridge to retire and there spent the last sixteen years of his life. It was across Cyrus' Atlantic Cable from a cablegram sent at Jonathan Field's law office in Stockbridge that Henriette learned of her father-in-law's death in 1867.

Laurel Cottage had a distinguished list of residents. Built by Jahleel Woodbridge in the 1700s, it was home to Matthew Arnold; Rachel Field; David Dudley Field's daughter, Lady Musgrave; and it temporarily housed St. Paul's Church.

It was at Laurel Cottage in 1850 that Herman Melville was introduced to Nathaniel Hawthorne. No biographer of either man has failed to mention the event. It was the meeting of two excellent writers. Hawthorne was forty-six, Melville was thirty-one, and each was at a high point in his career. ***The Scarlet Letter*** was published and ***Moby Dick*** was nearing completion. Regardless of how momentous the occasion may seem in retrospect, the other guests that day, Tuesday, August 5, 1850, gave far more space in their letters and diary entries to the menu and entertainment. Mr. Hawthorne's journal reads:

> Rode with Fields [Hawthorne's publisher, James Fields] and wife to Stockbridge, being there to invited by Mr. Field of Stockbridge [David Dudley] in order to ascend Monument Mountain. Found at Mr. Field's, Dr. Holmes [Oliver Wendell, Senior] and Mr. Duyckinck of New York; also Messrs. Cornelius Matthews and Herman Melville. Ascended the mountain: that is to say, Mrs. Fields and Miss Jenny Field, Mr. Field and Mr. Fields, Dr. Holmes, Messrs. Duyckinck, Matthews,

Laurel Cottage

Courtesy of the Stockbridge Library

Melville, Mr. Henry Sedgwick and I, and were caught in a shower. Dined at Mr. Field's. Afternoon, under guidance of J. T. Headley, the party scrambled through Ice Glen.[20]

James Fields wrote to Longfellow and said:

I have just got back from the Berkshire Hills where we have been tramping over the soil with Hawthorne, dining with Holmes, hunting up the mountains with Headley, and sitting in all manner of dangerous places with Melville.[21]

Later, in his journal, Hawthorne mentions Melville:

I met Melville the other day and like him so much that I have asked him to spend a few days with me before leaving these parts.

Melville wrote a two-part article for Duyckinck's ***Literary Reviews***, the August 17 and August 24, 1850 issues, called "Hawthorne & The Mosses." It is not clear whether Melville wrote the article in haste between the 5th and 17th giving it then and there to Duyckinck or if he wrote it before meeting Hawthorne. Melville himself made both statements. What is certain is that he wrote it anonymously and that it "represents possibly the most positive critique one author ever wrote of another."[22] The August 5th social gathering at David Dudley Field's Laurel Cottage was the genesis of a literary friendship that reverberated in both men's work.

In the 1870s, David Dudley built Eden Hill. He built on what had been simply called "The Hill" when Stockbridge was divided into the hill and the plain; it was then called Field Hill, and today is called Prospect Hill. When he bought the land, John Sergeant's

Courtesy of the Stockbridge Library

Laurel Cottage

Mission House built in 1739 was the only structure on it. (The house has since been moved to Main Street.) Windermere, Henry and Henriette Field's house, was down the road as was Henry Ivison's Bonnie Brae.

In ***Country Life***, August, 1933, Eden Hill is advertised for sale. The ad reads, "Acquired by the bank through foreclosure — Unusual opportunity to obtain immediate possession of a 265 acre estate — main house with six master bedrooms and five baths, reception and billiard rooms, library, dining and breakfast rooms with large fireplaces — servants' quarters — dwellings for caretaker, gardener, and chauffeur." It adds that it may be "especially suitable for a private school." The estate period had been foreclosed upon.

Today Eden Hill is the Congregation of Marians of the Immaculate Conception.

When David Dudley Field's daughter, Lady Musgrave, sold Laurel Cottage, she did so on the condition that two trees planted by Matthew Arnold would never be cut down. Today, it is unclear if those two trees stand, but Laurel Cottage is gone and in its place on Main Street are the Stockbridge town tennis courts.

HEATON HALL

(Stockbridge)

Courtesy of the Stockbridge Library

Heaton Hall under construction

Heaton Hall opened its doors on June 25, 1904. It was owned and operated by the Red Lion Inn which was situated less than two city blocks from it. The Treadways, owners of both, named Heaton Hall after their son, Heaton Treadway. The architect was Harry Weeks of Pittsfield. Heaton Hall, painted grey on the outside, contained several dining rooms, the largest being 45 by 63 feet. The main floor also contained an assembly room to the right as one entered, and on the left parlors and a writing room. The office was 26 by 50 feet. Also on the main floor were smoking rooms, private dining rooms, and maids' rooms. The interior was cypress and furnished with leather and wicker, hard wood floors, and rugs rather than carpet. Missing were the antiques and the home-like atmosphere of the Red Lion. At Heaton Hall, "Everything is new, fresh, and modern," ***The Berkshire Resort Topics***, reported. A concern about fire in such a large wooden structure caused the decision to house the kitchens in a separate building to the rear of the hotel and to house the boilers in a separate brick building near the kitchens.

Heaton Hall did not burn. It was torn down in the 1960s. A resident recalls that there was so much material from razing Heaton Hall, that no dump would take it. After negotiations, it was carted to the state of New York for disposal.

On the site today is award-winning senior housing. The exteriors of the buildings are grey as was the hotel and the name has been retained following the tradition of the Berkshires.

Photograph by Mimi MacDonald

This inn has been in continuous use since 1773. The guests at the inn over the years are as intriguing as any of the guests at the cottages. They include Presidents Cleveland, McKinley, Theodore Roosevelt, Coolidge, and Franklin D. Roosevelt. The inn can also boast of literary guests: Nathaniel Hawthorne, William Cullen Bryant, and Henry Wadsworth Longfellow.

It was owned by the Plumb family and then by the Treadways. Mrs. Plumb was an antique collector, and The Red Lion, then as now, was known for its gracious homelike antique furnishings. The Plumbs left the Red Lion in the Treadways' hands and ran another inn in Pittsfield, The Maplewood. The Treadways ran two hotels, The Red Lion

The Red Lion Inn

30 THE RED LION (Stockbridge)

and Heaton Hall.

Mr. and Mrs. Treadway lived across from the Red Lion in the corner white house that is now part of the Austen Riggs Center. Mr. Treadway was a congressman. A present day visitor to the Berkshires is a history professor. He tries with every new crop of doctoral students, to interest one in writing a dissertation on how little an elected official can do in Washington and still be returned to the capitol by the voters. The professor would like the willing graduate student to use Treadway as the prime example. He was loved by the voters and returned year after year, although no one knows of one single thing he did in Washington except to sing. Evidently, he loved to sing and at one point, started a singing group. No one can remember if it was a choir or a barbershop quartet.

It is great fun to stay at the Red Lion. The food and service are excellent. One never knows who will be in the lobby—the Kennedys or Paul Newman. ***The Berkshire Eagle*** carried a small article that Phil Donahue and Marlo Thomas called for a reservation during the season and were told there was no room at the inn.

Located on Main Street at the heart of Stockbridge, it deserves its popularity. The present owners, the Fitzpatricks, have some things in common with the owners of the past. Mrs. Fitzpatrick is a collector of antiques, and Mr. Fitzpatrick was elected to public office—a state senator.

Courtesy of Riverbrook School

Blueprint of Konkaput Brook

Photograph by Mal Guralnick

31

KONKAPUT BROOK
(Stockbridge)

Konkaput Brook was the home of Frederic Crowninshield. The architect, George De Gersdorff, was the brother of his son-in-law, Carl. The plans for the house are dated 1903. The Crowninshields owned the property prior to that date, and it is thought they lived in a little cottage at the back of the property before the big house was built. This cottage is near the stream that runs through the property. The stream was called Konkaput Brook and hence the name of the Crowninshield cottage.

Frederic Crowninshield was a painter. His son, Frank Crowninshield, was well-known in society for his wit and charm and was the first editor of ***Vanity Fair Magazine***. If there was a formal art studio in the house, it is not there today. But when the present owners were shown through the house, there was one room described as "Mr. Crowninshield's workroom." It was more a library. Painted on the walls was a border that followed the ceiling and outlined the doors with chains of green, silver and gold leaves interspersed with flowers, blue urns, and green figures. Over the door were the words, "Italia • Patria • Secunda." The art work was done by Mr. Crowninshield and the inscription translates, "Italy, my second home."

From 1914 to 1936, Frank Crowninshield occupied the editor's office at ***Vanity Fair***. "Somebodies of the very smart, frivolous and sporting kind gathered in Crowninshield's drawing-room office."[23] His office there, reminiscent of his father's workroom, was more of a library. And, very like the library at Konkaput Brook, Frank's ". . . door was painted too—a silver leaf background with figures in green and lots of long narrow leaves."[24]

The Old Corner House situated

Konkaput Brook

Photograph by Mimi MacDonald

The Corner House

on Main Street, Stockbridge, can boast an interesting succession of inhabitants. One of its first occupants, Madam Dwight, gave the ground for the Stockbridge Library on condition that the structure would set back far enough so not to obstruct her view of Main Street and the goings-on.

Edward Crowninshield, Frank's brother and Frederic's son, lived above and ran an antique store on the first floor. Miss Agnes Canning lived across the street. Frank Crowninshield called her, "The last of the traffic cops of society." A spinster, she was also the last survivor of her family. Her father, A. W. B. Canning, had come to Stockbridge in 1841 as principal of The Stockbridge Academy. The family had always occupied the same house on Main Street. By the time Edward Crowninshield became her neighbor across the way, she was so ghost-ridden that she could not sleep in her own house. She kept two rooms open on the first floor and a tiny kitchen area. She turned to Edward, and arranged to rent a room in his house. "At night she let a bedroom in the Old Corner House across the way in order to sleep," a relative explains.

The third Crowninshield child, Helen Suzette, married Carl De Gersdorff, and they had a house on Old Meetinghouse Road, Stockbridge. For two reasons there has always been some confusion about the Crowninshield cottages of Stockbridge. First, because there were a total of four Crowninshield houses. Second, because when Frederic Crowninshield lived in the little house by the brook, before he built Konkaput Brook, he called that "Crowninshield Cottage." After his father died, Frank lived at Konkaput Brook, and called it "Crowninshield Cottage."

Today, Konkaput is the Riverbrook School. The Old Corner House is the Norman Rockwell Museum, and the De Gersdorff house was destroyed by fire.

Crowninshield Cottage

Courtesy of Riverbook School

32 STRAWBERRY HILL
(Stockbridge)

Strawberry Hill was built by Lydia Field Emmet in 1905. The architect was Louis Metcalf, the brother of Susan Metcalf who shared the house with Lydia until she married Pablo Casals. Nathalie Sedgwick Colby said, in her book ***REMEMBERING***, that she thought they had the most fun up on Strawberry Hill of anyone in Stockbridge.

By 1925, Mrs. Rosina Emmet Sherwood had a house, Sherwood Cottage, on the hill, too. There she gathered with her daughter Rosamond and her son, Robert Emmet Sherwood, Pulitzer Prize-winning author of ***The Petrified Forest*** and other works.

Both Lydia and Rosina were artists. The family produced ten female artists. What was astonishing, in the nineteenth and early twentieth centuries, was that they were self-supporting female artists. Lydia never married, and said she was able to earn $20,000 per year from her work, a respectable sum at the turn of the century. After her husband lost his money, Rosina supported the whole family with her portraits. A third sister, Ellen, once remarked, after her husband lost his money in the 1929 crash, that she was able to keep him in polo ponies by selling her works. Rosina's daughter, Rosamond, recalls the change in economic circumstances in both families with pleasure. "It forced the members of the family to do things. Too many of the women of the day did nothing much at all," she says. Such extraordinary women probably did have a very good time up on Strawberry Hill.

The sisters were the first cousins of Henry and William James. Henry was close to his cousins. He was said to be in love with another cousin of the Emmets, Minnie Templeton. She died young, and James never married. Henry James sent Rosina first editions of all his books. On the inside cover, he would write little notes that began, "This is what I was trying to accomplish in this book . . ." and he would go on to describe his specific intent to her. "I think Henry James, more than anyone," Rosina's daughter says, "could turn a camera on his times and record them."

The Kobbes moved into a third house on Strawberry Hill, and called it Hillfield. One of the daughters, Marie Kobbe, was also an artist. Eventually Hillfield became an Emmet/Sherwood house as well because Miss Rosamond Sherwood bought it after her mother died. Rosamond took her mother's belongings from the New York House and put them into Kobbe cottage. Miss Sherwood recalls standing on the front lawn and watching as the house burned to the ground. She remembers thinking that it was as if the entire period was going up in smoke before her eyes. The house held not only her memories of fun in the cottages, but the pictures of the people of the era that her mother had painted and all the first editions with the words of Henry James, the gifted chronicler of his times.

Miss Sherwood is an artist in her own right, a champion golfer, and a woman of her times. She once remarked, "I would never have imagined calling Miss Choate, Mabel, although I knew her well and was a guest in her home. One didn't call people by their first names. Today, as I walk down the street, boys working on the road, call out, 'Hi, Rosie.' " She smiles. "Those were wonderful times, and I'm not sure that we haven't lost something, but I'm not at all sure that it isn't better today."

Hillfield, and the treasures it held are gone, but Strawberry Hill exists today, and is Miss Sherwood's home.

Photograph by Robert Owens

Linwood as seen from Naumkeag

33

LINWOOD

(Stockbridge)

Charles E. Butler, Esquire, purchased eighty acres and began building the unpolished marble house in 1858, the year he retired. The cottage was completed in 1859. It was modeled after poet N. P. Willis' house built six years earlier at Cornwall-on-Hudson. Mr. Willis' house had become quite fashionable; perhaps the Butlers visited there or perhaps a description of the widely publicized house had reached them.

He was fifty-years old the year building began. He had survived his first wife, by whom he had six children and married Susan Sedgwick, the niece of Catherine Sedgwick. The house was named after Catherine's 1835 novel, ***The Linwoods.***

Susan was said to be kind and gay, while Mr. Butler was remembered as arrogant, stern, and just. Just, he might well have been, as he was the senior partner of the law firm, Butler, Evarts, Southmayd and Choate. Linwood is next door to Southmayd's place, and from the front door of Linwood, Mr. Butler could look straight across the valley and watch as Naumkeag, the cottage of his junior partner, Mr. Choate, was being built.

At nineteen years of age, the story is told, he was offered two jobs by two New York lawyers. The first lawyer told Butler that if he worked for him, he would become rich; the second said if he worked for him, Butler would become a lawyer. Charles E. Butler took the second position and became a rich lawyer.

Ellery Sedgwick remembers him as "the ogre of my childhood." When Ellery would come to Linwood for dinner, Uncle Charles would stare at him and demand, "Have you brought your dinner with you? If not—down into the coal bin with you." Such humor, if humor it was, was inexplicable to a child and frightening. But adults remember him as the plutocrat of Stockbridge, donor of St. Paul's Episcopal Church, and a man to consult and listen to.

Having married a Sedgwick, he was buried in the "Pie" when he died in 1897.

Of his six children, one daughter, Virginia, left $100,000 for the upkeep of St. Paul's Episcopal Church's rectory. Helen Butler left the southeast quadrant of Monument Mountain for the enjoyment of the public. A third daughter, Lillian, married John Swann and built the house on Main Street, Stockbridge, that some townspeople have called the prettiest of all the cottages in Stockbridge. In turn, her daughter married Percy Musgrave. By whatever quirk of justice, when Mr. and Mrs. Musgrave were divorced, the house, Linwood, was awarded to the husband, and left the Butler family. The children stayed with the father, so that, one of the two astronauts on the first shuttle space walk, F. Story Musgrave, grew up at Linwood.

The caretakers of Linwood were as interesting as the owners. George and Laura Seeley were the children of the superintendent. George was interested in photography. His photographs have the appearance of paintings due to a developing process of his invention. His subject was very often his sister, Laura, and his backgrounds and scenery were often sites on the Linwood estate. Not particularly remarkable to his neighbors and friends in Stockbridge, his photographs gained Seeley a national reputation. Some are at the Metropolitan Museum of Art in New York; others have been auctioned at Parke-Bernet.

Today Linwood is owned by the Norman Rockwell Museum. The board of directors hope to move the collection from the Old Corner House to the Linwood estate.

Mr. French's studio

Photograph by Robert Owens

34

CHESTERWOOD

(Stockbridge)

Chesterwood was the home of Daniel Chester French, the sculptor. He is probably best known for his statue of Abraham Lincoln in Washington, D.C. and the Minuteman in Concord. A tour through the house and his studio will demonstrate the extent of his work far beyond these two well-known statues.

Chesterwood was begun in 1900 and completed in 1901. The architect was Henry Bacon of New York City. The house is a two story Georgian Revival house. The studio is separate and a few paces from the house. Mr. French bought the land in 1897. In 1898, two years before he built the house, he built the studio. Bacon also designed the studio. The men knew each other because Bacon had designed the Lincoln Memorial in Washington, D.C. that houses French's statue of Lincoln. It is has a high ceiling and gives the impression of enormous space and light. Since many of his statues were commissioned for the outdoors, the studio is equipped with railroad tracks and a flat-bed car so that Mr. French could roll his works outdoors and determine how the light would effect them.

In an inglenook at the front of the studio there is a couch where Mr. French rested. At the head and foot of the couch are built-in book shelves. Here, Daniel Chester French rested from his labors, read and entertained guests. The back workroom, where plaster models were cast and tools were stored, has a much more intimate feel. It is smaller and darker. It is almost as if, reflecting upon the respective proportions, that the studio was built for statues and the workroom built for a man.

"I live six months of the year up there. That is heaven," Mr. French said of the time he spent at Chesterwood. The view from the porch of Chesterwood is certainly heavenly as is his garden. Past the garden are woods, and in the woods, there are carefully laid out walking paths of different lengths.

Today, Chesterwood is a National Historic Site operated by the National Trust for Historic Preservation. There are tours through the house and studio conducted by guides who are informative and entertaining. There are special events such as "Christmas at Chesterwood" and special exhibits like a recent sculpture show set in the garden and the woods. There is also a gift shop.

The front garden at Chesterwood

Photograph by Robert Owens

35

THE SOUTHMAYD PLACE

(Stockbridge)

The Southmayd Place was built by Charles F. Southmayd who was a law partner of Messers. Evarts, Butler, and Choate in New York City. At the turn of the century, Mr. Southmayd purchased property from Henry Wadsworth Longfellow. The property was known locally as Oxbow beause of the bend in the river at that point. Longfellow never built a house on the property.

The house Mr. Southmayd built was "a wood house with a tin mansard roof; a good example of a Victorian house," says Mrs. Franz, now 93. As a girl she was the caretaker's daughter and resident of Southmayd's because when the Southmayds were in New York, the caretaker's family lived in the house. "I think we enjoyed it more than he did. Anyway, we lived there longer. He and his sister only came from New York a couple of weeks in the late summer or fall. We had it the rest of the time." Mrs. Franz remembers each room as being a monotone with heavy Victorian furniture. The bedrooms were red or blue or orange and one was green. In the green bedroom there was a green chamber set with goldleaf border fully two inches," she recalls, "and, oh, I loved that set." Even little things like perfume bottles or glass trays would be the same green, blue or red as the room. The parlor was brown and gold with black walnut furniture. "The windows had shutters not curtains and often the shutters were closed, making the house dark."

Southmayd's place never had a name as far as anyone recalls. It is not one of the most lavish of the cottages, and yet seems filled with drama, or perhaps it is melodrama. A dark tale of unrequited love, battles, though fought with the weapon of words, fear, and unfulfillment are played out against austere sets in Stockbridge and New York. The hero is a self-denying man unused to public displays of affection, perhaps unused to affection in any form; certainly no lover, frightening to children, living with his sister, choosing for himself the heavy, dark, and serious backdrop of Victorian and medieval decors. Not a man to engage in romance or derring-do; Mr. Southmayd's drama is not

Photograph by Mimi MacDonald

Southmayd's Place

made up of things done, but the things left undone. It is the drama of loss and frustration. It is more the psychological drama found in Henry James, who thought there was more interest in the nuance of a raised eyebrow than in epic adventures

Our hero introduces himself: each year Southmayd sends the same message to his tailor, "Two suits like the last." For sixty years there is no change in the message, thus there is no change in the look of the man.

He has a dialogue with Joseph Choate:

"Mr. Choate, it is the duty of every lawyer to accumulate and save his entire professional income."

"But," says Choate, "it isn't everybody who can do that for we must live."

"No," answers Southmayd, "that doesn't follow; that is not at all necessary."[25]

Mr. Southmayd walks through the village feared by the children. In New York, in 1862, he redecorates his law office. Joseph Hodges

Choate writes to his wife, "Mr. Southmayd, of course, has chosen the medieval style for his office."

In August 1874, he attends the wedding of the oldest daughter of his law partner, Mr. Evarts. Choate writes, "Mr. Southmayd even went so far as to kiss the bride, the first woman, as we guessed, that he had treated so in 20 years at least."

Mrs. Franz recalls seeing a red handkerchief when she was a girl. "It was red with two holes burned into it for eyes. We had that red bandana handkerchief for a long time." Her mother told her it belonged to the Gentleman Burglar.

When the Gentleman Burglar comes to Southmayd's and stands over Charles as he sleeps, it awakens him. The burglar says, "Be very quiet and I won't harm you."

At that minute, Miss Southmayd calls out from her room, "Charles, what is it?"

"Nothing," he replies, "just go to sleep."

When Edith Wharton experienced a similar alarm at a hotel in Europe, she said, "Let no one ever speak to me of fear who hasn't awakened to find an intruder looming over her."

Charles, in an effort to protect his sister, replies "nothing" to her anxious question, but he is very much disturbed by the incident. A man of few pleasures, he is never quite able to enjoy the house at Stockbridge again.

"Mr. Southmayd was a morose and unpleasant man because he was jilted," says Mrs. Franz. She considers, "or, he was jilted because he was unpleasant."

Jilted may not be quite the word. From first meeting, he is in love with Miss Butler, one of the daughters of his partner Charles Butler, but she never returns the affection. He is in her company—girl and married woman—and never in the way he wishes to be. It is even unclear that she knows of his affection. He never marries, and when, in later years, he gives a small piece of jewelry to a spinster lady of Stockbridge, it is the subject of general conversation and a snicker or two.

At his office, he does not fare much better. Although he prepares the briefs on which Choate bases his most famous case—the unconstitutionality of income tax—Southmayd is not the one who presents the case before the Supreme Court. Choate is considered the more persuasive speaker and it is he who wins the day in court and the personal glory. In July, 1911, the cautious, caustic, opinionated, brilliant, and lonely Mr. Southmayd died.

Although Mr. Choate often cast Southmayd as an object of humor in his letters, his eulogy stands as a deeply felt accolade. Choate also wrote of a dream he had where in the sad Southmayd dies and is reborn "the jolliest of babies." It was as if Choate were not dreaming but wishing for his partner. The man who spilled his wine out so no one else would enjoy it, generously saved the Sedgwick house when the family had severe economic times; the man who inspired jests equally inspired accolades, was a sad man who met an obstacle to fulfillment at every turn. Although he could not enjoy his summer cottage at Stockbridge after the burglary, he refused to sell it. He confided to Choate that he hoped when he died that it would burn to the ground. Southmayd's home stands to this day and is a private residence.

Searles Castle
(Barrington House)

Photograph by David Frank

36

SEARLES CASTLE

BARRINGTON HOUSE
KELLOGG TERRACE
(Great Barrington)

Searles Castle is in Great Barrington. It is beyond the proper geographical limitations set down for this book. To go beyond those limits requires a very good reason. Searles Castle is a good reason In the idiom of the last century, Searles' was a "cottage," but to our modern eyes and ears, castle is the right word. That is probably the reason the name, one never used by the owner, stuck.

Searles Castle is to a castle what the Gilded Age aristocrats were to the British landed gentry: a copy in form but not substance. A castle was a war machine, it was built, not for beauty or comfort or leisure, but for defence. When Mr. Searles found he could not even defend himself from the noise of the Great Barrington trolley, he put up the wall that surrounds the house today. When he found he could not defend himself against the curious who knocked on his front doors asking to see the house, he moved. The British landed gentry were both titled and supported by their country estates, that is, their entire support came from the land; the American country cottages were a result of money made elsewhere.

The present day name is a complete misnomer. Neither was the cottage a castle, nor was the builder Edward Searles. In 1883, Mary Hopkins, the widow of Mark Hopkins said to be the richest man of his day, returned to her hometown, Great Barrington. She hired Stanford White to build a summer cottage. Herter Brothers had been the decorator for her San Francisco home, and Edward Searles worked for Herters. Although he was twenty years her junior, she developed a deep affection for him. The house was originally to be named Kellogg Terrace after the two aunts who had left Mrs. Hopkins the Great Barrington property. The initials K. T. are still visible on metal flags on the roof of the cottage. Initials or no, in that way, and many others, the house would ultimately bear Mr. Searles' imprint. The name was changed to Barrington House, reflecting the name of the town rather than a family name of Mrs. Hopkins. Stanford White was replaced by Henry Vaughan, an architect more malleable and likely to follow Mr. Searles' suggestions.

The building required three years, several million dollars, and a private railroad built solely to bring the marble used in the house from the quarry. The result was spectacular, and was enjoyed by the then Mr. and Mrs. Edward Searles for a total of four seasons until Mrs. Searles' death in 1891.

Barrington House offers the twentieth-century visitor the opportunity to understand one aspect of the nineteenth-century concept of the decoration of houses. When we think of household decorations today, we expect the ornamentation to be mobile; decoration is that which is below the ceiling, above the floor, and inside the walls. Anything else, we call architecture. That is distinctly not the nineteenth-century viewpoint. Mrs. Searles would have expected the permanent architectural points of the building to afford decoration. Mr. Searles, a decorator, would have accepted as his responsibility, things like the sixteen matched Italian marble columns that support the entrance hall; the twenty-odd oil paintings worked into the concert hall ceiling; the installation of the organ in the concert hall; the mantle, fifteen foot mirror, and the painted ceilings and walls of the Versailles room (the replica was built in Europe, dismantled, and reconstructed in the Great Barrington house), and the bronze front doors caste in Munich. The line between the role

Courtesy of The Great Barrington Public Library

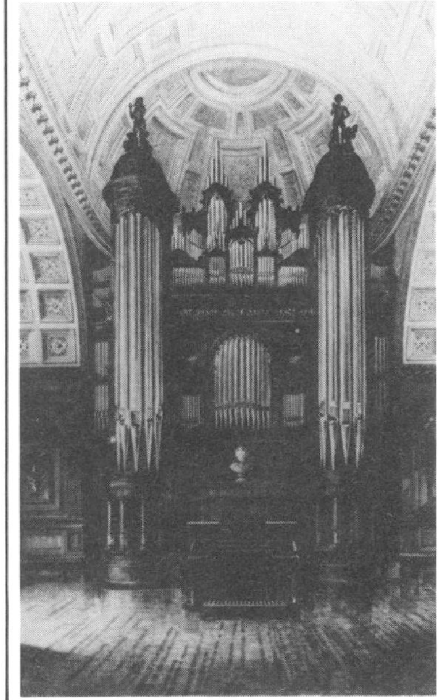

Etching of the organ

Mantle in the Versailles Room

Photograph by David Frank

of the decorator and the architect was subtle. The result of the collaboration between Vaughan and Searles was an example of the nineteenth-century ideal that architectural decoration should be a permanent part of the building. Specifically, the result caused a sophisticated twentieth-century woman to mistake a photograph of the butler's pantry for the library. It is not surprising in such a house, that at the Christmas Eve housewarming, the guests ate their dinner with solid gold tableware.

Unfortunately, the house was stripped of many of its treasures. The front doors are gone as are the oil paintings that were worked into the ceiling of the concert hall. The main staircase railing that was made of wrought metal is not there, nor are the original pillars. Most of these treasures were taken by Mr. Searles to his house in Methun after Mrs. Searles died. Others, they say, were sold by subsequent owners.

The great houses of the Berkshires are often in transition. Uses change. As you read this, Searles Castle may be in such a transition period. It has been a historic site with guided tours. At other times, the carriage house has been a restaurant. There have been periods when tea dances were held in the marble atrium of the great hall, and operas and concerts have been staged in the concert hall. Recently there have been plans to use Barrington House again as a conference center as was done years ago, to convert it to condominiums, or to sell it to Kripalu Center, the "macrobiotic educational center" that now owns Shadow Brook. In response to the latter, ***The Berkshire Eagle*** was moved to write that such a possibility "underscores the ironic fact that Berkshire County's major monuments to conspicuous consumption seem to have a particular appeal to prospective tenants dedicated to the simple life."

If you have the opportunity to tour the house, do so, but follow the guide closely; Barrington House is truly that castle of fairy tales—the one so large you can get lost in it.

Courtesy of The Great Barrington Public Library

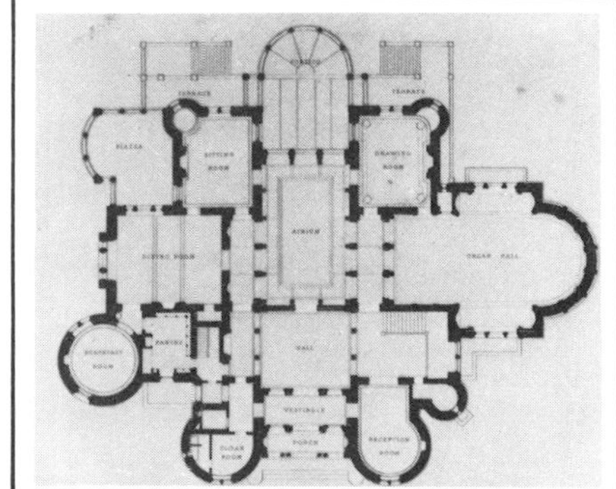

Floor plan of Barrington House

Etchings of bedroom and dining room

Courtesy of The Great Barrington Public Library

37

BROOKSIDE
(Great Barrington)

William Stanley purchased Brookside, from David Leavitt. For years the house had been a showplace with its own art gallery. In 1904, now the property of Mr. Stanley, the wood house burned to the ground. Mr. Stanley hired architects, Carrère and Hastings, to build a fireproof mansion, the basic material of which was concrete. The cost of the new Brookside was $175,000. The house included an enormous, yet graceful, music room and library. Across from the house, an Italian landscape architect created a loggia with sixty-seven marble pillars. Each one had to be waxed and wrapped every year so they would withstand the Berkshire winter. Across the facade of the loggia were faces of criminals worked into the stone that served as the gargoyles of Brookside. Between the loggia and the house was a garden that was a showcase for a number of statues, primarily of young boys and girls.

On June 1, 1908, the property was sold to William Hall Walker, a friend of Stanley's, who bought the cottage because William Stanley was insolvent.

William Stanley, born in 1858, was an electrical engineer of great talent. His inventions and discoveries included the alternating-current transformer, alternating-current motors, and the alternating generator. In short, Mr. Stanley was engaged in the business of producing power; he made electricity usable. In 1885, Stanley worked for George Westinghouse at his plant in Pittsburgh as an employee, but was forced to leave Pittsburgh for health reasons. In 1886, he demonstrated his alternating current by lighting the Main Street of Great Barrington, and George Westinghouse came to Great Barrington to watch the lighting demonstration. By 1888, he was a consultant under contract to the Westinghouse Company.

Courtesy of Library of Congress

By 1890, it had occurred to Stanley, that if he patented his inventions himself, he would make more money than by selling his services as a general consulting engineer for Westinghouse. A share in his new company, the Stanley Manufacturing Company of Pittsfield, rose from one hundred to three thousand dollars in a few short years. But from 1895 on, the

Garden at Brookside

Stanley Company was involved in constant litigation. The problem was with the Westinghouse and General Electric companies who wished to drive him out of business. The suits were brought by the larger companies for infringement of patents. By 1905, control of Stanley's company had passed to General Electric. In 1907, an adverse decision in the Westinghouse suit regarding the "Telsa patents" drove him completely out of business. (Nikola A. Telsa had built an electric motor in 1888 which Westinghouse manufactured.) By 1908, he was forced to sell Brookside to Mr. Walker. William Hall Walker was a retired railroad man. In 1915, in a renewed effort to save Stanley's enterprises, Walker also bought out Stanley's other business not affected by the lawsuits. That business made Stanley vacuum bottles—what we call thermos bottles. Stanley never realized much profit from this last idea; he died in 1916.

Today, Brookside is the Eisner Camp.

Stockbridge Bowl

Photograph by Todd Ehrlich

AFTERWORD

In 1982, an article in ***The Berkshire Eagle*** began with the words, "America is perennially the new world." The reporter meant, I think, that as a people, we have no interest in our own historical roots. That may be true, and yet . . . I have visited historic sites and stood together with others in our vacation clothes, cameras dangling, waiting for the old houses to speak to us and give up their secrets. We have walked through the great halls and ballrooms in little knots of curious people willing the house to tell us: what was it like to live then and there; what did the people who ate and slept in one and two hundred rooms think and do and what happened to them next, and what was it like, on the servants' day-off, to eat a hard boiled egg alone in a forty-foot dining room hung and draped and decorated with fabulous wealth? Yet the houses stood mute. In order to give the houses a voice, I have mixed figures and facts and fancy.

I don't believe we are without any sense of or interest in our past, but directly, or by inference, the Gilded Age has always been examined in comparison with modern times. Perhaps at the same time that we accept the convention of enlightenment through comparison, we recognize that it is not quite fair. "History" Julius Caesar cautioned, "is written by the victors." That means that the "historians" of the Gilded Age were members of the post World War I American middle-class state. They had a way of life and new values to defend. Even if the historian was of the economic upper class, he was influenced by his membership in a middle class, or "classless," country. One wealthy woman recalls that the only time she was struck by her mother was when she referred to the "class" of a friend. Her mother said, "This is America, there are no classes." The historians wrote about the Gilded Age to defend the rightness of a new way of life and deny that there was loss associated with change. The Gilded Age has not been treated kindly. It was a time and a people that left a deep mark on our economy and society, but they did not survive intact. Ours seems to be the first generation willing to look back on the period and seriously try to understand it. We have been willing to renovate the houses, admire the clothes, seek out the literature and music of the period. It was my intention that this be a guide to a vanished era. The last word belongs to a house in Pittsfield for a reason that will become clear.

Arrowhead was the home of Herman Melville. Whether the two are connected or not, Melville bought the house after meeting Nathaniel Hawthorne at Laurel Cottage. Melville was a resident until 1863. It was at Arrowhead that he wrote ***Moby Dick.*** In a letter written in December, 1850, Melville says:

> ***Do you want to know how I pass my time? I rise at 8—thereabouts—and go to my barn—and say good morning to the horse and give him his breakfast. (It goes to my heart to give my horse a cold one, but it can't be helped.) Then, pay a visit to my cow—cut up a pumpkin or two for her—and stand by to see her eat it—for it's a pleasant sight to see a cow move her jaws—she does it so mildly and with such a sanctity. My own breakfast over, I go to my workroom and light my fire—then spread my M.S.S. on the table—take one business squint at it, and fall into a will. At 2½ p.m., I hear a preconcerted knock at my door, which (by request) continues till I rise and go to the door, which serves to wean me effectively from my writing, however interested I may be.***

Arrowhead is a historic site with tours daily. I went to Arrowhead on a spring day in 1979 to see the desk at which Melville wrote ***Moby Dick***. The tour guides were filled with anecdotes about life at Arrowhead. In the basement and back of the house, is the Berkshire County Historical Society. For whatever the source of such small satisfactions, the journey ends where it began. It was in that basement that this book was first conceived as my family and I looked at the inventory photos of the Berkshire cottages.

Courtesy of Lenox Library

The entrance hall at Erskine Park

Appendix I: ENDNOTES

Foreword: TO THE TRAVELER

1. Recently, the Lenox Library published ***A Pride of Palaces,*** a collection of Edwin Hale Lincoln photographs of the great estates. On page 56, there is a picture of a room supposedly in Shadow Brook. It is actually a room in Elm Court and held Emily Thorn Vanderbilt Sloane's writing desk.

Chapter I: THE VILLAGES

1. Cleveland Amory, ***The Last Resorts,*** Harper & Brothers, New York, 1952, p. 11.
2. Katharine Abbott, ***Old Paths and Legends of the New England Borders,*** G. P. Putnam's Sons, New York and London, 1907, p. 238.
3. Donald G. Mitchell, ***American Lands and Letters,*** Charles Scribners' Sons, New York.
4. ***The Berkshire Hills,*** compiled and written by members of the Federal Writers Project Administration of Massachusetts, Berkshire Hills Conference, Inc., Funk & Wagnell's Company, New York & London, 1937.
5. Nathaniel Hawthorne, ***American Notebook,*** Randolph Stewart, Editor, Yale University Press, New Haven, 1932.
6. Henry David Thoreau, ***A Week on the Concord and Merrimac Rivers,*** Entry for Tuesday, 1849.
7. Henry Wadsworth Longfellow, ***Longfellow;*** Vol. 2, Journal Entry for August 2, 1848.
8. Henry James, ***The American Scene,*** Harper and Brothers, New York, 1907.
9. George A. Hibbard, "Lenox," ***Scribner's Magazine,*** Volume XVI, Number 4, October, 1894, p. 420.
10. Amory, op. cit.

Chapter II: TWICE TOLD TALES

1. George A. Hibbard, "Lenox," ***Scribner's Magazine,*** Vol. XVI, No.4, October 1894, p. 433.
2. Anson Phelps Stokes, ***The Stokes Journal,*** privately printed, New York, 1915.
3. The book, by Lucille Kallen, is called ***C. B. Greenfield: The Tanglewood Murder,*** Windham Books, New York, 1980.
4. Frederick Platt, ***The Gilded Age: Architecture and Decoration,*** Harcourt & Brace, New York City and London, 1976.
5. Nathalie Sedgwick Colby, ***Remembering,*** Little, Brown & Company, Boston, 1938.
6. Ibid.
7. Ellery Sedgwick, ***The Happy Profession,*** Little, Brown and Company, Boston, 1947.
8. Anson Phelps Stokes, op. cit.
9. ***The New York Times,*** September 10, 1893.

Chapter III: TO THE MANOR BROUGHT

1. Anson Phelps Stokes, ***The Stokes Journal,*** December 26, 1893, p. 50.
2. ***The New York Times,*** May 27, 1894.
3. Blum, Catton, Morgan, Schlesinger, Stampp, Woodward, ***The National Experience,*** Harcourt, Brace and World, Inc., New York, 1963, p. 432–3.
4. Ibid, p. 433.
5. Russell Lynes, ***The Tastemakers,*** Grosset & Dunlop, New York, 1949, p. 132.
6. Andrew Carnegie, ***The Gospel of Wealth***, 1901 Reprinted, ***The Gospel of Wealth and Other Timely Essays,*** Cambridge, Massachusetts, 1962.
7. Mark Sullivan, ***Our Times,*** Vol. 1, Charles Scribner's Sons, New York and London, 1937, p. 283.
   A reporter, under pressure from his city editor, gained entrance to the house

Courtesy of Arrowhead

A four-in-hand in front of Frelinghuysen cottage

Courtesy of Arrowhead

Victoriana

and asked to see Mrs. Astor. It was the occasion of Mrs. Astor's annual ball. A servant took refuge in the formula, "Mrs. Astor is not at home." When the reporter asked to see Mrs. Astor's secretary, the butler called Mr. Ward McCallister. He told the reporter that, "Mrs. Astor never gives out the names of her guests." When the reporter asked Mr. McCallister for the number of guests, he replied: "There will be 400. There are only 400 persons in New York Society, you know." Thus the phrase was born, the newspapers did the rest. That story has been told and retold so often that it is raised to the height of an American legend alongside of Paul Bunyon and Pecos Bill.

8. Thorstein Veblen, ***The Theory of the Leisure Class,*** The Macmillan Company, New York and London, 1899, p. 84.
9. Ibid, p. 74.
10. Edith Wharton and Ogden Codman, Jr., ***The Decoration of Houses,*** 1902. Reprinted, W. W. Norton & Co., Inc., Toronto, 1978.
11. Veblen, op. cit.
12. Mrs. H. O. Ward, ***Sensible Etiquette of the Best Society,*** Porter & Coates, Philadelphia, 1878, p. 474.
13. W. D. Howells, "An Opportunity for American Fiction," ***Literature,*** New York, May 5, 1899.
14. Ibid.

Chapter IV: DISCRIMINATING DIVERSIONS

1. JoAnne Olian, ***The House of Worth: The Gilded Age 1860–1918,*** The Museum of the City of New York, 1982, p. 3.
2. Chard Powers Smith, ***The Housatanic,*** Rinehard & Company, Newport & Toronto, 1946, p. 387.

3. Constance Cary Harrison, "American Rural Festivals," ***Century Magazine,*** Vol. L, No. 3, July 1895, pp. 323–333.
4. Ibid.
5. Anson Phelps Stokes, ***The Stokes Records — 1889–1891,*** Volume 3, privately printed, New York City, 1915.
6. The Lenox Club, ***Constitution,*** 1874.
7. Emily Holt, ***Encyclopedia of Etiquette,*** Vol. 1, Nelson Doubleday, Inc., Oyster Bay & New York City, 1901, p. 109.
8. Mrs. H. O. Ward, ***Sensible Etiquette of the Best Society,*** Porter & Coats, Philadelphia, 1878, p. 164.
9. ***Town Topics,*** New York City, September 17, 1891. The editor prefaces the letter: "The following letter from Lenox, which I picked up in the aisle of the Madison Square Theater last evening after the performance, and which was evidentally dropped by a Murray Hill girl, gives such a capital idea of life at that most fashionable autumn resort, that I print it in full." (Ibid., September 10, 1891.)?
10. ***The Berkshire Eagle,*** June and July issues, 1905.
11. Nathalie Colby, ***Remembering,*** Little Brown & Co., Boston, 1938, p. 110.
12. ***The New York Times,*** April 5, 1899, front page.
13. Colby, op. cit., pp. 109–111.
14. ***The Berkshire Eagle,*** December 28, 1893, p. 7.

Courtesy of Rosamond Sherwood

The Emmet sisters often pairted children like this one by Lydia Field Emmet

Chapter V: THE CARETAKERS

1. Thorstein B. Veblen, ***Theory of the Leisure Class,*** The Macmillan Co., Ltd., New York and London, 1899, pp. 68–9.
2. Louise Griswold, "The Way to Solve the Servant Question," ***Century,*** Vol. LIV, No. 4, February, 1898, p. 636.

Chapter VI: THE BUILDERS

1. ***From Max Weber,*** Ed: H. H. Gerth & C. Wright Mills, Oxford University Press, New York, 1946, p. 188.
2. DeWitt, Mallary, ***Lenox and the Berkshire Highlands,*** 1902.
3. Ernest Bowditch, Unpublished Journal, "From the Office," The Bowditch Papers, The Essex Institute, 1916.
4. Mrs. Schuyler Van Rensselaer, "Country Dwellings," ***Century Magazine,*** Vol. XXXII, No. 1, May-October, 1886, pp. 3–5.
5. George William Sheldon, ***Artistic Country-Seats,*** 1886–87.
6. Ernest Bowditch, op. cit.
7. Mrs. Schuyler Van Rensselaer, op. cit., p. 19.
8. Ibid, p. 206.
9. Ernest Bowditch, op. cit.
10. Henry James, ***The American Scene,*** Harper and Brothers, New York and London, 1907, p. 54.
11. Library of Congress, Manuscript Division, Frederick Law Olmsted Collection.
12. Sarah Cabot Sedgwick & Christina S. Marquand, ***Stockbridge: 1739–1939,*** The Berkshire Traveler's Press, 1974, pp. 238–9.
13. R. W. Lewis, ***Edith Wharton: A Biography,*** Harper & Row, New York, 1975, p. 94.
14. From a typed manuscript given to me by Mrs. Anson Phelps Stokes, Jr., dated January 6, 1977. Presumably it was written for the purpose of publication in a periodical. Whether it was published, and what the name of the gardener who wrote it was, was not known.
15. Letter to Madeline from Mrs. George De Gersdorff, May 21, 1917.

Chapter VII: DOES OUR PAST HAVE A FUTURE?

1. Frederick Platt, ***The Gilded Age: Architecture and Decoration,*** Harcourt & Brace, New York City and London, 1976.
2. ***A Monograph of the Works of McKim, Mead and White, 1879–1915,*** Arno Press, New York, 1977, Introduction.
3. Wesley Towner, "The Elegant Ones," ***Good Housekeeping,*** April, 1959, p. 219.
4. Richard L. Williams, "The Reds Pet Blueblood," ***Life Magazine,*** 1959, p. 36.
5. Towner, op. cit., p. 227.

Part II: TOURING THE BERKSHIRE COTTAGES

1. Note: Since this was a composite card, it is unclear if the figure represents the total cost incurred building Allen Winden.
2. Note: The contractor was Joseph Clifford's Sons and the carver who charged $145 was John Evans and Co.
3. "The Summer Colony at Lenox," ***Munsey's Magazine,*** Vol. XVII, Number 5, August, 1897, p. 678.
4. Louis Arnold, ***American Country Houses of the Gilded Age,*** Dover Press, 1983, p. 4. (Reprint of George William Sheldon, ***Artistic Country-Seats,*** 1886–7.)
5. In early reports (1903–4), Overleigh is spelled as above; later it is also spelled Overlee.
6. Note: Each generation of Morris' has a Newbold, but "to avoid the Junior or I, II, III, we have a system," Mr. Stephen Morris explains. "My grandfather was A. Newbold, my father Newbold, my brother Augustus Newbold. Now I have a nephew, we just start all over again."
7. Nathaniel Hawthorne, ***The Wonder Book,*** 1851, p. 4.
8. U.S. Court of Appeals, 8th Circuit, No. 5255, p. 15. ***Rose Pastor Stokes, Plaintiff in Error*** vs. ***The United States.***
9. James R. Mellow, ***Hawthorne His Times,*** Houghton Mifflin, New York, 1980, p. 318.
10. Ibid, p. 322.

Courtesy of Arrowhead

Dining room at Villa Virginia

11. ***The Letters of Herman Melville,*** Ed: Merrell R. Davis and William H. Gilman, Yale University Press, Inc., 1960, p. 349.
12. Ibid, p. 142
13. Katharine M. Abbott, ***Old Paths and Legends*** of the New England Border, G. P. Putnam's Sons, New York and London, 1907, p. 272.
14. According to the recent dissertation of Judith Hull, a doctoral candidate at Columbia University, letters were sent from Mr. Ward to Mr. Upjohn wherein he complains that the workmen are too slow.
15. To protect privacy, the true prices of many of the estates, land or houses, were not recorded after 1890. The records of land transfers listed the costs as "$1.00 plus other valuable considerations." The vast estate purchased by Anson Phelps Stokes from Samuel G. Ward is listed as costing "$1.00 plus." Therefore the land purchases made by Mrs. Iasigi may not have cost $1.00 and $11.00.
16. The books written about Henriette Deluzy-Desporte include ***The Strange Case of Lucile Clery*** by Joseph Shearing—(also titled ***Forget Me Not*** and ***Lucile Clery: Woman of Intrigue.***) ***All This & Heaven Too*** by Rachel Field, ***The Marble Fawn*** by Nathaniel Hawthorne, ***Crime of Passion*** by Stanley Jerome, as well as influencing ***Vanity Fair*** by William Makepeace Thackeray, and ***The Turn of the Screw*** by Henry James.
17. Kings Prosecutor, November 17, 1847.
    (Two spellings appear in the text because Henrietta Deluzy changed her name to Henriette Deluzy-Desporte when she came to America.)
18. Loomis, Stanley, ***A Crime of Passion,*** J. B. Lippincott Company, Philadelphia & New York, 1967, p. 190.
19. Stockbridge Library, Historic Room.
20. Nathaniel Hawthorne, ***The American Notebook,*** Houghton, Mifflin & Co., New York, 1900, pp. 496–7.
21. The Mr. Headley that both James Fields and Nathaniel Hawthorne refer to, was author of ***Napoleon and His Marshals,*** a book perhaps not read today, it went to fifty editions during Mr. Headley's lifetime.
22. James R. Mellow, ***Hawthorne His Times,*** Houghton Mifflin, New York, 1980, p. 324.
23. Jeanne Ballot Winham, "Flashback," ***Vanity Fair,*** December, 1983, p. 140.
24. Ibid, p. 143.
25. Edward Sanford Martin, ***The Life of Joseph Hodges Choate,*** Charles Scribners Sons, New York, 1920, p. 12.

Courtesy of Mrs. Olivia Stokes Hatch

Shadow Brook, 2nd floor landing

Appendix II: COMPILATION OF COTTAGE INFORMATION

The following may aid in using the list. Spelling of several of the cottage names has varied over the years. I have chosen the spelling used by the Columbia University, Avery Library Index to Architectural Periodicals. If an entry appears in parentheses, it indicates it is the same property that has been given a new name by a subsequent owner.

The second column lists the name of the cottager, not necessarily the original owner or builder of the house. Although most cottages were built by the cottager, if the cottager bought an existing house, the slash that divides the third column separates the year the cottage was built from the year it was renovated.

There is conflict about the correct building dates of the cottages. One reason is that it took from one to three years to build a cottage. Some writers have used the date on the plans; others have used the completion date. The date given here is the completion date. Wherever that date is in dispute, the date given is the one used by ***American Architect and Building News,*** a contemporary architectural magazine. If then the date is still in dispute, but an educated guess can be made, that approximate date appears in brackets.

If in column four it is indicated that the house no longer exists, there still might be information in column five. This indicates what exists on the site of the former cottage. If [NR] appears in column five, it indicates that the house is listed on the National Register of Historic Buildings.

(LENOX)

COTTAGE	COTTAGER	YEAR BUILT / RENOVATED	STANDING	PRESENT USE
Allen Winden	Charles Lanier	1881	No	Berkshire Christian College
Ananda Hall	Cortlandt Field Bishop	1924	No	Razed
Bellefontaine	Giraud Foster	1897	Yes	For Sale
Belvoir Terrace	Morris Ketchum Jesup	1886	Yes	Arts Camp
Blantyre	Robert W. Paterson	1903	Yes	Inn
Brookhurst	Newbold Morris	1905	Yes	Private Home
Coldbrooke	John S. Barnes	1882	Yes	For Sale
Cushman Cottage	Charlotte Cushman	1860/1875	No	The Brunell Avenue Development
(The) Dormers	Richard T. Auchmuty	1870	Yes	Private home
Eastover	Harris Fahnestock	1910	Yes	Resort
Edgecomb	Miss Sophie Furness	1880	Yes	Nursing Home
Elm Court	William Douglas Sloane	1885	Yes	Vacant
Erskine Park	George Westinghouse	1893	Razed	The Ponds at Fox Hollow
(Holmwood)	(Margaret Vanderbilt Baker)	(1919)	(Yes)	(Time-share resort)
Ethelwynde	Mrs. Robert Winthrop	1875/1890	No	Razed
Fairlawn	Mr. Charles Kneeland	1837	No	Razed — The Kneeland Development
Fernbrook	Thomas Shields Clarke	1904	Yes	High Point School
Frelinghuysen Cottage	Frederick Frelinghuysen	1881	Yes	The Bible Speaks
Groton Place	Grenville Winthrop	1901	Yes	Boston University Summer Music School
(The Elms)	(William Ellery Sedgwick)	(1858)	(No)	(Razed to build The Elms)
(The Elms)	(Mr. W. Robeson)	(1887)	(Yes)	(Renovated to create Groton Place)
Gusty Gables	Miss Mary DePeyster Carey	1880	Yes	Private home
Highlawn House	W. B. O. Field	1910	Yes	Private home and farm

COTTAGE	COTTAGER	YEAR BUILT / RENOVATED	STANDING	PRESENT USE
(Highlawn Farm)	(W. D. Sloane)	[1880s]		
Homestead	The Misses Appleton	1885	No	Fire
Interlaken	David Wolfe Bishop	1888	No	Razed
Maplehurst	Mrs. Joseph M. White	1880	No	Razed to build Ananda Hall
Merrywood	Mrs. Charles Bullard	1883	Yes	Music Camp
(The) Mount	Edith Jones Wharton	1902	Yes	Historic site
Oakswood	Samuel G. Ward	1878	No	Razed
Orleton	Harley T. Proctor	1912	Yes	The Gateways Restaurant
Overleigh	Samuel Frothingham	1903	Yes	Avalon School
(The) Perch	Fanny Kemble Butler (Mrs. Owen Wister)	[1860s]	No	Razed — plaque marks spot
Pine Acres	Mrs. William C. Wharton (Edith Wharton's mother-in-law)	1885	Yes	Three Gables Restaurant
Poplars	Henry White / Samuel Frothingham	—	No	Razed
Rockwell Cottage	William O. Curtis	1804 / 1906	Yes	School
Shipton Court	Mrs. Edwards Spencer	1885 / 1900	Yes	Seven Hills Resort
Spring Lawn	John C. Alexandre	1904	Yes	The Bible Speaks (college)
Stonover	John E. Parsons	1875	No	Razed
Ventfort Hall	George Halle Morgan	1893	Yes	For Sale
Whitney Reservation	William C. Whitney		No	October Mountain Preserve
(October Mountain)	(Harry Paine Whitney)	/ (1909)	(No)	
Windyside	Dr. Richard Greenleaf	1875	Yes	The Lenox Club
(The) Winter Palace	Cortlandt Field Bishop	[1900]	Yes	Private home

Courtesy of Arrowhead

Hagyard's drugstore

COTTAGE	COTTAGER	YEAR BUILT / RENOVATED	STANDING	PRESENT USE
Wyndhurst	John Sloane	1894	Yes	For Sale
(Blossom Farm)	(Henry Ward Beecher)	(1853)	(No)	(Razed to build Wyndhurst)
(Wyndhurst)	(General John Rathbone)	(1869)	(No)	Razed
Yokun	Richard Goodman	1794/ 1880	No	Razed to extend Ananda Hall
(STOCKBRIDGE)				
Beckwithshaw	Leonard Forbes Beckwith	1892	Yes	Desisto School
(Bonnie Brier Farm)	(Dan Hanna)	/(1919)	(Yes)	
Bonnie Brae	Henry Ivison	1879	Yes	Private home
Caldwell House	John Caldwell	1902	Yes	Austen Riggs Center
Chesterwood	Daniel Chester French	1901	Yes	National Historic Site [NR]
Clover Croft	Mrs. Oscar Iasigi	1890	No	Fire
Eden Hill	David Dudley Field	[1870s]	Yes	Congregation of Marians of the Immaculate Conception
(The) Elms	Timothy Edwards/ Charles M. Owens	1772 /[1880]	Yes Yes	Austin Riggs Center
Highwood	Samuel Gray Ward	/[1846]	Yes	Private home
Hillfield	Mr. & Mrs. Kobbe	1790	No	Fire
Konkaput Brook	Frederic Crowninshield	1903	Yes	Riverbrook School
Lakeside	Charles Astor Bristed	1894	Yes	Private home
Linwood	Charles E. Butler	1858	Yes	Norman Rockwell Museum
Naumkeag	Joseph Hodges Choate	1886	Yes	Historic Site [NR]
Oronoque	Birdseye Blakeman	[1892]	Yes	Boston University Summer Music School
Shadow Brook	Anson Phelps Stokes	1893	No	Fire
(Brook Farm)	(Anson Phelps Stokes)	(1891)	(Yes)	(Berkshire Country Day School)
Strawberry Hill	Lydia Emmet & Mrs. Pablo (Susan Metcalf) Casals	1905	Yes	Private home
Sunset	Henry Martyn Field	[1877]	Yes	Private home
Swann House	Mrs. John (Lillian Butler) Swann	1899	Yes	Austen Riggs Center
Tanglewood	William Aspinwall Tappan	[1852]	Yes	Tanglewood Music Festival
Villa Virginia	William H. Clarke, Esq.	1915	Yes	Private home [NR]
Wheatleigh	H. H. Cook	1893	Yes	Inn [NR]
Windermere	Henry Martyn Field	[1860s]	Yes	Private home
(GREAT BARRINGTON)				
Barrington House	Mrs. Mark Hopkins	1888	Yes	For Sale
Brookside	William Stanley	1904	Yes	Camp

Courtesy of the Berkshire Eagle

Interlaken,
David Wolfe Bishop's
cottage

Appendix III: ARCHITECTS OF THE COUNTRY ESTATES

The following list groups the houses under the architect who designed them.

ARCHITECT	COTTAGE(S)
Adams and Warren	Overleigh
Henry Bacon	Chesterwood
Leonard Forbes Beckwith	Bonnie Brier Farm
Carrère and Hastings	Bellefontaine
	Brookside
	Groton Place
George De Gersdorff	Konkaput Brook
Delano and Aldrich	Stonover
	Highlawn House
A. W. Longfellow	Clover Croft
Wilson Eyre, Jr.	Fernbrook
G. E. & G. Fountain	Caldwell House
Hiss and Weeks	Villa Virginia
Hoppin and Koen	Brookhurst
	Eastover
	The Mount
Guy Lowell	Spring Lawn
McKim, Mead and White	(began) Barrington House
	Homestead
	Naumkeag
	Oakswood
	(renovated) Yokun
Louis Metcalf	Strawberry Hill
Peabody and Stearns	Allen Winden
	(renovated) Coldbrooke
	Elm Court
	Wheatleigh
	Wyndhurst
Robertson and Potter	Blantyre
Rotch and Tilden	Ventfort Hall
Robert S. Stevenson	Swann House
Richard Upjohn	Highwood
Henry Vaughan and Edward Searles	(completed) Barrington House
H. Neill Wilson	Shadow Brook
	Interlaken

INDEX OF PHOTOGRAPHS

INDEX